Reviews

Chris Epting, Huffington Post Contributor Author and award-winning
journalist
In my opinion, it is a remarkable collection of both stories and artifacts that
allows people to experience exactly what it was like to live and work through
one of the most tumultuous artistic periods in modern history, alongside
some of the most iconic musicians the world has known.

maun1965 reviewed Out of Our Heads April 18, 2017
This is a terrific book -- fun, informative and a very interesting read.
And it's different. Not your typical retread on the Rolling Stones and some
of the big events that shaped our culture and have now become part of the
history of Rock n' Roll and the 1960's. If you want the real story on Altamont,
read this book. Ron Schneider tells the inside story and backs it up with documents and timetables that challenge and ultimately refute most of the mythol-
ogy that now surrounds the historical record of the event.
"Out of Our Heads" places you inside the inner circle of the Rolling Stones as
they're launched on the chaotic rocket ride that propelled them past simple
pop-stardom and into superstardom as The Greatest Rock n' Roll Band in the
World.
This book is filled with great stories that haven't been told before including
some fascinating anecdotes about the Beatles (They thought about acquiring
the movie rights to The Lord of the Rings trilogy). It also has charming stories
about John, Paul, George & Ringo and includes separate drawings that both
John and Paul made for Ron during a business meeting that gives you unique
insight into their thoughts on Apple, Ron and the business side of the Beatles.
If you love the Rollings Stones and the Beatles, your bookshelf is probably
crammed with slick, glossy books about these two great bands. Do yourself
a favor, instead of buying the next one that comes out with the same retold
stories -- buy this one, it's unique.

Gazza reviewed Out of Our Heads April 17, 2017
First class read from beginning to end
Fantastic read. Ronnie presents an affectionately written and witty first hand diary of life on the road with the Stones in the mid 60s and again from 1969-70, the at times chaotic behind the scenes dealings that resulted in the 'Gimme Shelter' movie (which he produced), the legal wrangles that dominated the final years of The Beatles and several other musical and cinematic ventures when he was employed by his uncle, Allen Klein. A welcome bonus is a large appendix of legal documents and correspondence which provide an excellent piece of context. There's an old cliche that if you remember the 60's, then you really weren't there. This book disproves it. Highly recommended!

PVOmaha reviewed Out of Our Heads March 31, 2017
Must read this book if you love music!
Best rock and roll book on the market. I never wanted to finish it.

Peter Schwab reviewed Out of Our Heads March 13, 2017
His account of what it was like being the business manager for these two groups was ...
First of all I never was a Rolling Stones fan. So you may ask why did I read this book. Since I was a Beatles fan I wanted to gather some insight about the Rolling Stones (and the Beatles too). Schneider's book gave me this and more. His account of what it was like being the business manager for these two groups was fascinating. It tells the story of what is was like being on the road with a very popular rock and roll group and all the things that it could or should happen. If you expected a "tell-all" book then this is not the book for you. Rather it is a day by day account of just what it is like to manage the stars, the promoters, the groupies and the travel from venue to venue. Schneider's account of all the happenings is a great read and one I can't imagine any Rolling Stones or Beatles fan will not enjoy.

Amazon Customer reviewed Out of Our Heads February 27, 2017
A MUST read!
Aptly titled, the book, to say the least, is an excellent insight into the music scene of the late 60s to the 70s, its ups and downs and the pains and pleasures. Ron managed the Beatles for ABKCO, his legendary uncle Allen Klein's company for many years and independently managed the Rolling Stones till the 70s. In 5 decades of my readings, I have rarely come across a book that is so well researched and documented - a must read for the fans as also everyone interested in the entertainment industry.

OUT OF OUR HEADS

The Rolling Stones, The Beatles and Me

by Ronnie Schneider

CLB
P.O.Box 15191
Beverly Hills, CA 90209

www.ronnieschneider.com

Ordering Information:

Quantity sales. Special discounts are available on quantity purchases by corporations, associations, and others. For details, contact the publisher at the address above.

Orders by U.S. trade bookstores and wholesalers.

First Edition

Library of Congress Control Number: 2017900212

ISBN 978-0-9981663-1-5 (hardcover-color-with Proof of Truth)
ISBN 978-0-9981663-3-9 (paperback-b&w-with Proof of Truth)
ISBN 978-0-9981663-2-2 (paperback-b&w)
ISBN 978-0-9981663-0-8 (epub)

Dedicated to the Fans

My Son, Eric Schneider, his wife Alicia, and grand kids, Addison and Evan
My Daughter, Holly, and grandson Ari Carpenter.
Their mother, Jane.

Significant other: Katia Bojilov Beebe

PHOTO CREDITS
unless otherwise stated

1965 tour-Gered Mankowitz
Photographs by Gered Mankowitz © Bowstir Ltd. 2016/Mankowitz.com

Cover, 1969 tour, Ed Sullivan and Altamont overview-Ethan Russell
©Ethan Russell All rights reserved http://ethanrussell.com/

Ondines with the Stones and Ringo leaving QEII-Tom Monaster
©Thomas Monaster http://monasterphoto.com/

"Stones" in the heart of darkness-Robert Altman
Robert Altman- "The Rolling Stones" at Altamont
©Robert Altaman http://www.altmanphoto.com/

ACKNOWLEDGEMENTS

Editors:
Mike Stax
Gerard Vanderleun

Notes from **Todd Stevens**

Cover:
Fernando Carpenter

A special thanks to:

Ethan Russell for the help and great advice!

Table of Contents

PROLOGUE

My story begins in a time of innocence: a time I played outside until it got too dark or Mom called me to supper; a time I didn't lock a door; a time your "mobile" phone was in a phone booth; a time the "F" word was treated like the "N" word now is. It was a time when people looked at one another instead of into their screens.

The 1950s segued into the mounting violence of the 1960s with the assassinations of John F. Kennedy, Martin Luther King Jr., and Robert Kennedy, the election of Richard Nixon, and the Vietnam War. Distrust of government grew, as did rebellion in the streets and on college campuses. Kids today are worried about affording college and paying their student loans; I was worried about being drafted and sent to die in Vietnam. In my hometown of Miami, I lived under the threat of a nuclear missile launch from Cuba. In the beginning of the '50s, life was innocent; toward the end of the '60s, life was becoming dangerous.

On the positive side, the birth control pill and the advent of "free love" couldn't have come at a better time for a short, chunky, shy young boy like me. Sex, drugs, and rock 'n' roll were the answer as my parents' pop music gave way to rebellious rock 'n' roll and, most significant of all for the burgeoning "counterculture," the British Invasion.

That invasion was led by The Beatles and The Rolling Stones. As the times began changing both bands played a significant role in the revolution that rocked society; they were, if you will, the soundtrack of the '60s. And I was right there with them.

—Ronnie Schneider

CHAPTER I

PLEASE ALLOW ME TO INTRODUCE MYSELF

I've always considered myself a Miami boy, even though I was born in Newark, New Jersey, on October 20, 1943.

As I lay on my front lawn looking up at the puffy white clouds in the Miami, Florida, sky, I saw elephants, dragons, and weird faces. I was 10 years old and chewing on a blade of green grass. I began to wonder how I got here, not the birth canal "how" but the universal "How and why was man and this universe, or our reality, created?" I pondered the use of a future time machine. I'd read the book The Time Machine where H.G. Wells seemed to think time travel possible. It seemed to me the real problem would be setting the time. What if 00:00:00 actually got you to the instant before the world began and poof! Time ceased to exist and so did you. But then, if you got to the precise second the world began, you still wouldn't know what was before that second. There would never be a factual answer. Never is a long time to a kid. I saw the possibility of driving myself crazy trying to get my head around the paradoxes of time and the logic of living. Why live and suffer (I was getting bullied) if you have to die anyhow? I had to come up with a solution. My solution was to stop thinking about it. There was no way I could ever know for sure! This life was it, and I should just have fun with it.

I decided that I would watch my life like a movie, let the events happen. I didn't want to ponder the epic question, "Is it fate or is it destiny?" I would just let fate or destiny bring things and events to me, and I would treat them as an opportunity knocking. Sometimes the knock would be the choice: Should I stay or should I go?

My father, Harold; me; my dog, Pepper; my brother, Jay; and my mom, Anne

My father chased jobs that took us from Newark, New Jersey, to Miami, Florida, to Los Angeles, California, and back to New Jersey. Then finally Miami again where he chose his last career, that of a mail carrier. He walked a route in Miami, and that's where I grew up.

My mother worked as well, doing various jobs that ranged from being a cashier at a grocery store to working for the FAA at the Miami airport, and finally as a dispatcher for the Miami Police Department. (A job that saved my ass twice!)

"You can be anything you want to be!" That's what my junior high guidance counselor told me after seeing the results of my ninth grade aptitude test. The counselor went further to say that with my high scores, I could be a doctor or a scientist. I liked the first option since even then I knew doctors made money.

And I needed money.

At the age of seven, Christmas had taught me about money, and the fact that my family didn't have much. We were living in a "temporary housing development" (shacks) set up in a park in Newark for returning World War II veterans. There was snow outside; it was the day before Christmas. My father said that we were Jewish and, therefore, would not be getting any Christmas presents.

My brother and I cried and carried on. "Okay, then what about Hanukkah and our eight days of candles and presents?" My father came up with some form of argument and sent us to bed. I soon realized that it had nothing to do with Christmas or Hanukkah; it had to do with us not having money.

My father made the point that it was up to me to take care of myself. That was stressed even more when I was eleven and needed cash for the weekend movie theater, and my father said he would loan me a quarter, but I had better get a job and take care of myself. I was too young then for a work permit. The day I could get a permit, I got a job at a local WT Grant department store.

What should I be when I grow up? What could make me money, so I could have fun?

Science really interested me—the challenge of discovering cures for diseases and solving other mysteries excited me. One of my favorite birthday gifts was a science kit with chemicals and a microscope. Through that microscope, I saw my first amoeba. It looked hungry.

For a junior high school science project, I decided to find out if I could feed a microscopic amoeba and make it so fat that you could see it with the naked eye. (I had my own weight problems at the time.) After a week of putting "food" (whatever I thought an amoeba would absorb) into a cup of stagnant water, I assumed I had accomplished my goal when I saw a small, dark speck floating in the water. I entered this project and its grand conclusion in the science fair. In retrospect, it may have been a speck of dust everyone was viewing instead of A Morbidly Obese Amoeba.

While dreaming of my future career in science I also fantasized about finding the cure for cancer. I had a mental image of my older self in an office in New York City, hunched over a desk, then holding up the test tube with my new discovery: "Ladies and gentlemen—the cure for cancer!" Unfortunately, due to my dark, pessimistic teenage view of life, I also envisioned a stray gunshot from the street coming through my window and killing me at that instant, dashing the test tube to the floor, my cure for cancer lost forever. Scratch "Research Scientist."

My next choice was to be a doctor. My Jewish mother, at least, would relish saying: "My son, the doctor!" An added advantage was that doctors made a lot of money, and that could give me freedom.

In reality, this dream of being a doctor was actually the dream of a thirteen-year-old boy searching for a future where I could see and touch naked women. A future where I would relish saying, "It's okay. I'm a doctor!"

On reflection, I quickly realized that all my patients would not be Playboy bunnies; they could be ugly, fat, and sick. Not only that, I would have to treat men, as well.

In addition: I had no patience for complainers or whiners! So, I could be a doctor, but I would only treat healthy, young, pretty women who didn't complain. All in all, not a realistic business plan. The dream was over. Scratch "Doctor to Playboy Bunnies."

While discussing my imaginary career options with my mother one day, she sensibly suggested, "My brother is an accountant. You could work with him." I met her brother, my uncle Allen, on his visits to Miami Beach and the Fontainebleau Hotel. As a teenager, I had babysat my cousin Robin, Allen and his wife Betty's daughter, on these visits. I enjoyed the family and now a guaranteed job with someone I knew sounded great. The job involved accounting and bookkeeping. Perfect—I was good at math and loved numbers.

When one thinks of accounting or bookkeeping, one usually visualizes some boring guy bent over a desk scribbling numbers. True enough, but those numbers represent, and indeed are, money, and accountants do deal with money. I felt if I was close to money, some of it could rub off on me. This was a career goal I could embrace.

I started with bookkeeping and accounting courses. I was lucky to have what I called then a "semi-photographic memory." I could read a book once and remember the contents for a long time. Since most teachers gave tests "by the book" I did well—as did my friends who sat next to me. In fact, my friends, during a university civics exam, placed pieces of paper on the backs of the chairs next to me, listing the odds of a good grade. The further the seats were from me, the longer the odds.

I enjoyed my bookkeeping classes in high school and as a consequence did well. We had a cost accounting classroom assignment that was supposed to last weeks, but I finished it earlier than everyone else, so I had spare time to do the bookkeeping for one of my teachers, who was also a lawyer. He paid me back later by getting me off when I had an automobile accident.

After high school, I decided to major in accounting and minor in law at the University of Miami. Accounting was working out well, especially auditing. I loved the challenge of making everything balance down to the penny. I loved finding that penny. Things were either in balance, or they were out of balance. I liked things in balance.

During the last semester of my accounting classes, we were given a Level II accounting exam, essentially a clone of the CPA exam one took after graduation. I scored the highest in the school, which brought an apology from my accounting professor. When handing out the grades, he said, "Mr. Schneider, I have to apologize to you. I always thought you were a wise ass who cheated to get your grades."

"No problem, sir, I just know who to copy from for the right answer."

During my 1963 summer vacation from the University of Miami and with some accounting and bookkeeping classes under my belt, I went to New York to work with my uncle.

My uncle was Allen Klein. I didn't know much about what he did, just that he was an accountant.

At the University of Miami business school, I heard the adage, "Business school teaches you the right way to do business. When you get a job you learn how business is really done." I was ready to learn real business from one of the masters, my uncle.

I set off in June for New York with three of my friends. We drove nonstop from Miami to New York City in my '62 Chevy Impala convertible. No sleep, twenty-six hours straight. I dropped one of my friends off in Brooklyn. Then I encountered New York and New Jersey traffic and drivers. These drivers didn't drive in lanes, but more like jockeys vying for pole position. I was tempted to turn around and drive back to Miami. "New York, New York. It's a wonderful town…"!

My timing, as it turned out, couldn't have been better. Klein had just taken over the management of the legendary singer Sam Cooke. As Cooke's manager, my uncle immediately shattered music industry precedent by taking the side of the artist instead of the record company. It was the first manifestation of a management style that would lead to Klein managing both The Beatles and The Rolling Stones.

At the start, I lived in Union, New Jersey, with my aunt Blanche and my grandmother Mimi (my father's sister and mother), and commuted by bus to Allen Klein and Company in Manhattan.

My uncle hated being alone and took pains to always have someone by his side as he went about his business. Klein's right-hand man was his attorney, Marty Machat. Marty was there to: 1) Draft the legal agreements that Klein created to stymie the record companies; 2) be his friend; and 3) join him for both lunch and dinner. Marty was also adept at handling talent and lending legitimacy to an accountant who, with the signing of Sam Cooke, had become a major manager in the music business.

My first summer of work there, he stuck me in a back office (i.e., supply room) filing "CCH Tax Updates." These tax code pages had to be inserted into many different binders to keep the tax laws up to date. It was tedious work, as each insert went to a distinct location in each binder. Other tasks included making copies, putting stamps on letters, and doing simple bookkeeping work.

As summer ended, I wondered if Allen was going to ask me back. I was confident in my work and knew I was a good accountant as far as school grades were concerned, but I wasn't sure of what my uncle thought. I went to Henry Neufeld, the head of the accounting department, and asked, "How'd I do?"

He smiled and whispered, conspiratorially, "We want you back."

I appreciated what Henry said, but knew that "we want you back" meant nothing unless Allen wanted me back. My uncle waited until my last day in the office to tell me to come back next summer.

I couldn't wait.

In my second summer, I was dispatched to do the bookkeeping for different clients the company represented. My job was to write up their checkbooks, which had to include all checks written and deposits made. I had to record the royalty income they received and the percentage splits that were relevant. There were writer royalties, performance royalties, and publishing royalties. A lot of these clients were in the famed Brill Building at 49th Street and Broadway in Manhattan. I remember walking down the halls there, hearing music: a piano playing, a guitar strumming, and the voices of songwriters pitching or creating their songs for singers or publishers. During this period, I did the books for Scepter Records (and its division, Wand Records), which had the Shirelles, Nancy Brown, the Isley Brothers, BJ Thomas, Dionne Warwick, and the Kingsmen of "Louie Louie" fame. Flo Greenberg had started the label—not bad for a bored housewife. Sometimes I would get a chance to talk to some of the singers; most of all I loved to walk and talk with Nancy Brown.

One of the nicest guys I recall meeting was Neil Sedaka. I would go to his office to do his books. His mother ran the office! I would sit at a nearby desk and write up Neil's income and his expenses. Neil would always be at the piano working on some new song that I would hear on the radio months later. Neil was both the perfect gentleman and son.

My uncle assigned me to the offices and the banal task of bookkeeping to see how I did while interacting with the talent and working at the business of entertainment. After doing this for a year, he let me join him when he worked with the other artists he represented.

The first of these was Bobby Vinton. Allen had done a groundbreaking record deal for Bobby and was managing his act, as well. In structuring Bobby's deal, my uncle got a large advance from the record company and then shrewdly leveraged that advance by buying an annuity. It was clever in terms of finance and publicity. The advance was $650,000. For $500,000, my uncle was able to buy a $1,000,000 annuity that guaranteed a monthly payout over 20 years and have $150,000.00 cash in the bank. He was able to announce "the largest record deal of the time"—$1,000,000 and Bobby still got a nice cash advance and a lot of great press. My uncle took a percentage of the deal.

Being in the background, I could watch Bobby rehearse as my uncle helped structure his show. My uncle's main premise was simple— "always leave the audience wanting more." Most talent doesn't know when to stop. If they have an adoring audience, they'll perform forever, so firm limits have to be set. Allen would help structure Bobby's live show, building excitement, leveling off, and then building to a wow closing. Next, there'd be a carefully planned encore. Then "Elvis has left the building!" Always leave the audience wanting more.

I joined Allen and Bobby on many shows in the Catskills and major clubs in New York. Vinton was an amazing talent. His father was a band conductor so Bobby had learned to play about fifteen different instruments. He would surprise the audience that came to see him sing "Mr. Lonely," "Blue Velvet," or "Roses Are Red" when he would break out a dozen instruments and play them. Another cute trick I noted from the shows was that every night when Bobby would introduce the band to the audience, he would say, "And let's hear it for our drummer; it's his birthday today!" That always got a round of applause, and I wondered what people thought when they came more than once to see his show.

Working with Bobby led to working with Sam Cooke.

Sam Cooke had originally hired my uncle to audit his record company, RCA, to see if they owed him money. At that time, record companies had a well-earned reputation for screwing the artists by playing fast and loose with royalty statements. One thing they did was withhold more money for "returns" than in the contract.

Returns were records that were sold to distributors and record stores that were later sent back because the store over-ordered. Rather than pay for the total records sold for a period the record company withheld a percentage of the money owed to cover this possibility. Sometimes they withheld up to 25% of sales, which, if you are a big seller, could amount to a lot of money.

That was the case with Sam Cooke. My uncle began the audit and found that the record company had withheld over $100,000, which wasn't provided for in the record contract. Now remember, this is 1963, when $100,000 was equivalent to $750,000 today. Imagine the feeling Sam had when Allen was able to hand him a six-figure check after he thought he had already gotten paid by the record company. Allen was his hero from that moment on, and Allen really cared about Sam. It was always personal with Allen. My uncle also structured another form of deal for Sam, a "buy/sell" agreement. Instead of just earning royalty income, Sam's company would manufacture the records and sell them to the record company. This created manufacturing income, which was taxed differently than royalty income.

Sam Cooke was a class act. He was a gentle guy with a sweet disposition and a voice like melted butter. Besides securing him an amazing record deal for its time, my uncle got bookings for Sam that were unheard of for black entertainers of that era.

Sam told me there were just two elements to his act. One: he would hop over the microphone cord, and two: he would bite his lower lip. That's all he needed. His voice did the rest. Those were great years. Allen, Sam, and J.W. (Sam Cooke's manager and partner) were very close friends as well as business associates. To celebrate their relationship, Allen gave Sam a Silver Cloud Rolls Royce.

It was the best of times, and then it all ended.

I was back home, in Miami, finishing my final year at the University of Miami, driving in my car, when I heard Sam had been shot and killed in a motel. Sam had been robbed at the motel and had run to the manager's office. Sam's pounding on the door frightened the old lady manager, and she shot and killed him. It was a very sad day. A major talent was destroyed for no reason at all. Allen was so upset that he hired private detectives to confirm the story of how and why Sam was killed.

In those early office days, we were a very small core accounting group. Henry Neufeld was the senior accountant running the office. I always had the feeling that Henry thought of me as a son. Joel Silver was next in line as to seniority. He was a big guy who was not only talented in accounting; he was also a fine basketball player, for our office rivalries. Alan Horowitz was the office manager and the guy who always asked for your receipts before reimbursing out-of-pocket expenses. Kenny Salinsky was my partner in crime and prank competitor. Adrian and Nancy were our receptionists. This was the office that took care of Bobby Vinton, Sam Cooke, Neil Sedaka, and several small record companies.

After graduation from the University of Miami, it seemed natural to move to New York. But that almost didn't happen. I'd put myself through college by working at the Grapeland Heights Library for $20 a week and gambling, playing Hearts, Gin, betting on Jai Alai, the dogs, and horses. Just before graduation, my best bud Joe Rose and I hit a Big Q (picking the winners of four races in a row) at the Biscayne dog track and won over $700 with a $2 bet. With this win, I was leaning toward staying in Miami and continuing as a professional gambler. I developed a system to bet on Jai Alai. I was winning consistently and making good use of my love of numbers.

Then I went to the Tropical Park Race Track, the big horse-racing facility in Miami, and took a long hard look at the professional gamblers there. Based on the look of these guys—scraggly, alcoholic, disheveled-looking losers—I rethought my romantic decision and realized that the odds were against me as a gambler. So I traded palm trees and sandy beaches for skyscrapers and concrete.

CHAPTER II

NO EXPECTATIONS

"You're going on the road with the Rolling Stones," said my uncle, the new business manager for the Rolling Stones.

It was October 29, 1965, I had just moved to New Jersey, and the office was in a flurry as the Rolling Stones prepared to leave for their fourth US tour.

Three months earlier, my uncle had signed on to represent the Stones in their record company negotiations. Since then, his role expanded into representing them on their tour. Andrew Loog Oldham, Rolling Stones co-manager, signed a short letter of agreement with my uncle that said:

You are hereby authorized to negotiate in my behalf as the producer of the Rolling Stones and the co-manager of said group for a new phonographic recording agreement… For your services, we agree to pay you Twenty Per Cent (20%) of the gross compensation paid pursuant to the agreement you negotiate. It is understood that your appointment hereunder is exclusive and can be revoked by you or myself by giving each other prior written notice of no less than 90 days.

So it began. I looked forward to meeting Oldham, the man who created the Rolling Stones' image. I had recently met another big image producer, Phil Spector. Allen introduced me: "Ronnie, meet Phil Spector." I turned to this dapperly dressed man in a white suit with a walking cane and offered my hand. He smiled, pulled a hidden rapier from the cane, and pointed it at me. "Hi, Ronnie". He sheathed the sword. I hoped my Oldham meeting would be different.

Image and marketing are the most important part of creating celebrity, but the biggest boost comes from having the talent to back it up. With the Rolling Stones, Oldham had both.

In October 1965, a giant billboard over Times Square was rented and painted black. At first, it seemed a waste of space and money. Then gradually over the passing days the following text, a poem by Andrew Oldham, slowly appeared:

*"The sound face and mind of today /
Is more relative to the hope of tomorrow, and the reality of destruction /
than the blind who cannot see their children for fear and division /
something that grew and related the reflection of today's children…
THE ROLLING STONES."*

Then their picture appeared at the top of the billboard.

The headlines in the press read, "Would you let your daughter marry a Rolling Stone?" This was Oldham capitalizing on a question he received from a British reporter that had become a slogan.

He had a hit. Society was in rebellion. It was called "the generation gap." The parents loved the Beatles; the kids loved the Stones. Oldham touched a nerve, and the band delivered. Screw society.

By the end of July, my uncle had the Stones sign the biggest British recording contract of its time with Decca in the United Kingdom. The deal included a $1.25 million advance and a higher royalty rate than the Beatles.

I began my new life.

My uncle didn't want to show any nepotism. To make sure no one could say he favored me, he paid me a salary of $60 a week in 1963 and had me start from the bottom. I was always a hard worker and didn't mind—most of the time.

With my meager salary and my 1965 Chevy convertible, living in Manhattan was out of the question. A car is a big problem in the city. So I settled into my new life in Newark, New Jersey, in a high-rise apartment complex next to Weequahic Park—the same park that housed the shacks we'd lived in many years before. I had a new roommate, and a building filled with airline stewardesses.

After a few months, I had fallen into a nice schedule. Up early, catch the bus into the city, and stop at Bickford's for my breakfast of two eggs over medium, hash browns, English muffin, and a cup of coffee. In the office by 10:00 AM. Leave work after 6:00 PM for a bus back to Newark. Get to the apartment and wait for girls to come by for a bite and whatever. Most weekends involved partying with the stewardesses.

In my first week at work, my uncle called me into his office with Candy Leigh. Candy, who was about five years older than me, was the ABKCO in-house public relations person. Candy had been a model and now, in addition to PR for Allen, had her own business, Call Candy, a telephone answering service. Allen told me that I needed some suits for work since growing up in Miami left me with a wardrobe that consisted of shorts, T-shirts, and flip-flops. He wanted me to go to a specific suit designer who dressed all the top businessmen, TV and film stars, and entertainers in New York. He instructed Candy to go with me to help pick out a wardrobe and gave me $400.00 to cover it.

One weekend my brother, Jay, came up from Miami to visit, and while he was in town, I got a call from Candy. She said that I should come over to her apartment in Manhattan to go over some upcoming work. I had no idea what we were going to discuss but figured that I had more to learn so I had my brother drop me off there. I told Jay that I would probably be about two hours, and he should wander around New York City and give me a call when he was ready to go.

Candy lived in a duplex ground floor apartment. It was very feminine with the walls painted in what she said was her favorite color, purple. We sat together on a rug on her living room floor and went over some papers. She was drinking large tumblers of scotch the whole time. After a couple of hours, my brother called, and Candy told him he should give us another hour. After she hung up the phone, she lay down on the rug next to me and kissed me. By now, she was a bit inebriated. We made out for a while, but every time I tried to take things further she stopped me.

After about an hour of this, my brother showed up. Candy quietly told me to send him back to New Jersey, and that I could always take a much later bus.

After he left, Candy and I resumed our "studies." After about thirty minutes, she got up off the floor and said she was going upstairs to her bedroom, and I should give her five minutes before coming up. That seemed even weirder to me, and I began to wonder what the hell was going on. First, she would kiss me then... nothing. Now she was inviting me up to her bedroom. All types of wild scenarios were running through my head.

"Come on up, Ronnie!"

Her bedroom had a purple and pink color scheme. She was wearing a floor-length nightgown and beckoned me over to her four-poster bed.

The sex was terrible.

When I woke up, Candy was still sleeping. I began planning on how to get out of there gracefully when she woke up and greeted me with a kiss. She turned on the television, and we lay in bed for a while, watching an early-morning children's show with Sheri Lewis and her sock puppet, Lamb Chop. We started swapping the characters on her show with different people in the office and were having a good laugh, which soon escalated into another sexual encounter. This time, it was great; we stayed in bed the entire day, talking, joking, having sex, and ordering food delivery. Eight o'clock Sunday evening rolled around, and I told her that I didn't want to impose, but I would love to stay over and have some more fun. She said I should go home, so I reluctantly left.

I went to the NY Port Authority and took a bus home. As I walked through the door, the phone rang. My roommate Butch picked it up.

"He just walked in."

Butch handed me the phone. It was Candy.

"Come back," she said.

For the next couple of months, we pretended to be just coworkers at the office. We would leave work separately and meet at her apartment. At dinnertime, Candy's dinner consisted of two gigantic tumblers of scotch while I tried to make do with whatever else was around. I tried vodka, but recalling my weight gain and general disgust with drinking, I gave it up and left the drinking to her. Our nights, lasting into the early hours of the morning, consisted of sex, her drinking, and intermittent conversation and laughter. It was great except for what it was doing to my work schedule.

We would wake up late and rather than run to work, we'd stop to have breakfast as the evening before usually hadn't involved any food. This made me late for work. Since at this time, I usually worked late with Allen, never leaving at 6:00 with the others, I discounted my coming in late. However, the rest of the office began to resent it.

To soothe their feelings, Allen declared that anyone late to work would be fined $10. Since I was only making about $80 a week, it became a problem that I turned into a joke. My fines were eating up my salary. I finally told Allen that I could follow the order and be on time, but that I would no longer stay late. If he wanted 10:00 to 6:00 office hours from me, and I was penalized if I was late, then fine, I would placate the office. Allen relented, and the fine went away.

Candy and I continued our secret relationship. She took me to Coney Island, and we rode the Cyclone. She took me to a spot underneath the George Washington Bridge, and we made love in the dirt next to the access road. She took me to Soho, and while walking the streets spotted a painting at an outdoor art show. It was a picture of two people walking under an umbrella in the rain. We decided it represented us. It was unique, but the colors were a bit off. We didn't get it.

Then one night, buzzed on alcohol, she surprised me with an oil painting set with a few canvases. "Let's paint a picture that shows us together," she said. We took out the heart red oil paints and proceeded to create our masterpiece of true love. When we were finished, we stood back to admire our creation, which showed us wrapped in each other's arms in a passionate embrace. It was magnificent!

But the next morning, when we woke up and took another look at our work, we couldn't even tell what it was. It just looked like a mishmash of red oil paint on a canvas. Instead of a masterpiece, it was a master mess.

"You will find someone your own age, and you will move on," Candy kept telling me as our affair continued. I always replied that everything was great, and nothing in the world could change it. I was happy with her; there was no need to find someone else. She should stop worrying and just enjoy what we had.

As it turned out, it wasn't another woman who brought an end to our adventure, it was the Rolling Stones.

Mick Jagger and Keith Richards flew into New York on August 15, 1965. I was sent to a marina on the west side of New York City, where I was told we would be taking a boat cruise together around Manhattan.

We looked so young. Me, Mick, and Keith

Onboard ship, I met Mick and Keith for the first time. We were about the same age, so that seemed an immediate plus. I liked them both right away. Mick was smoother and more of a charmer while Keith struck me as a "real" guy, who wouldn't suffer fools.

Luckily, I wasn't born with the celebrity adoration, kiss-ass, or rumor-mongering genes. By now, I was used to working with artists and evaluated and related to people as human beings, not celebrities, so I soon connected with the future monsters of rock and their rolling cohorts. We talked for a while about school and our backgrounds and connected on our attitudes toward life.

The yacht pulled up to the dock near Shea Stadium, where the Beatles were scheduled to perform later that day. Mick, Keith, Allen, and I walked to the Beatles' dressing room entrance, which was crowded with well-wishers and celebrities. There were a couple of security guards, but they were surrounded by fans. Mick and Keith walked ahead; I followed and got past the guard. I heard Allen call out from behind me as the security guard stopped him, "Ronnie! Ronnie!" I turned around, looked directly at the guard and yelled, "He's with me!"

The guard let Allen through, and we were all in the Beatles' dressing room. We would laugh about my "He's with me" line many times later.

In the dressing room, I first met the Beatles, not knowing that I would be working with them in the future. After about an hour in this crazy zoo where we couldn't talk as there were so many people jammed into the small space, it was time for the Beatles to go on stage. We headed to the side of the stage where we stood leaning against a large chain-link fence to watch the show.

As the Beatles mounted the stage, the roar of the audience was louder than the sound I heard as a kid in Miami when the city was almost destroyed by Hurricane King. We could see that the Beatles were playing and singing, but all we heard was the screaming. We stood there for a while, realized we wouldn't be hearing any music that day, and left for our walk back to the yacht.

CHAPTER III

WILD HORSES

October 28, 1965: New York City, Hilton Hotel

Kicking off the 1965 tour, the Stones held a press conference at the Hilton Hotel in the Penthouse suite. After the event, I spent the night in Manhattan with Candy with the thought that the next day work would be getting back to normal. The Talent would be on the road and I could get back to my desk and adding machine.

This is a shot by Gered Mankowitz of Brian and Bill descending the penthouse staircase at the Hilton to join Mick, Keith, and Charlie at the microphones to meet the press.

Everything was as expected when I got to the office the next morning and sat down at my desk to continue my daily work. Even with the heightened action for the tour going on in the office, my responsibilities remained the same as the day wore on. That was until my uncle called me into his office around 3 o'clock.

"Ronnie, get packing," he said. "You're going on the road with the Rolling Stones, and you'll be leaving immediately. You'll represent me in the box office. Your job will be to collect the money and oversee the tour. You'll share a room with the tour photographer, and, for now, you are in charge of these two suitcases for Keith."

I was handed two standard Samsonite suitcases. When opened, one was a record turntable, and the other became a right and left speaker. While on the road, Keith would buy hundreds of records and make very good use of these suitcases.

I had a few hours to pack and get ready. But, although I lived in Newark, my clothes weren't there; they were at Candy's apartment on 71st in Manhattan. While this was geographically closer, the situation presented a problem—I didn't have a key to her apartment, and nobody in the office could find out about our affair.

Candy was in a closed-door meeting with Allen, Andrew Oldham, and the other tour planning people. Time was running out, and I was contemplating having someone get a note to her when Kenny Salinsky came out of the meeting and said that Candy had a letter for me. He handed me an envelope and went back to the meeting. I opened the envelope and found her apartment key. Many years later, Kenny told me that he had figured out at that moment I was living with Candy. "I could tell that the envelope had a key in it," he said, "but I never told anyone in the office."

When I got back to the office with my one suitcase, Jerry Brandt, the William Morris agent handling everything agency-wise for the tour, pulled me aside for a quick tutorial on dealing with promoters.

"Don't trust them!" he instructed me. "You have to check the ticket numbers to confirm the advance sales and box office sales." This was important as quite a lot of the dates were advertised as $5 advance and $8 at the door. If I didn't get to the box office in time to get the on-hand ticket numbers (the distinct number that identified each ticket), the promoter would be able to say that everything had been advance sales. I had my marching orders.

This was not only going to be my first tour, but my first airplane adventure as well. We were driven to a small airport, and I saw a little twin propeller airplane sitting on the tarmac.

We boarded the plane and as I sat nervously gripping the armrest, my knuckles turning white, Bill Wyman looked over and asked, "What's wrong?"

I told him about it being my first flight and Bill called over to the stewardess and explained to her that I was nervous. She sat down next to me, took my hand, gave it a squeeze, said that all would be fine, and held it as we took off, and I lost my flight virginity. Actually, I wasn't that scared; I was more excited, but I did milk the situation. My first flight, my first trip outside the United States, and oh yeah, I was with the Rolling Stones.

Part of the entourage was Bob Bonis, as the road manager, and on the bus with the other acts was Mike Gruber. Mike also acted as the advance man, traveling a day ahead of us. For different dates our promotions guy, Pete Bennett, showed up. The Stones referred to him as their "Mafia Promo Man."

The Stones also had their own personal road manager with them, the inimitable Ian "Stu" Stewart. Stu had originally been the band's piano player, but had been ejected at Andrew's suggestion because he didn't have the right image (and because six band members were too many). He stayed on as the band's driver, road manager, and conscience, and continued to play keyboards on their records. [1]

October 29: Montreal, Canada, Forum

It wasn't until we were at the airport ready to fly to Canada from NYC for the show in Montreal that Keith pulled me aside.

"Ronnie, I don't have my passport," he revealed. "I left it in my room!"

It was too late to go back to Manhattan to get the passport, so I had to use what I refer to as razzmatazz. The moment we arrived in Canada, I headed straight to the immigration desk and asked if I could present all the passports together, because we were running late. After glancing at the growing size of our party and assessing the potential melee, the officer agreed, and I went about gathering everyone's passports. With a lot of fast talking, I was able to deflect any accurate count of the people in relation to the number of passports. Keith strolled behind my back, shielded by one of the larger guys in our party, and sneaked onto the plane.

The minute we walked out of the airport in Montreal it began to snow, adding an eerie, almost magical atmosphere to our arrival. Maybe it was black magic, though, as that night's show did not go smoothly.

---

1   When the Stones were inducted into the Rock and Roll Hall of Fame in 1989, they requested Stewart's name be included

As soon as we arrived at the Montreal Forum for the show I went straight to the box office. I had a look at their invoice for the ordered printed tickets and did a quick audit of what was on hand and what was really advance sales. I asked the guy in the ticket booth if they had any cash on hand to cover any overages, and he said not to worry as they had cash in the box office safe. This instinctive questioning of the ticket takers would help me at later dates when promoters would say they didn't have the cash on hand to pay what they now owed.

I left the ticket booth and went backstage to the Stones' dressing room to hang out while they got ready to play. Keith asked for a piece of paper and began writing down a list of songs for that night's set. This would be a ritual at every venue. Whereas most other groups, including the Beatles, played the same songs in the same sequence night after night, the Stones would often change the set around, playing the songs in the order that felt right for that particular audience, city, or night.

Typical 1965 Set List
Everybody Needs Somebody to Love
Around and Around
Time Is on My Side
I'm Movin' On
Little Red Rooster
The Last Time
I'm All Right
Satisfaction
Route 66

Finally, it was time for them to go on stage and for me to deal with the box office, which had closed just before they were going on.

I didn't know what to expect on my first foray into the promoter's office. I was a numbers guy and I thought it would be simple. Something along the lines of, "You sold 10,000 tickets at $5 a ticket; that's $50,000. You paid the Stones $10,000, which is 20% and equals the terms of the deal. There is no overage due so thank you and good-bye."

Unfortunately, that was not going to be the case for any of the shows. I found out representing Allen Klein in the box office was going to be a more complicated proposition. Allen had removed comp (complimentary) tickets from the promoter agreements. "Comps" are the tickets promoters give to the press, friends, family, politicians, radio promotions, and so on, and the promoters were not charged for them. My uncle changed the contracts to forbid complimentary tickets for any of the Rolling Stones dates. There would always be a computation to get the money for the comp tickets that the promoter had given out, and this would always cause a confrontation.

That was the lesson I learned in my first box office.

I noticed that the promoter had deducted fifty-eight press and promotional tickets from the gross sales. Now, I would have to claim money from the promoter that he hadn't counted on paying. The promoter, who was about twice my age, resented this.

"I'm not giving you anything, you young punk!"

I pointed out the clause in the contract he had signed and once again demanded the money.

"How about I break your fuckin' arm instead?"

He relented and paid.

As I left the box office to go backstage I realized I didn't hear any music. I ran to an entrance to the arena, opened the door, and saw the place was going crazy. The fans were rioting and had surged to the front of the stage. I didn't see the band. I had to fight through the mob to get backstage. I pounded on the dressing room door and screamed in my recognizable voice, "It's me!" The door opened and once inside we barricaded the doors. I was told that the fans had rushed the stage, and everyone ran for their lives. It got so bad Stu had to chase some kid who was trying to steal Keith's guitar while someone else stole a drum from Charlie's drum kit.

We were trapped in the dressing room for a couple of hours before things quieted down enough for us to get out to the airport and head back to New York. Even then, I was worried that we wouldn't be able to get Keith back into the States without his passport. When we got to immigration in New York, I again tried my Montreal gambit, explaining that I represented the group and handing over a pack of passports. It worked. I still have the vision of Keith sneaking behind everyone else as the group passed through immigration.

The show would start like this:

And end like this:

Now I knew why they called it rock 'n' roll!

October 30: Ithaca, New York, Barton Hall, Cornell University (matinee)

There were other bands traveling with us: Patti Labelle & the Bluebells, the Rockin' Ramrods, the Vibrations, the Embers. Mike Gruber was hired as the road manager for the other bands, and traveled with them on the buses during short hops. For longer trips, they flew with us on the plane.

If Montreal was an example, then with the Ithaca afternoon date, I knew what to expect. That routine held true for most of the tour.

Every show was going to be a race to beat the clock, from the moment the

Stones got on stage to the minute they left.

Every show would be a confrontation with an angry promoter and a fight to get it all done on time.

Every show was short, and the promoters would be complaining about the amount of time the Stones were on stage. I told the Stones that they should try and play at least thirty minutes. Some of the shows were done in twenty-five minutes. Afterward, the promoters commented that they would put a guaranteed playing time into the agreements.

And every show brought another possibility with it: riots. The crowds got worked up to such a state of excitement that they wanted to get closer to the Stones. This led to their jumping on stage and grabbing the boys. This was something that always brought a quick end to the shows. I don't think they intended to hurt the Stones, just grab a piece of their clothes or hair as a souvenir. Nevertheless, being torn to shreds by fans, no matter how adoring, was not any Stone's idea of fame.

October 30: Syracuse, New York, War Memorial Hall (evening)

By the third show, I'd learned to keep an ear out for the music. If it stopped, that indicated something had gone wrong. So I always had to have one ear listening to the promoter complain about the agreement, and the other cocked for the sudden silence that signaled a riot in progress.

No matter what, I would collect the cash and deposit it in a bank as soon as I had the chance. Back then that task wasn't as simple as now. Banker's hours in those days were usually 9 to 4 PM weekdays, closed Sundays, and maybe open until noon on Saturday. There were many days I couldn't make it to a bank and had to lug around up to $30,000 in a raggedy brown briefcase. I wanted to make sure that I didn't look like I was carrying anything of value so my battered old briefcase fit the bill.

Another duty, no matter what, was to call my uncle in the morning to go over the receipts and events from the night before. He would ask, "Are the Stones happy? How is the audience? What are the expenses? What did the promoters say? Any problems? Call me tomorrow."

October 31: Toronto, Canada, Maple Leaf Gardens

It was a bumpy plane ride to Toronto, and the Vibrations, sitting in the back of the plane, got very sick. At the Maple Leaf Gardens show there were, again, fights and rioting. To aid in our escape, we sent out a decoy bus. The bus was supposed to drive as if we were hiding behind the seats and thereby divert the crowd. When the bus drove off, it was surrounded within seconds. We were told later that the driver was unable to pull forward and the crowd eventually pushed the bus over. We stayed in the dressing room for another couple of hours before it was safe to leave.

November 1: Rochester, New York, Memorial Auditorium

Sometimes before and after the shows I had to try and get one or more of the Stones to sit down and speak with disc jockeys or other radio show personalities to promote the tour and their album. The Stones hated this to a man. They created the music, and they played the music and didn't think they should have to, as they put it, "do commercials."

"Keith, I have DJ such and such from KWCA," I'd say. "He'd like to have a few words with you about the upcoming show. Here, take the phone."

"Let Bill talk to him; I'm busy," would be Keith's reply as he walked away to sit and strum his guitar. Bill would be nowhere in sight.

Gered captured one of the few times the boys didn't mind an interview and, not surprisingly, considering the attractive interviewer; Bill was front and center.

Things got even crazier in Rochester. The show was stopped after seven songs, and Brian was injured during the melee on stage.

The fans seemed to go to the shows to vent and gain their Satisfaction. When the lights went up, they had their own stage to perform on. I had thought that a darkened arena would be more conducive to the violence, but the opposite was proving to be true.

After the show, we flew to New Jersey. The limo picked us up from the airport there and started to drive us back to our hotel in Manhattan. The driver turned around and informed us that we would not be going back to the City Squire Hotel.

"What?!" I exclaimed.

He went on to explain that the management of the City Squire had packed up all our rooms and moved them, exactly as they were, to the Lincoln Square Motor Inn. After we'd left the City Squire for the show in Rochester, the management found they had a problem. Girls were offering to have sex with the hotel staff to gain admittance to the Stones' rooms. Rather than fire their entire staff, they chose to move us to another hotel.

When we got to the Lincoln Square Hotel, I went up to my new room and found a girl standing in the small window in my bathroom, looking like she was going to jump.

"What are you doing?" I asked. She said she was committing suicide since her boyfriend was cheating on her. Her boyfriend was a DJ, and she had come to the Stones' rooms to get even and decided to jump instead.

"I'm tired," I told her. "If you jump from my window, I will have to deal with the police all night long and not get any sleep. Go to someone else's room."

This seemed to make sense to her. She climbed down from the window and talked to me for about an hour before she left in a better frame of mind.

We had the next day off. Keith went out record shopping and bought hundreds of 45s. He bought all types of music and would sit in his room and play through all the records, one by one. I asked him why and he explained that there was nothing new in music; there are only so many chords and notes. The records, though, gave him ideas in different ways to present them.

Later that evening we went out to a couple of nightclubs. The Stones were personally invited by Steve Paul to his hot nightclub, The Scene. Most times the Stones ignored these invites, but decided to go to this one.

"The Scene" was, as its name implied, quite the scene. The place was packed. I was standing next to Keith and Brian. Next thing I knew Brian was getting into a fight with a guy next to us. In a flash, Keith grabbed the guy's arms and pinned them behind him. Just as fast, Brian picked up a large beer mug and smashed it in the guy's face. Faster still, we left "The Scene." I asked Brian why he hit the guy since Keith had him immobilized, and he said, "I didn't want him hitting me back if I hit him, and Keith took care of that, so I hit him."

November 3: Providence, Rhode Island, Auditorium

Having a fun time.

Once again, I was in the box office, one ear listening to what song was playing—or indeed if they were playing. Luckily, there were no problems at the Providence show, and I could leave the box office to enjoy a few minutes of music.

I headed to the back of the auditorium to listen to the songs and check out the reaction of the audience. The Stones had just started "Little Red Rooster," and I saw the look on the fans' faces. They seemed hypnotized.

Then the band moved on to "The Last Time" and I sensed a different vibe grow, as the audience related to their own last times.

Everything changed, as everything always did, when the Stones started "Satisfaction." The crowd was suddenly gripped by a wave of energy that sent me rushing backstage to be ready, in case they wanted to get closer to the Stones, and we had to get the hell out of there.

November 4: New Haven, Connecticut, Loews State Theater (two shows)

Patti LaBelle, Sarah Dash, Cynthia Birdsong (later to join the Supremes), and Nona Hendricks made up Patti LaBelle and the Bluebells. I had a crush on Sarah Dash, or "Inch" as she was nicknamed, and sat next to her on the plane whenever I could. Patti LaBelle usually sat next to us.

Often, to pass time on the flights, I would sit and write imaginary love letters or poems. Back in school, I had found out that if I mastered a couple of drawings (a horse's head with the mane, a boat, a jet plane, and a weird small creature) and wrote poetry, I could grab a girl's attention as they looked over my shoulder at what I was doing. Like any guy, I craved the attention of girls. As I wrote these poems or did my drawings, I noticed Patti was making notes. I asked her what she was doing, and she said she was copying my love letters to use as her own. She bragged that she sent the same one to all her boyfriends.

November 5: Boston, Massachusetts, Garden

Another great night without any hardcore events other than the fans throwing stuff on the stage, like teddy bears.

November 6: New York City, Academy of Music

Andrew Oldham joined my uncle for the Academy of Music show. By this time, the tour operations and shows were under control. Most of the problems that had surfaced in the early shows had been taken care of. We had become a well-oiled rock 'n' roll touring machine. The minute Andrew got there, though, I knew it was going to be a different situation. He immediately began causing problems.

Artists' managers and artists' lawyers both seem to have a desire to demonstrate their worth to the artists they represent. This is best accomplished by creating problems and then solving them, thus showing how indispensable they are.

Andrew's first comment at this show was, "The stage rug has to be cleaned!" He then pointed out a few other issues, and I was soon dashing about trying to rectify these complaints.

Andrew in "get it together" mode.

My uncle jumping in to help protect the Stones from the fans who leaped on stage. It was always personal to Allen.

November 6: Philadelphia, Pennsylvania, Convention Hall

Before the date, I had met with the promoter and learned that he was an Orthodox Jew. Because of this, he told me that I would not be able to be in touch with him during the Saturday show, but not to worry. I worried anyway, but we were able to settle any of the minor problems we encountered.

We returned to Manhattan that evening, and Mick and Keith invited me to go to a club with them in Harlem. We took a limo to Harlem and descended some steps into a small basement club. The place was packed! We were escorted through a sea of black faces, ours being the only white ones, to a small cocktail table in the middle of the room.

As a white guy, I felt I got a pass since I was with Mick Jagger and Keith Richards, and they were definitely recognized. Everyone was seated elbow to elbow. Once settled, a pint bottle of whiskey was passed to Mick from the people sitting next to us. There were no glasses and I didn't see any waiters, just the people in the audience passing small bottles of alcohol from table to table. Mick took a swig, passed it to Keith. When Keith passed it to me, I put the bottle straight to my mouth and took a swig.

Meanwhile, there were sounds from the stage as the band's horn section began warming up. An announcer came out, and the next thing I knew, there was James Brown. This was the 1965 James Brown. Brown was at the top of his form, and I was lucky to see such an amazing show. On stage, Brown worked his ass off with his legs and feet moving at the speed of light.

I think he collapsed to the floor of the stage at least eight times in feigned exhaustion. The first couple of times an assistant would come out, drape a cape over James, and partially lift him to his feet before James would come back to life and start another song. About the seventh time, two men would begin to carry him off, only to have James once again revive himself and perform another song to the screaming audience. Nobody wanted to see him leave the stage. He was pure magic.

November 7: Newark, New Jersey, Symphony Hall/Mosque Theater (two shows)

After the Newark show, we were staying at the City Squire in Times Square. Gered Mankowitz, the photographer, and I had the room next to Brian's. There was a knock on the door and Mick and Keith came in giggling mischievously. "Bob Dylan is coming to see Brian," they told me. Keith took an empty water glass from my bathroom and put it to his ear and against the thin wall separating our room from Brian's. Then Mick picked up my room phone and placed a call to Brian's room.

"Mr. Zimmerman for Mr. Jones," Mick said to the operator in a fake American accent.

The phone rang in Brian's room, and Mick and Keith were giggling as Mick attempted to carry out a conversation with Brian in his best imitation of Dylan's voice.

"Mr. Jones, I love your music, and you look beautiful on stage. You should be the leader of the Rolling Stones," was all Mick could get out before he fell to the floor laughing.

We could hear Brian screaming from the other side of the wall. "Leave me the fuck alone! I know it's you, Mick!"

After the teasing, Keith asked me to join him for clothes shopping. He had just received a royalty check and was basking in the pleasure of having some money in his pocket. Andrew Oldham recommended a men's clothing shop, R. Meladandri, and that's where we went. Keith spotted a colorful array of button down dress shirts. He picked up a bright yellow one, a dark green one, and a dark blue one and said to the clerk, "I want one of every color. I'll take the shelf." "Absolutely," said the salesman. Caught up in the moment I walked over and took a look at one of the shirts. I held up a finger and was about to say I'd take a couple when I looked at the price. I passed.

Keith's time at the crap table of life was starting to pay off.

November 9: New York City

I was back in the office on November 9 taking care of business during a break in the tour when, just after 5 PM, the power went out. We stalled around the office wondering what was happening, until Allen told us to go upstairs to the 48th floor and have dinner at the restaurant on the top of the Time-Life Building. As the power was out, we were served whatever was going to go bad and didn't have to be cooked.

We ate by candlelight, hoping and waiting for the power to come back on. It didn't and after a couple of hours, we were told to walk down to the street. Yes, walk down 48 flights in the pitch black. As our small group entered the stairwell, we learned that Candy had an insane fear of the dark. She was screaming and screaming. I wrapped my arms around her and tried my best to console her, but I had a very scared young woman by my side as we made our way slowly down the darkened stairs guided by candlelight, matches, lighters, and the security of the handrail.

When we got to the street I whispered to her if she wanted me to take her home since she was so freaked, but she said, "No, go to the hotel."

When I arrived at our hotel, I made my way up the stairs to my room and found Brian, Bob Dylan, and some large guy that I think may have been Dylan's bodyguard. Dylan was strumming a guitar, and they seemed to be jamming. The room was illuminated by a candle sitting on a dish in the middle of the bed. After greeting everyone I went to check out some of the other rooms where various parties were inevitably going on.

When I returned to my room with Gered later, it was empty and there were burn marks and soot on the sheet where the candle had been.

November 10: Raleigh, North Carolina, Reynolds Coliseum

The flights on our small charter plane were fun when the flying conditions were calm. When it wasn't a long enough flight to play cards or Monopoly, I would sit next to Sarah Dash of the Bluebells, and we would chat. Sarah was the first black girl whom I was attracted to. Her voice was amazing, and she was a doll.

It was in Raleigh that we experienced a dose of real down-home 1960s Southern racism. Sarah and I decided to stroll around the town. She wanted to do some window shopping. We stopped in front of a shoe store window. Sarah was shorter than me, and I welcomed the opportunity to drape my arm over her shoulder as she looked at the shoes. Then, suddenly, somebody smacked my arm, knocking it off her shoulder. I spun around and saw a couple of old guys quickly moving on, muttering something under their breath. Sarah was used to it; I wasn't. The Civil Rights Act was enacted in July 1964; it was now only a little over a year later.

It got worse.

When we got backstage the cops warned us that the black acts weren't allowed in the Stones' dressing room, nor were the whites allowed in the "coloreds'" dressing rooms. The Stones would have none of this. They immediately went to Patti Labelle and the Bluebells' dressing room and then on to the Vibrations.

I saw the cops, glowering with their billy clubs in hand, and I cornered the promoter.

"Control the cops," I demanded. "Get them out front to set up security. Keep them away from the talent."

November 11: NBC Studios, New York City Hullabaloo TV show

The Hullabaloo Show opened with footage from the Stones feature film that would later be entitled Charlie Is My Darling. I met Brenda Lee backstage and felt that she was flirting with me. I figured it was because I was with the bad boys. I had loved her voice and was flattered, but that was it.

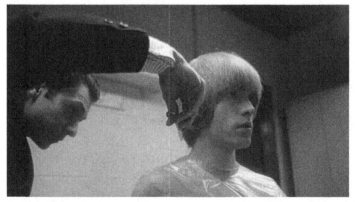

Photo by tour photographer Gered Mankowitz from the Hullabaloo Show. Brian getting a haircut before the show.

November 13: Washington, D.C., Coliseum

In D.C., we had a quick bite at a hotel restaurant. Afterward, I stepped away from our table to go to the bathroom, and a man grabbed my arm and asked me for an autograph.

"I'm not in the band," I told him. "You don't want my autograph."

"I don't care! You're with them; I want your autograph!"

I protested further, but he didn't relent, so rather than prolong the ordeal I scribbled "Mickey Mouse" in my illegible scrawl. They never asked anyone from the group for a signature.

This would not be the last time that would happen. To all you autograph collectors, including those local politicians who insisted on autographed Rolling Stones photos, pushy promoters, the press—all those who received autographed photos during the '65 thru '70 tours—I signed all the Stones' signatures on the majority of the photos given out. They had no patience backstage for signing photos, so rather than fight the myriad requests, they gave me their photos signed the way they wanted them signed, and I copied them as best I could. With the Stones, the music came first.

November 13: Baltimore, Maryland, Civic Center

As we were leaving the Civic Center, Stu came over to me and was really upset. The dulcimer that Brian had just bought had been stolen, and he wanted more security for the equipment and the group. I told him that we could not afford additional security, but I would contact the promoters and have them provide better protection.

November 14: Knoxville, Tennessee, Civic Coliseum Auditorium

If time permitted, after I left the box office, I would walk through the audience from the last row to the first, up and down the aisles. I wanted to get a feel of the fans' reactions to the Stones, to the songs, and to the performances of the other groups.

Each of the band members had their own individual following of fans. There were the fans of Mick, the lead singer with those big lips and gyrations; fans of Keith, who were more of the bad-boy lead guitar fans; fans of Brian, the pretty-boy artistically driven musician; fans of Bill Wyman, the quiet, stone-faced, intense bass player (Bill got more women than anybody, mostly because he wanted to); and fans of Charlie, the drummer—drummers always have their own following.

When I shared these observations, the Stones would tell me to shut up. They didn't care—that was their attitude. In many ways, the Rolling Stones was just a job for them. They got up on the stage and went to work, and when they left the stage, they were individuals again.

November 15: Charlotte, North Carolina, Coliseum

The Bluebells had a manager/chaperone who traveled with them, Mr. Montague, whose responsibility was to protect them from the untoward advances of men. In most cases, men meant the Rolling Stones—and me. It was interesting to sit at dinner with the Bluebells and watch as the boys tried to make moves on them. Bill would try at Nona and Cynthia to no avail, as far as I know.

Sarah and I liked each other. I would dream of kissing her. Then, one night we met in the hotel hallway; she had gotten out of her room, away from the watchful eyes of Mr. Montague, under the pretext of getting ice. Next to her room was a door leading to the staircase exit for our floor. I met her at that door; we opened it, stepped into the stairway, and nervously we kissed. It's interesting, the things we remember and can still feel.

Sarah later told me I was her first Jewish boyfriend. She was my first African American kiss and girlfriend.

November 17: Memphis, Tennessee, Mid-South Coliseum

After the show, we flew to Miami for a stay at the Fontainebleau Hotel. It was a chance for the group to get some R & R—rest and recreation, for a change, as opposed to rock 'n' roll. The hotel rented Sea-Doos, small Jet Ski boats that a single person could sit on, like a motorcycle.

Keith, Brian, Gered, Anita, and I hopped aboard our little seacraft and followed the rental agency's recommendation to proceed about a hundred yards offshore where the boundaries were marked by two buoys. We raced around the buoys peacefully, for a while—until Anita decided to play bumper boats.

Suddenly, she came barreling toward me and rode up and over my left foot, at the same time smashing into my boat. She continued this game, chasing a few other riders. Needless to say, the boat operators were upset and whistled us in. We heard them scream that we would shortly be running out of gas and should head for shore.

We turned our boats around and headed in. As I arrived on shore, I noticed that the agency guys were running around blowing their whistles and screaming. It seems that Brian had not heeded the warning and was heading straight out to sea. They sent a motor boat after him and caught up with him just after his gas ran out. He was sitting on the Sea-Doo, bobbing up and down on the ocean swell, staring up into the sky.

When they got Brian to shore I asked him what he was doing. "I was following the birds," he said. Later, I learned that he and Anita had taken LSD that day, which maybe explains things.

At about 11:00 PM I got a call from the hotel front desk saying that there were complaints about screaming and the sound of fighting from Brian and Anita's room. The hotel sent a manager to investigate. He'd knocked on their door; they hadn't answered; could I please do something? My knowledgeable answer would have been "no" but I assuaged with "I'll see what I can do." I called Brian's room.

"Brian, I'm getting complaints from the front desk about yelling coming from your room," I said.

"We're just having fun," he answered.

That wouldn't be the last time a hotel front desk would call about the yelling coming from Brian's room when Anita was with him.

November 20: Shreveport, Louisiana, State Fair Youth Center

On these earlier tours in '65 and '66, the costs offset any profit from ticket sales. In some cases, the costs were more than the profit. One of the largest expenses was Charlie Watts' phone bill. While Mick, Keith, Brian, and Bill were out doing "things" during the tour, Charlie would be in his room on the phone with his wife, Shirley, back home in England. International phone rates in those days were astronomical, and the cost of these lengthy long-distance phone conversations far exceeded Charlie's share of the income. I would tease Charlie, but always envied his devotion. Charlie and Shirley are an example of true love, still together after everything the world, fame, rock 'n' roll, and The Rolling Stones could throw at them. That's a rock 'n' roll triumph and an example for more to copy.

November 21: Fort Worth, Texas, Will Rogers Memorial Center

The only way to get on stage at the Memorial Center was via a trip down the center aisle of the auditorium. The fans would never have let the group make it to the stage in one piece so security improvised, and an armored truck was provided to get them to and from the stage.

Armored car delivery

November 21: Dallas, Texas, Memorial Auditorium

We had a day off and Keith suggested that since we were in Dallas, we should go horseback riding. I loved the idea and found a place to rent horses about thirty-five miles out of town.

The stable insisted that we have one of their people as our guide. They selected a cute, young woman. Unfortunately for her, we didn't want a sedate trail ride. We wanted to gallop, to play cowboy. The landscape was desert, dotted with a lot of brush, large cacti punctuated by small hills made up of jagged black rock. We galloped together until the girl told us she had to stop and go to the bathroom.

She wagged her finger at us. "Don't you guys dare move. I will just be a short distance away."

She rode away for about fifty yards and then got off her horse. After she had squatted down behind a large bush, we counted to ten…

"Giddyap! Giddyap!" we yelled, and pushed our horses forward, charging toward where she was squatting.

Our defense for this course of action was that, obviously, we were the cavalry coming to the rescue of a damsel in distress. She didn't see it that way, pulled up her pants, got back on her horse, and said, "Time to go back."

A plus for the Dallas concert was that we were staying in a top hotel in Dallas, and it had a renowned chef in the kitchen. The Stones had a large suite, and we gathered there for lunch after an exhausting day. We had ordered almost everything on the menu and after finishing eating, we became giggly and began piling all the leftover food in one big mound in the middle of the table on top of a hamburger bun.

Brian liked a sunny-side up egg on his hamburger, and this led to all of us experimenting with variations on this theme. Everyone was suddenly a chef and added their own chosen garnish to this new food creation. Everything that was on the table became part of this monstrosity. The result was a giant hamburger with everything on it, including prunes, very sophisticated and considering what artisan things some hamburgers have become, very much ahead of its time.

The Dallas promoter had arranged for the local chapter of the Rolling Stones fan club to have a visit while we were eating. This chapter was headed up by someone's domineering mother who walked around the table regarding us like animals in a cage, all the while chattering away to the fan-club members as if we weren't there. The mother finally asked if there was something special that the Stones liked to eat, and they remarked that they loved the hamburgers, especially the rare and yet highly renowned Prune Burger. Without a pause, the woman picked up the food mess that we'd created and took a big bite to show her troop that she was eating what the Stones ate. Mommy dearest.

November 23: Tulsa, Oklahoma, Assembly Center

A lot of my friends had gone to law school in Tulsa, and they were lined up by the stadium door entrance. This was the time of the Vietnam War, and a lot of young men went on to law school simply to avoid the draft. In my opinion, this had a far-reaching effect on American society. This large number of young men who attended law school to avoid the draft had to have something to do after they graduated, so they became lawyers and started this country on its course to becoming the world's most litigious society. All these draft-avoiding lawyers had to make money somehow, so they started suing everyone.

November 24: Pittsburgh, Pennsylvania, Civic Arena

Memories of dancing to Dick Clark's American Bandstand brought a smile to my face when I saw the Pittsburgh date was shared with Dick Clark's Caravan of Stars. With the Byrds, Bo Diddley, and Paul Revere and the Raiders, it was a great show. It was also a scary show, for the Stone you'd least expect to be attacked: Charlie Watts.

I was on the left side of the stage, behind the curtain, watching the show, when a quick movement at the back of the stage caught my eye. One moment, I saw Charlie and the next, he was gone. A curtain covering an entrance at the back of the stage was closing. In front of it sat an empty drum kit. The stage was built against a large hall entranceway. The drum riser was about three feet from the stage floor. Some girls got backstage and had climbed up behind Charlie. They grabbed him, pulled him off his stool, and disappeared behind the curtain. They were as surprised as Charlie and when they hit the ground, they ran off. Everything stopped until Charlie climbed back, and the show went on.

November 26: Detroit, Michigan, Cobo Hall

We would often pull out of the arena in our limo and find a line of cars waiting for our exit. It's in these situations that your limo driver matters the most. Some of our drivers got upset when they saw they were being followed and would try to escape the pursuing fans. The driver would go faster, and the fans behind us would go faster.

Depending on our mood, it was either, "You gonna let that little kid beat you?" or "Take it easy! Don't get us killed racing these kids."

When people get a hit of adrenaline, they seem to get superpowers. You have no idea how strong a teenage girl can be with all that adrenaline. After a wild, mad chase to the airport, we got out of the limo, and a girl who had been with a group that was chasing us ran over and grabbed the middle post between the front and rear door of the limousine to avoid being pulled away from us. It took five big men to pry her hands off that post.

On another occasion, as we got to our charter airplane, a large group of fans who had followed us grabbed Mick just as he was about to climb up the drop-down stairway to the plane. We kept screaming at Mick to protect himself as we battled through the fans. Mick began assuming comical karate poses and flailing the air. As he couldn't hurt a fly, his efforts at intimidation were to no avail. Security finally pulled the girls off Mick, but he did lose some clothes and hair.

Pursuing fans weren't the only problems we encountered while traveling in limousines. One time a Lincoln limo was taking us to our hotel, and we stopped at a red light. Brian was in the middle seat in the back, and I was sitting on his right. Suddenly, he reached over me, grabbed the door handle, and began climbing over me to get out of the car.

"Brian! We have a show! Stay here!" I screamed, imagining a Brian-less Rolling Stones show.

"Don't worry, I'll be back!" shouted Brian, as he hopped out of the car. "I have to see Jim McGuinn. He's in town with the Byrds." And true to his word Brian made it back in time for the show. Just.

Time to go on stage. Mick, Keith, Charlie, and Bill were walking out of the dressing room when I felt a tug on my elbow. Brian pulled me to the side and whispered, "Please watch out for me. I think someone dosed me with acid [LSD]." And then he walked out the door. I watched him, figuring it was 50/50 on whether someone dosed him, or he took it himself. It didn't matter; there were no problems during the show and after the show Brian went directly to his room. We didn't see him until the next day for the sound check.

November 28: Chicago, Illinois, Arie Crown Theater, McCormick Place (2 shows)

Sometimes when we arrived in a city, we got a police motorcycle escort from the airport to our hotel and then after the show back to the airport. These "escorts" were usually thrilling, harrowing events. The motorcycle escort would leapfrog intersection to intersection to stop traffic. The minute we went through a light, that officer would jump on his motorcycle and speed up to pass us to get to another intersection, past the one where another officer was holding off traffic. These guys were flying by at way over 100 miles an hour.

When we weren't going over 100 miles an hour, games were a good way to ward off the boredom of travel. To while away time on the plane, we played cards and Monopoly. I don't recall that we ever finished a game of Monopoly. Nor did money play a part in the card games; just the teasing and usual guy banter took place.

Brian and I at a game of Monopoly

Eating on the plane wasn't a pleasure. No catered dining for us on that tour—we got airplane food. Our charter service picked up our meals at the airports where we landed. They used the same food and catering services the commercial flights used. Only The Vibrations had a cure for the bland, plastic-covered, plastic-tasting food. They carried hot sauce with them, and no matter what they were served, they covered it with that.

November 29: Denver, Colorado, The Coliseum

When we arrived in Denver the governor of Colorado declared November 30 "Rolling Stones Day." It was par for the course. The Rolling Stones received a lot of "keys to the city." They would have a meet and greet with the local politician, and he would declare it a "Rolling Stones Day" and give them a key.

Keith, Charlie, and I went horseback riding in Denver. Gered took pictures of that day:

"Is this the posse or is this the gang?"

November 30: Phoenix, Arizona, Veterans Memorial Coliseum

We had time in Phoenix to shop and take care of sundry things. I got back to my motel room and was sitting on my bed next to an end table going over our schedule when I heard a weird sound. I looked around and noticed a small hole had suddenly appeared along the baseboard.

"Keith, what the hell are you doing?" I yelled through our adjoining room door.

"Testing a Derringer I just got."

"Keith! You just shot a bullet into my room! You could have killed me!"

"I couldn't kill you," he yelled back. "I shot it into the wall just a few inches off the floor. The worst would be I shot your ankle."

December 3: Sacramento, California, Memorial Auditorium (2 shows)

I was in the box office going over the numbers with the promoter when suddenly the music filtering into the office from the stage stopped. Another crowd riot, I surmised, and ran out to see what was going on.

However, there didn't seem to be a riot. Instead, I noticed a look of fear and shock in people's eyes. I got backstage as fast as I could and was told that Keith had been electrocuted. I got a hold of Stu, and he told me that Keith's guitar had touched the microphone stand, it wasn't grounded, and he was knocked unconscious. The medical people revived him. They said that Keith would be fine. Keith was upset, but anxious to get on the stage.

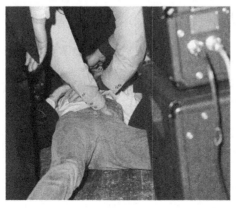

I don't know if it was because of Keith's brush with death or something else, but after all had quieted down, and we were back at our motel, Mick asked me to sit and have a chat with him in his room.

"Ronnie, do you think I should marry Chrissie?" he asked me, referring to his girlfriend Chrissie Shrimpton.

Stunned, I replied, "I don't know anything about the two of you together, but I do know one thing about marriage that I can give you my opinion on: Don't get married here in California, you have to split everything if you get divorced!"

December 5: San Diego, California, Community Concourse, Convention Hall

There were no fans at our hotel when we arrived in San Diego. Bill called my room, and he was upset. He needed to get laid. He said he had been on the phone with some local fans, but they wouldn't be at the hotel for hours, if at all. He couldn't wait. He wanted to get a cab and go looking for a hooker, and he wanted me to join him on his quest.

We got a cab and after a couple of awkward minutes of obtuse, but obvious, discussion, the cab driver revealed that he might know a girl and drove us nearby to meet her on a corner. She leaned into the passenger-side window, noticed how harmless we were, and asked Bill if he ever had a toothpaste blow job.

"No," Bill answered quickly, "but I'm willing to try."

December 5: Los Angeles, California, Sports Arena (evening)

The Los Angeles Sports Arena was the last date of the tour. We ran from the limo to the back entrance with the fans in pursuit because the driver didn't know where to go. A cop outside the stage door grabbed Brian by the hair, screaming at him, "No fans allowed!"

As the suit-wearing guy, I yelled at the cop, "He's in the band!"

The cop let go of Brian and whacked me with his night stick. "You're not in the band!"

The band went on, did a great show to a responsive LA audience, and….

Just like that, the tour was over.

CHAPTER IV

PAINT IT BLACK

Brian signed my tour book with a personal poem. I loved that he took the time. I loved the Star of Hawkeye—his compliment to me as a Jewish guy with balls…

Recam, Redeye,
Hawks, Lap,
and Shooting Moon
may your soul rot
in Shit

Keith Richard

there is a man who also
sings with his fingers
bitten tho' they may be
they are not so bitten
that they don't see the
black and white
and the up and down of
our lives
that politicians play with

keith
richard

Keith signed my tour book referencing my sophomoric lessons. He also drew a figure
representing someone "shooting a moon" on his guitar.

If anyone were to lay odds after the tour, I am sure that all the money would have been on the Rolling Stones corrupting the short, chubby little Jewish guy who grew up in Miami. Judging by what Keith and Brian wrote in my tour book, it was a two-way street. Maybe the obscenities they scrawled were their way of acknowledging the tawdry, childish stuff I had represented and the fact that they got the humor. Or it could have been them jumping into the sophomoric prank pool. We didn't influence one another; we just shared a common distaste for convention. Convention was boring; it still is.

With the tour over, everyone was planning on what to do next. The captain of our airplane charter told me that he was heading back to Florida and to let him know if any of us wanted a ride. He could drop us off anywhere along the route. I asked everyone. Keith said he wanted to go on an overnight horseback camping trip in Scottsdale, Arizona. He was in touch with a ranch there, and they would take care of everything. Keith invited Gered and me—or at least we were the ones who wanted to go. Our charter captain agreed to drop us off.

Keith brought with him a custom-made Colt.45 that he borrowed from record producer Lou Adler. When we arrived in Scottsdale, we went to a western outfitting and gun store where we duded up for our adventure. We bought Winchester rifles, chaps, and cowboy hats—black for Keith and me, white for Gered. Unfortunately, I didn't buy cowboy boots; instead I had my Bally loafers, which were not the best choice for the wilderness, as I soon learned.

A shot by Michael Roberts from Black Star

Next we headed for the ranch in Scottsdale where Keith had made arrangements for our adventure. There we were introduced to our cowboy guide and told that he was the person the movie studios went to when filming cowboy movies in Arizona, specifically John Wayne movies, and I believe he also worked with John Ford. He had the grizzled, sun-worn face of a real cowboy.

We were given horses to choose from and mounted up. A while into our ride we had to cross a creek that was about thirty feet wide and only a couple of feet deep. I rode my horse into the creek and he stopped and started pawing the water. I looked over to our guide and asked, "What's going on with my horse?"

"He's going to take a roll in the water," he replied.

Immediately I tried to get my horse to move forward, but instead he dropped down on his side and took a roll in the shallow water. I managed to jump off, but so much for my Bally shoes.

Later, we learned that our steeds were voice-trained horses for feature films. You could say, "Back up," and the horse would back up; the same with "stop" and "go."

Gered, Keith, our cowboy guide and Me -shot by Michael Roberts from Black Star

After a couple of hours riding, we stopped to take a rest and play cowboy. We tied up our horses and tried out our Winchesters, using our hats as targets. Instead of being afraid of getting shot, we were more afraid that our horses would run away. Keith took out the Colt.45, fired it once, and it jammed. We went back to the Winchesters: pump and fire.

I love this shot that Gered Mankowitz took and was surprised and pleased to find that it was used inside the Rolling Stones "More Hot Rocks (Big Hits & Fazed Cookies)" album cover.

As a kid who grew up with great cowboy films like *High Noon*, pumping a Winchester rifle and aiming and firing at the imagined bad guys was a fantasy fulfilled: it was every kid's BB gun at Christmas. I think it felt the same for Keith.

We rode the entire day and finally got to a location set up for us with tents, a fire, and a chuck wagon. We sat around the fire and ate food that tasted amazing. It was probably just beans, but any food eaten while camping or in the wild always seems to taste better.

Too tired to care that Keith had the rifle pointed at me!

Sitting around the campfire, we talked about our adventure before crashing into our tents for a sleep that was ended early in the morning by the sound of a gunshot. Startled, we jumped from our tents to find our guide with a gun in his hand.

"What happened?" we asked.

"A bobcat was stealing our bacon, so I took a shot at it," said our guide.

We saddled up and rode back to the ranch and reality.

From the ranch, we drove straight to the Phoenix airport to take a commercial flight home. We didn't shower or change clothes and went covered in dust, dirt, and cactus needles. We checked in at the ticket counter and were told that we couldn't check our rifles, but they would carry them on board for us and leave them outside the pilot's cabin. Rifles leaning against the wall next to the pilot's cabin are a sight I don't think anyone will see again.

By now, everyone in the world knows how durable Keith Richards is, not only for the music he has helped create, but also for his ability to survive heroin addiction—or "the big boy" as he sometimes called it. I don't know why Keith invited me or Gered horseback riding and camping with him that day, and I never asked. We were a poster of opposites: Gered, an artist, a photographer with an eye, a gentle, sweet guy; Keith, an artist, a guitar player who wrote songs and created sounds that captivated audiences; and me, a sarcastic, joking, dirty-minded, number-loving accountant. I think what keeps Keith alive when those around him are dropping from the same indulgences is all the life he has experienced.

Gered said to me recently, "It makes me laugh how Jewish you and I look, in spite of the setting and the chaps, and dear Keith looks like Billy the Kid!"

CHAPTER V

RIDE ON, BABY

Returning from the '65 tour, I went to my apartment in New Jersey and didn't spend another night with Candy, until ten years later. I returned to an office that was getting ready for the Christmas and New Year's holiday break. I was in bliss; not only had I survived my first tour representing my uncle on the road, I was rewarded with a raise and a $400 Christmas bonus. I couldn't wait to spend it. I bought a gold watch.

With the start of the New Year, I was back at my desk doing royalty breakdowns for the different recording artists and independent record companies Allen represented. After being on the road with the Stones, and in control of my own destiny, I had to step back into the accounting role. Those days were filled with numbers on pale green worksheets and the never-ending division of a two-cent royalty between the writers of the songs and their publishers. My only contact with the Stones was as Allen's intermediary in sending telexes and money to them at Allen's behest.

One day a large, brown-paper-wrapped oblong box was delivered to my desk. It had my name and office address on it. I didn't recognize the return address and had no idea what it could be. I opened it to find a large black cape with a blood-red silk lining and high collar: a Dracula cape. I put it to the side of my desk. Three days later, Keith Richards stopped by and asked, "Did you get the cape I had sent to you?"

"I didn't know who sent it, but I would never throw out a Dracula cape," I said, handing him the box.

He opened it, pulled out the cape, and swirled it over his shoulders, making menacing poses with a big smile on his face. During this time, I learned an interesting lesson from my uncle. I was writing up the ABKCO expenses when I noticed that his limo driver bought new tires every six months and always paid cash for them.

I sat down with my uncle and told him, "Your driver is screwing you. He's probably getting a kickback from the tire guy or not even buying new tires."

Allen looked at me and said, "Good."

"Good?"

"At least I know where he is stealing from me. If I stopped letting him 'get tires' he would have to find another way to steal from me. I can accept this."

It was Monday, March 7, 1966. Allen told me to get on a plane for a one-day trip to Los Angeles. I was to go straight from the airport to the RCA recording studios and take the Stones to a doctor's office for an insurance policy physical. If the trip to the doctor ran late, I could spend the night and return the next morning. I took a change of clothes on a hanger, threw it over my shoulder, and headed off to the airport.

I went directly from LAX (Los Angeles airport) to RCA Hollywood recording studios on Sunset Boulevard. There I met the Stones and hung around listening to them finalizing their recording session, while stressing the point that we had to go to the doctor's office.

The boys in the studio with Ian Stewart, ever unsmiling and always with a job in mind, looking on. This was the Rolling Stones, the original group, caught together by Gered Man-kowitz.

Getting them ready to leave together was not an easy task as they were in a recording studio mindset and didn't want to be bothered with a touch of reality such as going to the doctor.

After their physicals, we went back to the studio where I stayed and listened.

Anyone who has not been to a recording studio may have this romantic image of how music is created. The reality, for an observer, is actually rather mundane. You sit and listen; they record; they talk to the engineer and producer. You sit and listen; they lay down a guitar track; they talk to the engineer and producer. You sit and listen, and so on.

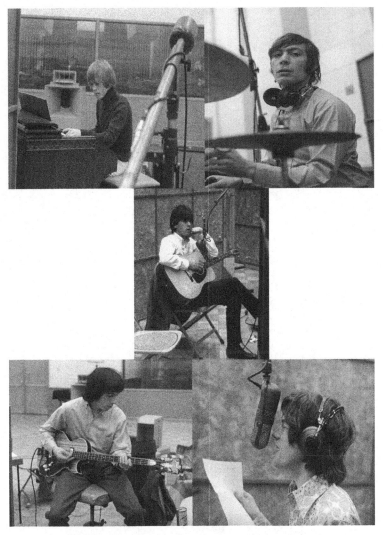

The only interesting part is watching the engineer at the control panel. All the lights, slides, levers, knobs, and other components of the control panel give you the ability to make believe you are watching the pilot of an airplane. Keith liked to sit there and work with the engineer.

There's no real excitement until you arrive at the finished song.

I sat and listened as they laid down a couple of tracks. Keith would play a bit. They would listen. Bill would play a bit, and they would listen. The creative process is not fast, as I learned in this first session with the Stones.

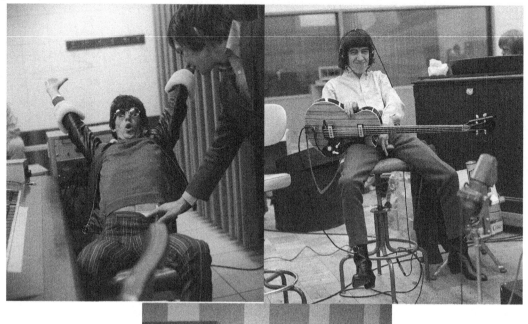

Sometimes the monotony got to everyone.

I left them at about 1 AM. I had reported to Allen earlier that the task was done, and since it was late, I checked into a hotel for the night and would catch the first flight back to New York.

I met a girl while at the recording studio. She was in the hallway, and we had chatted. Later, she went with me to the hotel. We spent the night, and she drove me to the airport in the morning.

About two weeks after I was back, Allen called me into his office.

"Ronnie, I accidentally opened this telegram addressed to you," he said, while I thought, "Yeah, sure! Why wait two weeks if it was an accident?"

He handed me the telegram, and it was from the girl, saying, "It was great meeting you and spending the night with you! Call when you come to LA again. Love…"

As I walked out of his office, Allen called after me, "When did you find the time?"

Six months passed. And then I was told that I was going on the road with the Rolling Stones again. This time I knew what to expect—the unexpected.

The '66 Tour Set List
Not Fade Away
The Last Time
Paint It Black
Stupid Girl
Lady Jane
The Spider and the Fly
Mother's Little Helper
Get Off
Of My Cloud
19th Nervous Breakdown
(I Can't Get No) Satisfaction
No Encores

By now, the Stones and I knew each other. They knew that I had their best interests at heart and would fight for them. These things are important to a celebrity. They want people who accept them for themselves and don't want something from them. ("I love you. Can you get me a screen test?") I didn't want anything from anyone, and I didn't judge.

In preparation for this tour, we used an advance man to assist the tour manager. His job was to get to the hotels days or hours before us, get the hotel rooms and keys sorted, and take care of any other problems that arose before our arrival. We wanted to walk up to the hotel desk, grab an envelope that had our name, room number, and key, and head off to the room.

At the start of this tour I asked Mick if there was anything I could do to help them while I was waiting for them to go on stage. He suggested that I try to find the lighting guy for the show and ask him to put a tight red spotlight on him when he was singing "Lady Jane." That was the entirety of lighting requests for the 1966 tour.

June 24: Lynn, Massachusetts, Manning Bowl

When we got to the Manning Bowl, we saw kids on a hill fighting with the police. The minute we got out of the limo we were hit with a horrible smell that burned our eyes. That was my first taste of tear gas.

Rioting, tear gas, and police; Lynn had it all, and it was only the first show.

One of the common tour problems that could never get sorted out was the limo drivers and their unpredictable grasp of directions. Arrivals were not the problem. We would get into the airports very late or very early in the morning, usually around 2:00 AM on the average. Those drivers would take us to the hotel without any difficulty.

Getting to the venue for the show was a different story. Many times, we would get into a long, black Cadillac limo to go from our hotel to the auditorium and after driving for a while, we would notice the driver getting nervous. It was always disconcerting as you notice the driver's furtive glances to the right and left as if he was waiting for some form of an answer to come from the road or above. "Should I go right? Should I go left?" It was about this time that Charlie would make a droll remark, a sarcastic, "Ronnie, really?"

"What's the problem, driver?" I would ask. They usually didn't answer; just a look right and left and finally a turn. The next stop was a gas station for directions.

The big-city limo drivers were cool until they offered you the movie screenplay they'd written as a celebrity driver, or the demo tape of their friend's band. The Stones were sharp and immediately recognized when the driver was a talker and trying to be their buddy in order to glean some gossip to pass along, so they invariably kept to themselves. If there was a partition in the limo, it went up.

Limos had other dangers. At first sight, the kids would charge for the car. Depending on our surroundings and traffic, the driver could usually get out of any danger, but in those instances where we were stopped for any period of time, the kids would assault the limo.

Usually, they would peer into the windows to see who was inside. When they saw it was the Stones, they would call out, and before long we would be surrounded. It was scary. The excited mob usually pushed the car from side to side, and we would begin to rock. Other fans wanted our attention by pounding on the windows, doors, roof, and hood of the car. We worried they would crush the limo and us. Some drivers would drive slowly and get us out of the mess while others freaked and stopped the car until our hollering got them to move.

June 30: Montreal, Canada, The Forum

The Forum was a hockey arena where the orchestra seats were on the skating rink floor, surrounded by a four-foot high wooden fence. The place was packed with an unruly crowd. I noticed a fight between two jean-jacketed guys to the right and in front of the stage. Two large, helmeted, leather-uniformed policemen grabbed the guys by the scruffs of their necks, pushed their heads down, and ran them head-first into the wooden fence. The stunned pugilists were lifted up and passed over the fence to other police and carried to a team dressing room behind the stage that was converted to hold people in need of medical attention.

During the show, I stayed in the audience and watched as different fights broke out. I was pissed to see spotlights search out the fights and light them, instead of the Stones on stage. I felt they were exciting the crowd and causing more problems. Later, I heard that the police were filming the crowds.

Adding to the beaten-up and knocked-out kids in the recovery room were the kids who passed out. Fans would surge forward, pinning people against the stage or wooden barriers in front of the stage, and quite a few passed out from lack of oxygen or just fainted from the excitement. They were handed over the tops of people's heads to be taken backstage.

By the end of the show, there were over forty kids in the recovery room, including the fighters, passed-out fans, and other unruly hooligans who had been sent there. The police soon realized they had made a mistake putting everyone together! These kids, revived, were now a mob rioting backstage.

We got out of there quickly.

Back at our hotel I was surprised to see two identical blonde girls at my hotel room door. They looked like cute female clones of Brian Jones.

"We know you are with the Rolling Stones, and we want your help," one of the girls said.

"What is it?" I asked.

"We're lesbians, and we've never been with a man! Brian is the prettiest boy we've ever seen, and we decided that if we were going to have sex with a man, it could only be Brian. We really mean it and would do anything to make it happen."

"You'll have to do me first."

"OK," they said in unison.

I marveled at their logic. I didn't take them up on it.

Brian's room adjoined mine and the next afternoon when it was time to head out for a sound check, I opened our adjoining door and walked in to tell him it was time to get up. In the darkness, I saw two similar blonde heads of hair with faces in the pillows.

"Get up, Brian, you'll have time for a bite and then off for the sound check."

I opened the drapes to let the sun in. It was only then that I saw Brian wasn't there; it was the two girls who had his hairstyle. I freaked at first, wondering where he'd gone. He was in the shower.

On non-show nights in Manhattan, we partied. I joined the boys for a couple of nights at Andy Warhol's downtown studio, The Factory. Here, you were surrounded by talented, captivating characters. To Mick, it was a mutual admiration society. To me, the art at these parties was the people. You never saw boring. From the art crowd I would be swept along to the photo crowd, photographer and film director Jerry Schatzberg's, for a star-studded party for the camera world.

Other nights we went to the nightclub Ondines' at 59th Street on the east side of Manhattan. Here I saw Jimi Hendrix perform his guitar magic, playing it behind his back, on top of his head, with his teeth. He was an amazing performer.

July 2: New York City, Forest Hills Tennis Stadiums

After a week on the road, Mick's throat became a problem. When he felt there was something wrong with his voice, he needed more consolation than a cup of tea with honey. In this photo, I am assuring Mick that I would have a throat specialist come and ease his fears.

Mick came over to me the minute we got backstage.

"Ronnie, my throat hurts and I don't think I can sing. I don't want to damage my voice."

I assured him I'd find a throat doctor. I got hold of the promoter and asked him to locate a throat doctor for Mick. The promoter told me he knew a doctor who worked with the opera and went to get him on the phone. In the meantime, I asked around and got everyone's home remedy.

"Tell him to drink hot tea with honey and lemon."

"Have him have a shot of brandy."

We got hot tea, brandy, honey, and lemon to the dressing room, and Mick had a hot cuppa and felt well enough to go on with the show. I managed to arrange an appointment with the opera's throat doctor. He gave Mick a shot, some throat-soothing tips, and a clean bill of health.

July 4: Asbury Park, New Jersey, Convention Hall

I was standing in the aisle along the back rows of the audience when I noticed Keith jerk back unexpectedly and then take his guitar and swing it like a golf club into his amp. The audience kept on being the audience without any change in yelling, and I rushed backstage. There I found Stu was carrying a guitar to Keith's stand and putting the smashed guitar away. Even as the show continued, Keith was still visibly upset.

"What's the problem?" I asked Stu.

"He busted a string," Stu replied.

"So?" I asked, wondering what the big deal was since it was a mechanical issue, and no one in the audience noticed. Stu didn't answer me, and I realized his silence implied "Ask Keith."

After the show, when I had a moment, I sat down with the still upset Keith.

"Keith, the fans don't know the difference," I told him. "Ninety-nine point nine percent of them don't know if you missed a chord or if your string breaks. I was in the audience, and I could tell you they didn't notice it at all." Keith was his own worst critic. All my logical reassurances couldn't quell Keith's rage at himself for breaking a string and, as he saw it, ruining the song. Much later, after he calmed down, he told me he stayed mad for so long because he was further pissed at himself for breaking his favorite guitar over the broken string. Stu sent it out to be fixed, but they both figured it would never sound the same.

On one of our days off in New York City, Keith brought his girlfriend, Linda Keith, to my studio apartment in Newark, New Jersey. We swam in the downstairs pool while tenants, my neighbors, stared at the long-haired guy. Then up the elevator to the roof with Alleghany airline blankets (thank you, stewardesses). We sat on the blankets, on the roof, in the dark, and watched the sunset from atop the twenty-second floor of my apartment building overlooking Weequahic Park. We sat in silence, but it was more of a moment. One of those moments when you don't have to speak.

July 4: Virginia Beach, Virginia, Under the Dome Theater

Sometimes, I would hear the sweet voice of Brian on the other end of the line: "Ronnie, I'm going shopping." Other times, Bill would call and ask if I wanted to join him shopping or walking nearby and tell me not to tell Brian or Mick and Keith. In a group, they teased Bill because he was around six years older. Guys are merciless. "Hey, geezer!" They would tease, but it was all in good fun: Kinda. He was still the "old guy".

On this night, Bill called me to his room in Virginia Beach. His door was ajar, so I walked in and this time he had two girls naked on a dining room table in his suite.

"Her girlfriend was feeling unloved," he told me, indicating one of the girls. "I told her I would bring her a lover."

Bill was standing at the head of the table with a naked girl lying in front of him with her legs spread. The other girl was at the foot of the table, lying back with her head next to her friend. I walked to the foot of the table and began taking off my clothes. In these instances, I was always nervous that I was not what the girl wanted since I wasn't one of Bill's bandmates, but none of the girls ever seemed to mind.

Bill turned out the lights. From that point on it was moaning and the sounds of bodies squeaking on a slippery wax table top.

July 6: Syracuse, New York, War Memorial Auditorium

We exited the Syracuse date via an underground tunnel that took us outside to our waiting limo. As we gathered together, we realized that Brian wasn't with us. "Where's Brian?" someone asked.

The cop leading us out said that Brian was being held for questioning.

"What? Where?"

We were astounded. Before the debate as to whether the rest of the band should leave and I and the road manager deal with the police, a couple of us were led back through the tunnel to an underground office where we saw Brian sitting off to the side.

A detective began questioning me about any political motive Brian may have had to disgrace the flag. The police complained that after the concert, Brian had grabbed the American flag from a flag pole, wrapped it around himself, and was dragging it along the floor as he was leaving the stage. The police took offense to this. While we were running toward the exit, they grabbed him and brought him to the underground interrogation room. I told the detective that it was more likely a fashion statement as opposed to a political one. Eventually, the police were persuaded that he was not trying to insult the American flag, and we were released.

Band Lived Up to Reputation In Flag Fracas Here in 1966

By WILLIAM LaRUE
The Post-Standard

It was late afternoon on July 6, 1966, and Mick Jagger was angry at the Syracuse police.

He thought officers had used excessive force to grab a fan who got too close to the Rolling Stones. And now Jagger and the band were being detained after accusations they desecrated the American flag.

A fuming Jagger plopped his feet onto a detective's chair in a room at the Public Safety Building.

"They're a bunch of Nazis, that's what they are," Jagger told a Syracuse University student newspaper reporter who was scribbling notes. "This is unbelievable. Just like in Germany."

It was clear that Syracuse police didn't much like the Stones either, especially the British group's long hair and rebellious manner.

CARL SINGLE/The Post-Standard

In 1966, the Stones used modest staging at the War Memorial.

But the real stir occurred when the late guitarist Brian Jones tried to walk off with an American flag that was hanging in a tunnel under the Onondaga County War Memorial where the band was performing.

Eventually, the band apologized and authorities decided not to press charges. But the flag incident made international headlines, adding to the Stones' reputation as one of the rock

(Continued on Page A-8)

The cops were waiting for us in Syracuse, and when they couldn't do anything during the show, they proved their worth by grabbing Brian.

July 8: Detroit, Michigan, Cobo Hall

Detroit shows were enjoyable for me, even though they usually resulted in major car chases. A couple of times, as we exited slowly from an arena garage, a fan would jump onto the back of the limousine's trunk. They would spread-eagle, grab the two sides of the back window, and hang on for dear life. The driver would try to drive away before we were descended upon by the mobs. As the driver picked up speed to escape, the fan would still be hanging on at 40 miles an hour. After we were clear of the crowds, the driver stopped and the kids dropped off of the trunk. We sped away.

July 9: Indianapolis, Indiana, State Fairgrounds Coliseum

Bill Wyman and I were in bed with a girl who insisted she wanted to be with both of us while reading poetry. Bill and I looked at each other with the same thought in mind: teeth. If she is going to be talking, her mouth is going to be moving, and neither of us wanted to be on the oral end of the engagement. In the spirit of things, we did take turns. She brought pages of a prepared poem to the king-size bed we jumped onto. We got naked and began playing around. When we had established a rhythm and a comfortable position, she started reading from her poem. It was hard not to laugh and to stay hard, but then again, it was a mix of sex and culture. "Poetry in Motion."

The girl fulfills her fantasy and goes back to her friends with bragging rights for having bagged a rock 'n' roll star. The rock star or lucky guy who is hangin' with the rock star just smiles and is thankful.

The only people who might be upset would be the parents.

And then I think of Chicago.

July 10: Chicago, Illinois, Arie Crown Theatre, McCormick Place

We were staying in a motel in Chicago since none of the hotels would have us. I made a food run and when I returned I noticed a car parked in front of Mick's door with a middle-aged man and woman sitting in it. I walked past them and up to Mick's room and knocked on the door.

"I'm busy!" Mick called out.

I went next door to Brian's and got the word out that we had food. I asked Brian if he knew what Mick was busy with and he replied that he was with two sisters.

"The weird thing, Ronnie, is that their parents brought them, and they are sitting in their car out front."

Later at the concert I did notice that the sisters were in the left-side first row, smiling and waving at Mick. At least they got front-row seats.

July 11: Houston, Texas, Sam Houston Coliseum

Mick Jagger is lead from dressing room to stage by protective Houston Police.

Mick being led to the stage by the Houston police as I assume my usual position over his right shoulder. Image from YOUNG HOUSTON MUSICIAN staff photographer Paul Wallace.

Before leaving for Houston, Texas, I heard the horror stories of how hot it could be inside the stadium.

"Figure on 115 degrees," I was told. "Very hot."

I called Allen and asked if it was okay that I didn't wear a suit and tie when I went to the concert.

"No, it isn't okay. You are my business representative, and you wear a suit and tie at every concert," he told me.

This was ironic since at the time Allen had given up wearing suits and usually sported a colorless knit shirt. But then again, I wasn't the boss.

Often we would be either taxiing to take off on a flight or in the air when the discussion would turn to picking a title for the posthumous album that would be released after the Stones died in a plane crash. They were sure it would win all the awards once they were dead. This fatalistic outlook on air travel had even been channeled into a song called "Flight 505" on their album Aftermath.

Common throughout the concerts was that the physically disabled were often assigned a front row. While this may have seemed like a kind idea, in reality it was a different story. Usually at the Stones concerts, at some point — usually the start of "Satisfaction" — the crowd would stand up and move toward the stage. This crush of people would push the front rows of fans forward until they were pressed against the apron of the stage or the barricades. This often resulted in people blacking out and having to be passed overhead to safety. Unfortunately, in deference to the disabled, the area on the front right or left stage was where they put the people in wheelchairs and crutches.

Front-row positioning also worked against the local politician who copped front-row seats to take his kids. Some of the funniest photos I have seen show a well-dressed politician in the front row with his fingers in his ears while kids are all around him screaming in bliss. The politicians always got out of there fast when the crowd surged.

Then there was "Gregory Lesion Verruca," the ultimate fan.

Keith and I created Gregory. We were discussing warts when Keith told me they were called "verruca" in the UK. With that, the conversation moved on to such scintillating topics as open wounds and moist lesions. From there we came up with Gregory Lesion Verruca, a fan stricken with leprosy but redeemed by an unending love of the Rolling Stones.

We would slip notes under one another's hotel room doors along with things like the tip of a hot dog. The note would say: While I was waiting to see you, I lost part of my finger. I want you to have it. Your Biggest Fan, Gregory Lesion Verruca.

We arrived at the Hyatt in Dallas, only to find that our rooms were already rented, and we needed another hotel. Our advance man's job was to be at the location prior to our arrival, make sure the limo drivers knew where we were going, have us checked into the hotel, our room keys in envelopes ready to hand to each person, and take care of any other problems that might arise. Our advance man kept telling me there would be no problems, guaranteed.

"But there are always problems."

"Ronnie, I guarantee there will be no problems."

"There are always problems. Just be sure you take care of them before we get there."

And so it became certain that there were problems unsolved when we arrived.

The advance man was running around ranting and raving about the hotel's incompetence. I didn't care about the past; I just wanted us to have rooms. We were getting the usual, "There's a convention in town; all the good rooms are gone, etc." I screamed at the assistant manager, and he made a call to another hotel and made the arrangements for us.

Mick came over to me and complained about our advance man.

"I thought it was his job to take care of this!" he said. "What the fuck? What are you going to do about it, Ronnie?"

The advance man was history before midnight.

Over the years, I have found that because I joke around, people don't take me seriously. They mistake my sense of humor for giving them a free pass on fucking up. They are wrong, as the advance man and others have found out to their surprise and, at times, regret. I expect everyone to do their job as well as I do my job, or else.

The road manager, Mike Gruber, took over for the fired advance man. We figured he could handle being ahead of us. Most of his duties overseeing the Stones were done by Ian Stewart. Ian was a hardworking, quiet, honest-as-the-day-is-long kinda guy. He took care of the Stones and their equipment. Stewart preferred not to be bothered by other people interfering. Stewart was the mama bear chasing the kids who messed with the equipment. Stewart was the dad you wanted to please. Stewart was that quiet guy who slipped onto the piano bench and joined in on Honky Tonk Women, Let It Bleed, or Brown Sugar. Stewart was the co-founder who stayed with his baby. Ian Stewart was a class act.

20th July: Seattle, Washington, Center Coliseum

As the tour gathered momentum, each city blurred into a mirror image of the previous city. We moved in a McDonald's and mini mall world, with all cities looking the same.

The Stones would perform,
then we would leave the show,
then get in our little airplane charter,
then fly to the next city and arrive after 1:00 or 2:00 AM,
then drive to the hotel or motel,
then settle into the rooms and search for food.
By this time, it was the dead of night and the only places that were open
were the local very, very greasy spoons. The available food was usually
fried chicken, beef stew, chili, burgers, and fries—the typical all-night diner
fare. Then we'd stay up another couple of hours unwinding.
Then we'd try to sleep.
Then I'd have to be up later that morning to get the troops together for an
afternoon sound check, usually around 2:00 PM.
Then we'd have time for some dinner and maybe a little relaxation before
the show.
Then, do the show, leave the show, board the plane, go to the next city, and
so on and so on. Wash. Rinse. Repeat.

July 21: Portland, Oregon, Memorial Coliseum

The Rolling Stones Threaten Cameraman

Portland, Ore.

The British rock 'n roll quintet, the Rolling Stones, rolled into town Thursday night, threatened a television cameraman with a "knuckle sandwich" and appeared later before some 10,000 hysterical teen-agers.

One young girl was carried out the Portland Coliseum by a policeman after trying to charge the stage.

At Portland International Airport, the Stones refused to talk with reporters after their arrival.

Mike Gruber, from the Rolling Stones' New York based publicity agency, said interviews "would ruin their image."

As the Stones started back up the steps of their chartered plane, a television cameraman asked the Stones' business agent, Ron Schneider, to stop blocking his camera.

Schneider and Gruber yelled at the cameraman, Carl Vermilya, to get his camera off the field and one of the Stones yelled from the plane, "Give 'im a knuckle sandwich, Mike."

A local promoter said the group would get about $18,000 for the one-night stand.

United Press

A tarmac confrontation with the press — "Give 'em a knuckle sandwich, Mike."

Just before the tour began, I decided I wanted a new car. I had been in a head-on collision in Miami during my first year of college (not my fault) but had failed to get enough money from the insurance company to buy a Jaguar. I had been test-driving all types of cars in the Corvette image and had fallen in love with the Jag E-type convertible. I had seen all the old dudes in Miami driving them, trying to project a more youthful image. That had been a goal: get a cool car while I was still young!

Pete Bennett was the guy I turned to for a deal. According to him, he knew everyone. He was an "I can get it for you wholesale" kind of guy.

"Pete, I want a Jag XKE convertible," I told him.

"Don't worry, Ronnie. I'll find one for you," he assured me. It was in Portland when I got that call.

"Ronnie, I found you a Jag; it's in Mount Kisco, New York. It's also the last Jag XKE convertible in the States, due to the dock strike in England. No one knows when that will end. You want it?"

"What color is it?"

"Maroon with a black top and I got you a great price, $4,200!"

"I'll take it," I said.

July 22: Sacramento, California, Memorial Auditorium (1st show)

We were in a small motel in Sacramento, CA. It was about 10:00 AM, and I was on the phone with Allen going over figures from the previous night's show. I was in bed with just a pair of black briefs on. There was a knock on my door: I let Brian and Keith in. I told them I would be a minute as I jumped back onto the bed to continue my conversation with Allen.

There was another tap at my door, and Keith let Mick in. Now, almost everyone was in my room, and there was another knock on the door. I heard "Room service!" Brian opened the door and four tables of desserts were wheeled into my very small single room with twin beds. I ignored it as Brian mumbled that he was hungry and had ordered it for my room before he came over.

As I continued my phone conversation with Allen, something whizzed past my head and hit the wall next to me. After it hit, it stuck for a second and then slid down the wall. I could tell that it was chocolate pudding. I scooped what I could off the wall and threw it. My response garnered a flurry of small dessert plates being thrown throughout the room. As I tried to keep from laughing, I told Allen I would have to call him back. And then the food fight began.

By the time it was done, there was strawberry shortcake, blueberry pie, coconut custard, chocolate pudding, rice pudding, lemon meringue pie, and any and all the gooey desserts from the typical room service menu on all of us and all over the room.

We decided that the best way for us to get clean would be to jump into the pool outside, between the reception building and the motel room building. It was about one hundred feet from my room. Everyone walked out of my room and headed for the pool. On the way, I saw a maid's cart a couple of doors down. I found the maid and told her that we had made a mess, and that we would give her a big tip to clean it up.

By the time I jumped into the pool, the water had a grease slick with all kinds of weird stuff floating in it.

As we soaked in the pool amid all the dessert debris, we watched the maid walk from my building to the reception building. A minute later, she strode with two other maids toward my room. I figured she'd brought them along to help her clean, but a minute later we saw the three of them walk back to the reception building. Next, we saw the maids with two guys in suits walking toward my room. Minutes passed. Now the suits came toward us in the pool. I got out and told them we were going to take care of the maids and apologize for the mess. They weren't happy.

Later that night at the venue, the Stones were backstage getting ready, and I was standing by the last row of the audience when the MC announced that before the show began, Mr. Whatever-His-Name-Was from the local motel had something he wanted to say.

Next, I looked on in disbelief as one of the suits from the motel took the microphone and told the audience something along the lines of "The Stones are rude, horrible people who have no respect for anything or anyone, and you kids should boycott the show."

You can guess what the reaction from the Stones fans was. They booed the guy off the stage and destroyed his faith in humanity forever.

I later got a bill for $3,325 for the motel room. I felt it was insulting. I refused to pay it. I spoke with the motel manager and told him I would pay a fair amount, but $3,325 was ridiculous. He told me that the room would have to be totally redone, and it would take a month. It seems strawberries are berry, berry bad (sorry) for the wallpaper.

Eventually, we settled for $300.

July 23: Salt Lake City, Utah, Davis County Lagoon

We were on our plane on the way to Salt Lake City, playing Monopoly. Bill was sitting next to me on my right; Keith was across from him; and Brian was facing me from his aisle seat. We heard a loud bang and then the sound of air hissing. A window on the plane had shattered as we climbed above the mountains.

The loud sound of the rushing air made us think we were going to be sucked out of the plane.

Brian jumped out of his seat and began running down the aisle, screaming. "We're all gonna die!"

I called out for him to get into a seat and buckle it. I looked over at Bill; he smiled and pointed to both our seatbelts; they were fastened. We weren't going to be sucked out anyhow. The sound we were hearing was the sound of the air coming into the plane through the cracked window, not going out. The captain increased the cabin air pressure, and the sound stopped. Some of us got headaches from the increased cabin pressure, but that was not as bad as being sucked into space.

We arrived at the venue to find that it was an amusement park, and the show was at the fairgrounds. The Stones went to the dressing room, and I went to the front gate. I saw that the boys on line were dressed in black pants, white shirts, and ties. I asked one of the kids on line why everyone was so smartly dressed, unlike the typical Stones fans. He told me that they were Mormons. I said my knowledge of Mormons was that they didn't drink or dance. He agreed, somewhat: "We don't drink, and we are not supposed to dance. But we do dance, and we love the Stones."

July 24: Bakersfield, California, Civic Auditorium (two shows)

We stayed in LA when we played Bakersfield. While we were in LA, we stayed at the Century Plaza Hotel, hung out by the pool and drank margaritas, or went up to the room and…

I got a call to bring some cash to one of the Stones' suites. Our road manager walked over to me and said he needed some money. Everyone in the room hollered out, "Give him some money, Ronnie!" I counted out some cash, and he went into one of the bedrooms. A few minutes later, he emerged with a shoe box, and everyone moved to another bedroom. When he opened the box, I saw what looked like a brick. I later learned it was a "Mexican brick" of marijuana. Pot smugglers formed them into bricks for stacking and shipping.

The brick was opened in a flash.

"Let's have a joint rolling contest!" someone suggested.

A couple of the girls in the room immediately went about cleaning the pot and within seconds, there were joints for everyone and whoever won was quickly forgotten.

July 25: Los Angeles, California, Hollywood Bowl

If I ever had a favorite venue (tied with Madison Square Garden), it would be the Hollywood Bowl. It is a fantastic place to experience a concert. The audience sits outside in a natural mountain bowl and looks down and across a semi-domed stage backed by mountains and a star-filled sky above.

Just like New York City, there is always a special excitement when performing in Los Angeles. The Stones show that night was great, and when it ended, the crowds still surrounded the exits of the Bowl. The promoters were concerned about our safety leaving and called in an armored truck. A large Brinks truck pulled up to the stage exit; we quickly jumped into the back of it, and they shut and secured the back door. We slowly pulled out, and the driver headed for the 101 freeway entrance across from the Hollywood Bowl. As we inched through the crowd, we heard the driver complaining about the fans blocking his way to the entrance ramp of the freeway. The kids followed us on foot and created a traffic jam that eventually brought us to a complete halt. We heard people climbing all over the armored car. Some even got onto the top of the vehicle. There was a large air vent above us, and we heard them pulling at that to get to us. They tore it off, but there was still a metal screen protecting us from anyone getting in.

After quite a long time, the fans finally gave up and dispersed. We went back to our hotel.

July 26: San Francisco, California, Cow Palace

We got to the Cow Palace on time for the show, but were kept waiting by the other bands playing. We were on a tight schedule as we were leaving for our last date in Hawaii, and had to get back to Los Angeles to make the flight.

The Jefferson Airplane was playing when we arrived, and I went to their manager and asked him to make sure they finished soon. When the Airplane broke into yet another song, I went back to him. He seemed to be placating me, but not paying attention, so I warned him that if they didn't end their set soon I would pull the plug on the electricity and end it for them. He told me to go screw myself and enjoy the show.

I waited and watched. The Airplane started another song. I found the person who had control of the power and told him to kill the stage and instrument power, or they could continue watching the Airplane since the Stones would be leaving to catch their own airplane. He pulled the power, and the sound went dead.

The Airplane left the stage, and the Stones performed. We left for LA in time for our trip to Hawaii.

July 28: Honolulu, Hawaii, Honolulu International Center

After the Stones played the final date of the tour, we found we couldn't get a flight to leave the island due to an airline strike. There are worse places to be stranded than Hawaii, so we figured we would take advantage of the island's amenities and see the sights. On our first night out, Mick, Keith, and I went to the Don Ho Show.

When Don Ho began singing his signature song, "Tiny Bubbles," he called out individuals in the audience to sing with him. That night he made a big push to get Mick to join him, but failed. Even with the fans yelling out for Mick to join Don, there was no way he was singing "Tiny Bubbles." To this day, I'm still trying to keep "Tiny Bubbles" out of my head!

Luckily, as we returned from the show to our hotel, another image comes to mind that can eradicate the song in my head. We had an enormous Samoan limo driver. He was squeezed into the driver's seat with the steering wheel against his chest. Someone pulled out a yellow-wrapped amyl nitrite ampule and popped it. Each of us took a sniff, and the driver asked what we were doing.

We explained that the popper gave you a head rush and was also great for sex. You popped it and took a sniff at the moment of orgasm. All sensations were enhanced, if it didn't kill you. At the very least, it will wake you from a faint.

He wanted to try it and asked if he could. Keith passed a capsule over as the rest of us wondered if it was a good idea for this guy to try it while driving us. Figuring to lessen the danger I said, "You have to keep both hands on the wheel. We don't want an accident."

"Sure," he said as he popped the amyl nitrite ampule, put the capsule under his nose, curled his top lip to secure it in place, and put both hands on the wheel. It was something to see, this huge man with a yellow ampule mustache under his nose, his eyes wide open, staring forward, hands at 10 and 2 on the steering wheel, and driving us.

"I like it," he remarked coolly and without further ado got us to the hotel.

"I like it" was the way Keith felt about horseback riding as Hawaii presented another opportunity for us. Jerry Brandt, the agent from the William Morris Agency, joined us in Hawaii. He, Keith, and I went horseback riding up a dormant volcano. At the top, we stopped with our horses overlooking the ocean. Below us was the aquarium where we could see a killer whale in a pool.

As our boredom increased I tried to come up with something to take our minds off being stranded. I rented a 35mm movie projector and per Keith's suggestion got a copy of One-Eyed Jacks, a film starring and directed by Marlon Brando. We had our own private screening in Keith's suite.

As the airline strike dragged on, Allen tried to work out a way to get me back to New York. I had been stranded for two weeks until the travel agency figured out how to get me back. There were no flights to US destinations, but there was a flight from Hawaii to Bermuda that made a stop at JFK airport in New York. I got that ticket and got off the plane in New York. Somewhere I still have a ticket that has the JFK to Bermuda leg, unused. The airline strike ended on August 19 after forty-three days.

Everyone went back to their regular lives. I wouldn't be on the road with the Stones until three years later. And then, under much different circumstances.

Here we are at a table in Ondine's nightclub in Manhattan after the Ed Sullivan Show. Mick is looking over the shoulder of Mike Gruber as he inserts an amyl nitrate capsule into a Benzedrine nasal inhaler. It is also a nice shot of a friendlier Keith and Brian. The girl next to Mike is Devon, who was a girlfriend of Jimi Hendrix. Brian's hand is bandaged after a glass door incident at the Ed Sullivan Show.

However, I did see the Stones again on September 11, 1966, when they played the Ed Sullivan Show. Our limo stopped in front of the stage door entrance to the Ed Sullivan Theater to let us out. A few fans noticed and called out to the passersby, "It's the Rolling Stones!" We found the stage door locked and after a few minutes of pounding with no answer, and with the fans growing in number, we ran to the front of the theater. Unfortunately, the glass-paneled front doors were locked as well. The fans found us and began to crowd around, the ones in the back, pushing to get a better view. As the crowd surged, Brian's hand was pushed through a glass panel. I don't know if he broke the glass trying to open the door, or if it was the result of the turmoil, but he was cut and bleeding. Finally, a guard on the inside opened the door, and we got in.

After the Ed Sullivan Show, we headed out to one of our favorite nightclubs in New York, Ondine's. One night after partying at Ondine's Brian asked me to come to his room. I walked into a very messy bedroom, and he motioned me over to the bed. With enormous flair, Brian lifted the comforter off his bed and onto the floor. On top of the bed was a white top sheet; he pulled this to the side and there was the bottom sheet with five obvious wet spots.

"Ronnie, I fucked Devon [Jimmy Hendrix's girlfriend and groupie] here." He pointed to one of the stains. "Here, here, here, and here," he went on, as he pointed to each of the wet spots. "Congratulations," was all that came to mind.

CHAPTER VI

FARAWAY EYES

At the end of November, Allen sent me on my first trip to London to have the Stones sign a formal management and publishing deal.

A large black Phantom V Rolls Royce greeted me at London's Heathrow airport. The driver opened the rear passenger-side door, and a giant cloud of sweet-smelling smoke preceded Andrew Loog Oldham. He stepped out of the back of the big black car dressed in a dapper white suit. I appreciated that he came all the way to the airport, over an hour's drive with good traffic, to greet me.

"Get in," he said, gesturing toward the rear of the Phantom.

The back of the Rolls was a darkened cavern, surrounded by sixteen speakers, as Andrew told me.

"Here." He offered me a giant spliff (a joint rolled with hash and tobacco). Lucky for me, I was already a pot smoker. After all, I was an accountant, a fact that came with its own set of built-in expectations I confounded. I might have been wearing a suit, but I wasn't "a suit." We went to Olympic Recording Studio in Barnes, London, a little studio that faced an alley. As I looked out the glass front door of the studio, I saw a hooker on her knees giving a guy a blow job in the alley. Not that classy a neighborhood.

At Olympic, I watched the Stones as they worked on some of the songs for their next album, Between the Buttons. There they were, each in his own cubicle of sound. I learned to just sit and listen as they made music, and watch how their songs were created. Keith would have a tune in his head that he would try to convey to the band, while strumming it out on his guitar.

Charlie would pick up a beat with the drums; Bill would come in with a bass line; and Brian would have some unique sound that he wanted to add. Mick, with his hand-written lyrics sometimes playing the harmonica or strumming a guitar, sat on a tall stool adding the vocal to the music track. Each Stone added something unique that eventually became the song. This is where I heard the sum becoming greater than the parts.

I got the Stones to sign and was back on a plane on December 1 with the completed contract in hand. The contract later became known as the Nanker Phelge agreement. I didn't know the details and was given the instruction to just bring it to them and have them sign it. (My having them sign the agreement was the reason, many years later, my uncle would contact me. He hadn't done so in a long time. He needed my testimony during a trial. I was the witness to the Stones signatures.)

I'm the guy over Ed Sullivan's right shoulder, and the producer is over Mick's shoulder.

Creating and recording the Stones' songs was one thing, promoting them was something quite different. When the Stones appeared on the Ed Sullivan Show on January 15, 1967, "Let's Spend the Night Together" was their current single. Conservative Ed Sullivan was against the lyrics and wanted Mick to sing "Let's spend some time together" instead. This evolved into a battle of wills that lasted for hours. The Stones felt their artistic integrity was at stake while Ed felt the moral foundation of his show was at stake. Then, I noticed a group of singing nuns in the audience watching the rehearsal. I requested they take a picture with the Stones. I had this vision of the Singing Nuns in their orthodox clothing surrounding the unruly Rolling Stones, thus putting the world in balance. Before I got an answer from the nuns, someone squealed to Ed. Ed and his producers wanted to have me thrown out of the building. They thought my idea was tasteless, and the Stones were Satan incarnate and shouldn't tempt the nuns. The nuns didn't seem to mind. Eventually, Ed and his producer were persuaded to let me stay without the photo being taken. The Stones relented and agreed to sing the changed words.

When we watched the show later, we were upset to find that the producers had drowned out the lyrics with the overdubbed screaming of the audience. The words hadn't mattered at all.

CHAPTER VII

LADY JANE

Fate or timing has a way of influencing the future.

"Who's that girl?" I asked my roommate Irv as we walked into a little diner on Lyons Avenue in Newark, NJ. "You said you knew all the pretty girls in Newark."

"That's Jane Gordon," Irv responded. "I used to date her. Want me to fix you up?"

"Sure," I said.

I was working with the Rolling Stones and had a lot of girls chasing after me. I was never sure if it was for me, my contacts, or my new Jaguar XKE. None of these factors influenced this eighteen-year-old girl from Maplewood, New Jersey.

Jane seemed to know what she wanted—and that was me. And I believed Jane. Jane and I, and our family and friends, had a fantastic wedding on February 5, 1967. When we'd gotten engaged in November, Jane told me we would probably have a yearlong engagement while she, her mother, and my mother planned a wedding. In December, Jane said they were unable to find a location for a wedding for at least two years, but when they went to a Maplewood wedding hall, the owners said that they kept February 5 open for their own anniversary party. It seems they loved Jane and her mother so much that they would let us have the hall for our wedding on their anniversary. Next thing I knew we had our wedding!

It was a show-biz bash. Bobby Vinton sang, and Pete Bennett played drums; we partied all night, and it was early the next morning by the time people started to leave.

Jane and I took our limo into Manhattan and stayed in the Honeymoon Suite at the Plaza Hotel. We got up early to catch a flight to the Bahamas for our honeymoon. When we drew back the bedroom curtains, we saw that New York was beginning to be engulfed in a blizzard. We rushed to the airport. Our flight left just as they closed JFK.

After one week in the Bahamas, we came back to New York to move into our new apartment on the Upper West Side. As we walked into the apartment, we noticed our TV and other things were gone. I ran into the bedroom and noticed the window facing the street was open and there were footprints on our bed. Jane freaked, and we went to stay at her parents' house in Maplewood. We got out of the apartment lease and began to look for a more secure place to live.

I went back to the office, only to be told by Allen that I would be going to London with him on February 18. Mick and Keith had been busted for drug possession at Keith's Sussex house, in Redlands, on February 12, and he wanted me there as someone of their age who could relate to their situation, try to keep them calm, and show our support.

It wasn't until the end of June that I went to the court with them. It was weird that after the judge was done speaking, they didn't lead the boys out of the courtroom; they led them down. There was a trap door that lifted up in front of the bench, and they were walked down to the basement jail.

On July 31, Mick was sentenced to three months' imprisonment for possession of four amphetamine tablets; Keith was found guilty of allowing cannabis to be smoked on his property and sentenced to one year in prison.

Due to a public outcry over the harsh sentences, both were overturned and the boys were let out.

Herman's Hermits

The Stones weren't the only UK talent Klein represented. It was his representation of Mickey Most, an English record producer who created hits for The Animals, Herman's Hermits, and Donovan to mention a few, that led to my first feature film experience.

Because of Mickey Most, Allen had a deal with MGM to produce a Herman's Hermits film. This was in the era following the Beatles' wildly successful films, A Hard Day's Night and Help! All the groups were looking for a theatrical venture to boost their star status. For the Hermits, Allen enlisted his old friend, producer/director Saul Swimmer, to head up the task as the producer. As director, Saul hired Morton DaCosta. DaCosta was formerly a stage director who had directed and produced several plays as feature films: Auntie Mame in 1958 and The Music Man in 1962. The Herman's Hermits film was titled after one of their most successful songs, "Mrs. Brown You've Got a Lovely Daughter." In the script, however, Mrs. Brown turned out to be a greyhound and her daughter, a puppy.

I witnessed an interesting method my uncle used to motivate the film's screenwriter, Norman Thaddeus Vane. To provide script changes requested by the studio, Allen locked Norman in one of the bedroom suites and told him he could not come out or eat until the edits were made. The writer complained, but this technique yielded results as pages were slid under the door for acceptance and lunch.

"You'll write all the checks, oversee the budget, and report to me every night," Allen told me. "You will pick up my per diem and save it for me when I come to the set."

And with that I was in the movie business.

My new wife, Jane, was still in New Jersey as I was beginning work in London. The rumor mills were running rampant as Jane moved back home with her parents. "They're getting divorced," "She left him," "He left her" were all making the rounds of the neighborhood. It wasn't much longer before Jane joined me in London.

We had recently bought a show champion, champagne-colored Afghan hound, Chica, as a pet. Afghans looked great, and many a head would turn when I was driving my Jag with Chica in the front seat. Jane would hear that her husband had been seen with a blonde in the passenger seat of his car. Sadly, though, back then England would quarantine pets for up to six months to keep rabies out of the country. So Chica wouldn't be joining us. After a short time in London, we went to a dog show and got another Afghan puppy. We named her Mia, and Mia was a bitch, a true bitch. She bit through electrical cords and dragged toilet paper throughout our London apartment.

Allen rented a small house for producer/director Saul Swimmer on Three Kings Yard, off Davies Street in London W1. The previous tenant of the house was director John Huston. I met Huston with my uncle when we were checking out the house. He was a really impressive guy with this great voice. I never forgot his powerful handshake and gritty "Hi, how are you?" At the end of the Mews was the apartment where Paul McCartney lived with Jane Asher.

A short distance from the house, at Three Kings Yard, was the 1930s/'40s movie star George Raft's Colony Club Casino. I would go for an evening of gambling. For entertainment, I sat at the blackjack table wearing a yellow and green satin Carnaby Street, Mr. Freedom Spiderman T-shirt underneath my white business shirt, tie, and jacket. Wishing for Spidey luck and further breaking the accountant image in everyone's mind.

Once I heard a racket behind me at the craps table while I was playing blackjack. Cubby Broccoli's wife (he did the James Bond films at the time) was going to roll the dice, and she wanted to bet £25,000. The pit boss signaled that she should sign a chit for the money; instead she threw her gold- and jewel-encrusted purse onto the dice table.

She rolled the dice and lost.

Sitting next to me on another night was the actor Telly Savalas, TV's Kojak. We were at the blackjack table, and I noticed he had half a pinkie finger. I never asked how he lost the other half. I always watched his films and TV shows to see if they ever showed his pinkie. Later, another player told me that Telly was a shill for the casino. I did notice that whenever he lost a pit boss would come by and give him more chips, and he never signed for them.

One night my uncle came to gamble with me. After a half an hour he was up £10,000 and walked away from the table. The pit boss came over and insisted we stay for dinner, their treat.

"Why is it my uncle won £10,000 and gets a free dinner," I asked, "while I lose everything every night, and I get nothing?"

They just ignored me.

Of course, the casino wanted to have him come back to lose what he had won. He did.

CHAPTER VIII

MRS. BROWN YOU'VE GOT A LOVELY DAUGHTER

Saul Swimmer and I worked together as he prepared to begin shooting the Herman's Hermits film. My first day on the movie set at Shepperton Studios was quite educational. I walked onto the set and saw all these guys sitting around doing nothing. I made sure they heard my voice as I began complaining about how time was money and there seemed to be a lot of lazy people on this set.

Saul grabbed me and told me that those were the carpenters and electricians. They had built the sets, and now they just had to wait until anything else was necessary. He explained I would have to get used to seeing a lot of guys sitting around as well as other wasteful work practices. At the time, trade unions were very strong in England. Work was supposed to end at 5:30 PM. In reality, union rules allowed the crew to wash their hands and clean up before they left. Work actually ended at 5:15.

Another rule: if you wanted the men to work overtime, all the crew had to agree. If one man didn't want to work, no one worked. This rule came into play during the shooting of a scene that took over two and a half hours to light. The shot was ready at 5:10 PM. We knew we were going to go over the time limit, and I was told to negotiate overtime with the men. We only needed fifteen minutes to get the shot, so I offered them an hour of overtime so we could get it. The cameraman had a date and refused to stay. I offered two hours, and he still refused. We didn't get the shot.

It took us another two hours the next morning to set up that same scene and shoot it. I hated the British film unions.

Before we got any shots, Saul was casting the film with the director. One person he wanted was a classical British actor, Stanley Holloway. Stanley Holloway was famous for his comic and character roles on stage and screen, especially that of Alfred P. Doolittle in My Fair Lady. At the time, Stanley was seventy-six years old, and we needed to get insurance for him. You needed insurance to get a completion bond; the bond guarantees that the film will be completed on budget. You didn't get the bond, you didn't get the money! We were concerned we wouldn't be able to get the completion bond because of his age, but Stanley took the physical and passed with flying colors. Furthermore, he loaned us his Rolls Royce for some shots.

Our first set was constructed to mirror Covent Garden, London's famous fruit and vegetable market near the Royal Opera House. The shot involved a musical scene with wheelbarrows of flowers, fruits, and vegetables being moved about and Stanley Holloway and the boys singing a song about how to sell them. Morton DaCosta seemed to be having a problem directing the scene and Saul kept complaining to me that DaCosta was really a stage director and didn't seem to know what he was doing.

After the second day of lost shooting time, Saul wanted me to join him on a phone call to Allen to explain the problem and back him up. I did.

Allen gave me an order: "Fire Morton DaCosta. He's putting us behind schedule."

That evening I went to DaCosta's house, which was in a mews in London. We had a cup of tea, and I told him that, unfortunately, things weren't working out and he was fired.

He stood up and yelled at me, "You can't fire me!"

I told him I was sorry, but I had been instructed to fire him, and he was fired.

"You are a young nobody and don't have the power to fire me!" he screamed.

Unfortunately for him, I did have the power. In the film business, the little guys are the ones who get their hands dirty, while the execs stay safely in their offices.

Saul took over as the director, and I was now a movie producer. I vowed to never be that lecherous casting couch guy and to never cheat on my wife.

A couple of months into the pre-production of Mrs. Brown I managed to break one of those vows.

Saul favored a cute, young innocent girl and gave her a break. Saul was honorable and never took advantage of his director position. He liked her in a "take her under his wing" way and gave her acting tips and a small part in the film.

One day she appeared at the door of my office at Shepperton asking to speak with me. After we'd talked for a while, she asked if she could use my executive bathroom. A few minutes later she shouted for me to come in to "see something." "Something" turned out to be her naked on her knees in the shower stall.

"Come here," she said and waved me toward her.

"You don't have to do this," I said feebly. "And I'm married," I continued, holding up my hand to show my wedding ring. She came over to me, smiled, and dropped to her knees again. Well, what can a poor boy do? So much for my vows.

I rationalized cheating by telling myself "what she doesn't know doesn't hurt her," "I tell them I'm married," and even that old chestnut "it's only sex." I even invoked an "across the ocean" rule: screwing around over 3,000 miles from home doesn't count.

After scenes from Mrs. Brown were shot and there was no further use for the sets, they were taken apart. After the first set was struck, the set construction crew got together and in a couple of days built a futuristic office. It was amazing to see rooms created in a week that take home construction months to complete. I decided that I wanted these guys to decorate my house.

While we were shooting, Saul wanted to check out Spike Milligan for a possible role. Spike was a very talented British comedian and comic actor in the same vein as Jonathan Winters. Spike had done a popular radio show, The Goon Show, with Peter Sellers and Harry Secombe. I appreciated his sense of humor; Spike had ordered his cemetery headstone to read, "I told you I was ill."

Spike's latest play, The Bed Sitting Room, took place after a nuclear war. The radioactive fallout was causing strange mutations in people, such as the play's protagonist, a man who thought he was turning into a studio apartment.

We went to see the play and meet Spike. In the UK, before plays or films started, everyone stood for the national anthem, "God Save the Queen," much like at a ball game in the States. During the intermission, people came down the theater aisles selling refreshments, drinks and candy.

The play itself was very funny with the interaction between all the characters. Spike would often step out of character and depending on his mood or what was going on locally, he would go off script and ad lib to the theater audience. We went to two shows. Each was different. Spike stepped out of character at one point and turned to the audience to discuss the latest football scores and then, bam, back into character and back to the script.

Saul wanted to use Spike in the film, but it became quickly evident that he couldn't be directed or controlled. Instead of staying in camera focus, he would start wandering and improvising a new scene. In thanks for our meeting and consideration, he suggested we use one of his friends and fellow comedians, Bob Todd, who is seen in all the Benny Hill TV show skits. Spike's friend was in the scene where Peter Noone is registering Mrs. Brown for an upcoming race. He was only supposed to take the money and say thank you, but when Peter handed him the money, Bob Todd stopped, brought the bundle of cash to his nose, and made a face as if he was smelling fish. He took a small bit and made it his own.

Since Mrs. Brown and daughter were greyhounds, the film had a lot of the scenes involving greyhound racing. We filmed at a couple of the greyhound tracks around London. I found out how lucky I'd been when winning at the dog tracks in Miami.

As I became friendly with different people at the track, they clued me in to how the races were fixed. The obvious ways were not the most usual ones. By obvious, I mean keeping the dog constipated or sand papering their paws. I knew of these through my experience at the tracks in Miami. What I didn't know was the most common trackside trick that did not involve the dogs at all. "It was that wascally wabbit!" as Elmer Fudd would say. The guy who controlled the speed of the rabbit could cause the slower dogs to be the winners. As the fastest greyhounds charged down the track, the controller would slow down the rabbit, the fastest dogs would slow, and the dogs behind them would bump into them and throw them off speed or for a tumble if they were rounding a corner.

CHAPTER IX

I'M INTO SOMETHING GOOD

My new wife and I began married life in London W1. It took some getting used to. We didn't have a refrigerator. Most British homes still used ice boxes. There were only three television channels and two of them were state-run. The TV fare sometimes consisted of a show that taught you how to train fleas for a circus or Badger Watch, which showed nightlife at a badger burrow. Everything closed after 5:00 PM on Sundays, and they didn't have a decent hamburger! The only place open on Sunday was Wimpy's, a hamburger franchise—but what they served didn't qualify as a hamburger.

We got a cook, Mrs. Turkish, who would take care of Saul and us for dinner. Her dinners were usually five-course belly busters. We were expected to eat all of it. She would stand over us like a Jewish mother.

"Finish your soup," she'd scold us. "You must have the pudding. Clean your plate."

This was our regimen for a week and a half before we told Mrs. Turkish to make only three dinners a week for us and stagger the days. We ate the leftovers on her off days.

Every morning Saul and I would have a driver take us to the studio unless we were on location. I liked our driver and when he would take us to a restaurant for lunch or dinner, we would ask him to join us. He always refused and when we asked why he replied that all the men in his family were chauffeurs. They were proud of their job, and they strived to be the best chauffeurs around. Chauffeurs did not socialize with clients.

In my office at Shepperton Studios, I would meet with the MGM accountant assigned to our film. Every night I would go over the budget numbers with Allen, allowing for a time difference of about eight hours. We went over every number, so we could make sure we stayed on budget.

The film shooting on the set next to us was 2001: A Space Odyssey. The director, Stanley Kubrick, had forbidden the MGM executives from viewing the film. They were blocked from the set. Not being an MGM exec, I walked over to the stage and could go in and peruse the carved wooden miniatures that would be transformed into seeming life size on the screen. I played with the circular space station as I imagined myself a member of the crew.

After a while, I was allowed into the inner sanctum of MGM at Shepperton. While I was with the MGM accountant, I listened to his rant against Kubrick. He complained that they had to fly Kubrick's maid, nanny, and family over first class. Probably because of his exec ban, MGM wanted to stick it to Kubrick in any way they could. They were going to examine Kubrick's expenses and find as many as they could show as income to Kubrick.

Toward the end of my time at Shepperton, I was asked into the MGM accountant's office. On his desk were a lot of camera lenses. One of them was an oval wheel that was about ten inches in diameter. There were different colored crystals sticking out from the wheel. The accountant told me that this was the lens that Kubrick used to shoot the ending of the film. When I saw the 2001 ending with the scattered multi-colored prism light horizon, it confirmed the lens offered was the lens used for the scene. The scene, according to the newspapers, that would have hundreds of LSD-taking fans on the floor of their movie theaters looking up at the screen. MGM offered the lens to me for £5. At the time, I couldn't think of a use or a reason to carry it in my luggage. I regret not getting it!

After a few weeks of shooting at Shepperton, we went on location to Manchester, Herman's Hermits' hometown in the north of England. Here, we were allowed to shoot at a fantastic estate. For the shoot, we were going to repaint and change some other aesthetics in the house and pay a rental fee.

We were going to get aerial shots of Manchester for the opening of the film and when the pilot volunteered to give me helicopter lessons, I leapt at the opportunity. I went for my first lesson on a small two-seated Bell helicopter. It had a Plexiglas bubble, so you seemed to be sitting in the air as you flew over the countryside. The pilot showed me the controls, which were few.

"Here's the stick that does just about everything," he said. "Pull it back."

And we were airborne. He showed me what to do and took me on a tour of the area outside Manchester.

"You see those little hills with those little lines leading from them?" he asked.

"Yes, so?"

He swooped down, and as we got closer, I saw that the lines were railroad tracks. He explained that the little hills were storage areas for bombs, and the tracks were how they were transported to that little mound. Here they stored the bombs during World War II to keep them safe from the enemy's bombardment of the city.

When our hour was up, we landed, and he announced that the lesson was over.

"But how would you like some fun?" he added.

"I'd love it."

He lifted the helicopter a few inches off the ground and pushed the stick forward, and we flew literally inches from the ground, building speed, faster and faster, and then he spun the 'copter around 180 degrees and we were instantly heading back the same way, just a few inches off the ground. It was exhilarating.

Living in a foreign country is much different than visiting for a week or two. You're not just a tourist. You get local. You make it "home." We would eat our meals at the house during the week because we would come back from shooting tired and cranky without the patience to go out dining. We would go out on the weekends. The film business has its favorite watering holes, and we were drawn to them. We would go to an Italian restaurant, Trattoria Terrazza on Romilly Street in Soho, which was responsible for introducing Italian food in London and making it trendy.

We had another favorite Italian restaurant in Soho, SPQR. Besides great pasta, they had the best T-bone steak. I would go with my uncle. We once took John Lennon there, and he signed and drew on their wall. The restaurant was owned by an Israeli husband and wife. Many times I would see Liberace eating there. One night the restaurant owner's wife came over to us crying, saying she didn't know what to do. Her husband had run away with Liberace.

"Shoot to edit" was a term I learned when the filming was done. I spent a lot of time in the editing room with Saul and the editor Tristam Cones. We were in a 12′ x 12′ darkroom. Strips of the film were hanging all around on hooks and there were barrels of footage in various places in the room. Tristam would be hunched over the Movieola (film editing machine) painstakingly moving an image back and forth to find the right edit. When he found the right section, he would take a razor blade, cut the frame, and piece it together with a strip of Scotch tape. He would then review the scene and move on and on and on. It was a tediously slow job, now done in seconds via computers. I observed carefully how scenes were spliced together and noticed how Saul would artfully create a smooth segue into the next scene. Jump cuts, fade out, fade in; I was paying more attention now. When I went to the movies later, I would notice the cuts, and sometimes it would ruin the film, especially when I recognized clumsy technique.

We finished the Herman's Hermits movie on schedule and on budget. Then the politics took over. Allen had been in a proxy war with MGM and had, unfortunately, backed the loser. At the time, I was told that to fulfill the contract obligations, MGM had released the film in Kentucky, where it played for a week. Then they shelved it. It was a cute, harmless film that today would be G-rated.

There would be no profits from this film that took all that time and money to make. Right then I started to hate the "business" of movies. I hated the odds. You wait until the film is released, and you wait, and you wait, and still may not make a penny.

When it was evident that we wouldn't have any further income from Mrs. Brown I asked Allen why he did it. He told me he didn't care about the profits. He'd already made money during production from his producer's fee of $150,000, plus a per diem of $1,500 per week as well as my salary and expenses in the film's budget. "It makes for a nice piece of change," he said, "and there is always the chance you have a hit."

He was right about money during production; I could save my paycheck and a lot of my per diem cash; the company paid for my food and board; and I got a raise.

It wasn't until a late evening in 2012 when my son called me to tell me Mrs. Brown was on Turner Classic Movies on TV that I finally got to see it.

I got the last credit on the screen roll of Mrs. Brown: "Assistant to the Producer."

I was happy to see that I did get a credit on the film. One credit I never received was for my vocal contribution to one of the Rolling Stones' songs. While I was living in London, I went to quite a few of the Stones' sessions. On July 26, 1967, I went down to Olympia, where Glyn Johns was engineering "2000 Light Years from Home," which would end up on the band's next album Their Satanic Majesties Request. (The Stones were challenged by the June 1967 release of The Beatles, Sergeant Pepper, not only the music but the album cover). They wanted a chorus of voices and eerie sounds and told everyone to get into the studio and sit on the floor around the microphone. I did as told and gave them whatever came out of my mouth. As a science fiction lover, I always felt that this was the perfect song for my screech. It was also Bill Wyman's opportunity to do more than be the bass player. Bill stayed away from the psychedelics and parodied the Stones' situation in the song In Another Land. It was released as a single the week before the album came out. Bill Wyman was always battling with Mick and Keith to get a song on an album.

CHAPTER X

TUMBLING DICE

After three and a half months of living in London, Jane and I left the UK for home on August 5, 1967.

We returned to Maplewood, New Jersey, to stay with Jane's parents until we got a new place in New York City. It felt great to be on home ground again. As we were crossing through the Lincoln Tunnel, my uncle's driver asked if there were anywhere we wanted to stop before getting home. Anything we had missed.

"Take us to Jimmy Buff's," we both said. "We need a sausage and peppers sandwich."

He drove us to the store in Livingston, NJ, and we bought a couple of greasy sandwiches. Two for ourselves and one for the driver to eat later. He had it wrapped in butcher paper and put in a brown paper bag. By the time he dropped us off, the grease had soaked through all the paper, and it made an ugly-looking brown paper bag. The next day the driver did not turn up for work. Stomach problems.

Jane and I decided that if Riverdale was good enough for my uncle, it was good enough for us. We found an apartment in a high-rise a couple of miles from my uncle's place off the Hudson River. I didn't like that it was in a high-rise. We chose a large four-poster wood bed and a nice new couch. We were new to high-rise living and found out the hard way that the four-poster didn't fit in the elevator or the stairway. The bed would stay in storage, and we couldn't wait to leave and find a garden apartment. And that is what we did. We saw a garden apartment in Riverdale just off the Henry Hudson Parkway and got it. We settled in Riverdale with our two dogs and a baby on the way.

At work, I got caught up in the Cameo-Parkway Records deal.

By caught up, I mean, screwed. Cameo-Parkway was a Philadelphia-based record label Allen was buying to make ABKCO a public company, without the usual rigmarole. It was a way to back into being publicly traded and a source for a lot of funds. The first thing Allen told me was that I could not buy any stock in the public company.

"I don't want anyone to be able to say that there was insider trading," he explained, "Absolutely don't buy any stock or give any info to family members."

This and the constant nepotism salary adjustments added to my disenchantment with Allen and the company. There was going to be a lot of press about Allen and Cameo-Parkway and the stock would definitely jump, but I respected my uncle's wishes and didn't make a move. Shortly after the announcement, the stock went from around twenty-five cents to eleven dollars. People made fortunes. My wife walked into our local drugstore and heard the owner tell her how he'd just bought a new house with the money he made on the stock. We heard these comments from a lot of people and felt like the only fools in the world.

I went back to London in the fall of 1967. While I was there, Allen wanted me to be on the lookout for possible recording studios for the Rolling Stones. Every time a cinema was closing, I was sent to check it out as a possible studio location. I would often bump into the Beatles reps who were doing the same thing.

On May 21, 1968, Brian Jones was busted, again, at his apartment in London for marijuana possession; he didn't want to return home. Emotionally he was a mess. His usual paranoia was increased tenfold by the fact that this was the second time he had been busted by an over-eager police department. Brian swore that this second bust was a police set-up, which was the main reason he didn't want to return to his flat.

Allen called me at the London Hilton and told me to put Brian into our corporate apartment that was reserved there. I called the front desk and told them I would pick up the key for the room. I did this without telling them who it was for. After I got Brian into the room, I went to my own room and got into the bathtub for a soak. While in the tub, I got a call from the hotel management, and they were freaking that Brian was there. I freaked right back at them and slammed down the phone. Minutes later, six hotel execs stormed into my room. It gave me a great opportunity to jump out of the tub, naked, and scream at them. I threatened them with the wrath of my uncle and the firestorm he would bring down on the London Hilton if they threw Brian out. They left; Brian stayed.

After getting dressed, I went to Brian's room. He was an emotional wreck, completely drained. He felt that the government was picking on him. He was crying, face down in the pillow. I held his hand as he fell asleep.

The next day I was in a meeting with four barristers and a Queen's Counsel (UK attorneys). We were sitting and talking about Brian's case, all business-like, and Brian walked into the room, padded over to me, and kissed me on top of my head. "Thank you for last night," he said.

The lawyer's mouths dropped open. They just stared.

CHAPTER XI

SILENT STRANGER

I was only seventeen when I first met Tony Anthony in 1961. He and his partner, Saul Swimmer, came to Miami Beach with my uncle to celebrate their making of a feature film, *Force of Impulse*. Tony is now best known as an actor/director/writer producing and starring in the successful "Stranger" series of spaghetti westerns; *A Stranger in Town* and *The Stranger Returns*.

In the summer of 1968 Allen sent me to Japan to work with Tony Anthony on his new spaghetti western, *Silent Stranger*.

I planned to leave New York and fly via the west coast for a July 7 arrival in Tokyo, but with Allen Klein, plans were often mere wishes. On July 1, my uncle and aunt were leaving for a trip to London. While Allen was getting ready to leave the office, he asked me to join him for the ride to the airport. I got in the limo with Allen, my aunt Betty, and their luggage. We were running late, and Allen had the driver call ahead. (At that time, airlines would hold airplanes, especially for first-class passengers.)

We arrived at the airport, and the ticket agent began to handwrite Allen's tickets as the airplane sat waiting on the tarmac.

"Ronnie, come with us," Allen said. "You can leave from London to Japan."

Turning back to the agent, he said, "Add a first-class ticket for Ronnie Schneider."

We walked across the tarmac to a waiting Boeing 727, climbed the long metal staircase, and entered first class to a loud "BOOOO!" from the passengers, who had been waiting on us for over forty-five minutes.

We arrived in London, checked into the Dorchester Hotel, had a bite together, and chatted business.

Jane arrived the next day. We left London July 3 via TWA. The flight wasn't direct; its next stop Bombay, India.

"Wouldn't it be cool to see Bombay?" I asked Jane.

"Yes." When the plane landed, we got off. We stood in line at immigration and watched as our plane left. We reached the official, and I handed him our passports.

"Where is your visa?"

"Visas? We don't need no stinking visas!" went through my mind, but I said, politely, "We just wanted to see your city and decided at the last minute."

"You need a visa to enter Bombay," he said, and signaled security. And with that, Jane and I had rifles pointed at our heads. "You will be escorted to a hotel where you will spend the night. You will be picked up at 5:00AM for the first flight out in the morning." And so it was. The next day we flew on, only to get off at the next stop for three ptomaine-plagued bedridden days in Hong Kong. While recovering from food poisoning I had a tailor come to our hotel room, and I left with three suits, two sport coats, and five custom-made shirts.

Next stop: Tokyo.

When I first traveled to London, adjusting to the country and the culture was easy. They spoke English; you could read directions and talk to cab drivers. The only difference was their very tiny spoons for sugar, and they boiled their beef. My next trip was to Rome, where they spoke Italian, but understood English. Their food was divine, and I look Italian. Tokyo, though, was a land with people I didn't understand and a diet of raw fish.

It was 1968; the streets of the Ginza section of Tokyo were packed, and we walked among throngs of people. For the first time in my life, I was taller than most of those around me.

After settling in, I met Tony Anthony at Toei Studios where we would be filming. We sat at a long conference table and went through the next business event, the Presentation of the Business Cards. This is a cultural ritual that you observe when doing business in Japan. You bow, smile, and hand the people your business card. They spoke English, and we discussed the filming of Silent Stranger. We would be shooting for approximately three months in

Kyoto.

Allen had made the deal with MGM to shoot the film in Japan since MGM had "blocked funds" (money that cannot be transferred from one country to another because of exchange controls). Our film was a way to get the money out: pay for the film in Japan with MGM blocked funds and reap the rewards of the money earned and parked outside the country. The total budget I would oversee was $1.6 million. MGM, to begin production, would wire $100,000.00 into an account I was to set up at a bank.

I went to a couple of the Japanese Tokyo branch banks to open the account. Each one told me the same story: I could open an account, but I couldn't touch the money for six weeks. MGM was wiring cash, and we needed it immediately. They smiled and said no. They said they could give us quicker access if it was wired into a savings account. Even with that, they would only allow us $10,000 to use until six weeks had passed.

This was unacceptable. We needed cash. The only American bank was Chase Manhattan, and they were located in Osaka. I had to take the bullet train from Kyoto to Osaka to set up the account. I did and Chase came through for us. The money was wired, and we started work on the film.

At the Toei Studio in Kyoto, we met our American producer, William Ross. Ross worked as liaison between our production and the studio. Bill was married to a Japanese woman and had been involved in other feature film productions in Japan. Today you often see him acting in vintage Japanese films such as The American General who helps fight off Godzilla, Mothra, and other assorted Japanese film monsters of that era.

Luigi Vanzi was our director. He surrounded himself with an Italian camera crew and Italian stuntmen. In all, there were six Italians. Tony, Lloyd Battista (American co-writer/actor), and I were the only Americans; the Japanese film crew was about thirty-five; and we had to have two Japanese translators, one for English and the other for Italian.

Communicating through a translator—or sometimes two of them—was a challenge. Immediate communication was impossible. Screaming at someone to make a point? Fruitless. Counting slowly to ten was all you could do while your tirade was being translated into who knows what.

Language and the culture were thought to be our biggest problems. It turned out that our real enemy was the weather. We started filming our outdoor shots, but unfortunately the typhoons came early. A typhoon is a tropical cyclone; it's called a hurricane in the North Atlantic. During the course of our filming in Japan we were hit by thirteen typhoons, plus one earthquake (my first) in Kyoto.

Here we are walking through a set that will soon be destroyed by a typhoon. You will note how the talent always treats the guy in the suit, especially a Hong Kong–made suit.

With the early arrival of the rainy season, our only option was to adapt. We had to do our shots in the rain. Unfortunately, you can't shoot in the rain and have it look like rain on screen. The rain had to be visible and consistent. To get that effect, we used fire hoses and cameras equipped with a device that simulated rain in front of the lens.

And then the rains came. My nice suits and cheerful demeanor were changed.

After we rebuilt the sets destroyed by a typhoon, we knew we were falling behind schedule and blowing through the budget.

And then the sets were destroyed a second time by another typhoon.

I believe that the look on our faces in this shot says it all! Luigi Vanzi, Tony Anthony, sitting, our translator, and me standing

After the weather destroyed our sets for the second time we had to get MGM's approval to rebuild. Tony phoned my uncle and my uncle phoned Robert H. O'Brien, the president of MGM, and Red Silverstein, the Southeast Asia Director for MGM. We had filmed quite a lot of footage, but there was no way we would be on budget or on schedule. So they sent the MGM studio execs.

They wanted to know how we were going to proceed as the weather was now totally against any outdoor shooting. The mornings would start with the sun out and by afternoon it would begin to rain.

Tony came up with a brilliant workaround. He suggested that we change to shooting nights. We didn't have to worry about the weather. We would have to shoot a month of six nights in a row in the rain. It was a miserable schedule, but it could work.

After a couple of weeks of shooting, I could see the toll the weather and other conditions were taking on our director. On my right is our Japanese production manager. Behind me is our American production manager. In front of me is Vincenzo Cerami, our writer, and the girl in the distance is one of our translators. Gigi, our director, is on the ground.

The structure of *Silent Stranger* was short vignettes, little skits that would try to add some humor. Lloyd Battista co-starred or co-wrote many of the spaghetti westerns with Tony. As Lloyd explained, "Because multiple languages were spoken in all the pictures we made, and humor was the most difficult thing to translate, our improvising would often give us what was needed."

Tony didn't want subtitles for the Japanese dialog. He wanted the audience to experience the perspective of a cowboy coming from the United States to Japan and dealing without knowing the language. The MGM execs lectured us on why we needed subtitles. Tony ignored them.

Allen kept complaining that we were behind in shooting and to stay on top of everyone to get on schedule. So I kept telling Vanzi, "We're behind schedule, speed up the shooting!" For a week, I kept hounding him: "We're behind schedule, do something!"

He finally had it with me, turned with the shooting script in hand, and asked, "How far behind are we?"

"Two days," I replied.

Vanzi held the script in his left hand, arm outstretched in front of him, then extended his right hand, and with his thumb and index finger plucked two pages randomly from the middle of the script. He dangled them in front of my face, tore them up, and threw them in the air.

"Now we are on schedule!" he told me, and walked away.

We lost additional time because we had to shoot two versions of the usual Japanese bath tub scene; the chaste—covered in a white sheet—version for those countries that fear breasts, and the topless version for the countries whose topless beaches we love to visit.

Tony's typically Italian machismo was never in question, but there was another side to his personality, too.

"Macachi! Macachi!" he would holler. Tony, this dirt-covered, rough, tough cowboy would be calling to his makeup man, Macachi.

"Where's my mirror?" Tony would yell.

Macachi would come running, carrying the mirror raised so Tony could see himself. Tony would primp, and when he felt it was right, nod, and got back to work. Macachi would silently walk away. Mind you, this happened every five minutes!

"Macachi! Macachi!"

Tony always cast characters to match his own character and was an equal-opportunity actor.

Tony's character, "The Stranger," never backed away from confrontation and Tony took this opportunity to set up great visuals of his face-off with armies of enemies.

If you aren't Bruce Lee with kung fu to defeat hordes of attackers, you need your own weapon. The Stranger figured the best thing to do was to carry a big gun.

Here we go over the big gun with the special effects guys.

By now, wearing suits was a thing of the past. I think that the little plastic umbrella that Tony is carrying kind of dilutes his macho image.

To effectively do some of the scenes, it was necessary for our stuntmen to become Japanese warriors. In the scene above they are discussing how the samurai would fight.

Like the action films of today there were a lot of stunts in Silent Stranger. As producer, I had to negotiate with the stuntmen for each of the stunts they performed. They would negotiate with me like they were selling something at a flea market. "Ron, we want $400.00 to jump off that three-story building." I didn't like putting a value on something that could break your neck, but to them, it was just a job, and I had to treat it as such. If I agreed to their immediate request they felt they had undersold themselves, so I had to come back with, "I'll pay you $300.00."

On one of our nights off we took our director to a bar in Kyoto. There was a group of Japanese men shooting pool. One of the men had his shirt off with a fantastic dragon tattoo on his back. Vanzi decided he wanted the man in our film. We sent our translator over. He came back to tell us that the man was in a rival gang to "our gang" at the studio. Both gangs would have to agree to let him in the film. Our production manager arranged a sit-down and the gang member, and his tattoo, made it into the film.

I already knew about "our gang" when paying bills. After the first week of shooting at Toei, I noticed a fee for security to a group I didn't recognize. I asked who this was for and was told it was a payoff to the gang that handled security for the studio. The gang had an office at the studio, and everything was in broad daylight. They billed you for not using their strong-arm tactics.

I was indignant and said I wasn't going to pay. I was told that was not a wise idea. Gangsters would block the camera; things would get broken or catch fire; and it would cost us a lot more to fix things than to pay for their "security" services. I relented and wrote the Yakuza a check.

Eating was something else. Here we are, Lloyd, Tony, and me dining in the executive dining room.

Food being important, our biggest catering disaster occurred on the day we had fried chicken. I sat down with a full plate of food, took a bite of the breaded fried drumstick, and immediately regretted it. You don't forget the taste of raw chicken with its blood running down your chin; I haven't.

The Japanese crew was always given Bento boxes. A Bento consists of rice, fish or meat, and one or more pickled or cooked vegetables, usually in a box. The cooks would make something different for the non-Japanese. Today they made us fried chicken. They covered the chicken in flour, dropped it in the deep-fat fryer for a minute, and we had their idea of fried chicken. It looked good but wasn't cooked.

As I jumped up to tell the cooks, my Italian crew came over en masse declaring, "Doctore, you can work us like slaves, you can curse us, you can spit on us, but you must feed us!" The biggest insult to an Italian was bad food. I told them I would take care of it and ranted at the caterer—which was easy with chicken blood dripping from my chin.

Tony's girlfriend, Luciana Paluzzi of James Bond Thunderball, came to our rescue. We built an outdoor fire and rigged a giant metal pot over it. She boiled water in the pot and made pasta. That calmed the Italians and they went back to work.

Scheduling the scenes to be shot was another problem. Because of the weather, we had to be ready to change the day's schedule, in case there was sun to pick up the shots needed to match scenes already shot days or weeks before.

One of the shots took place on one of the oldest bridges in Japan. The director wanted this to be a great visual. Luigi shot scene after scene of the bridge: he shot the bridge alone, the bad guy running on the bridge, and the soldiers walking across it. Until Tony exploded.

"Stop with these artistic bullshit shots!" he screamed. "Get me on the bridge and let's leave."

Luigi ignored him. Later, he explained his attitude toward the actors:

"Actors are cattle. I tell them where to stand, what to say, what to do, and I whip them with a stick to keep them in line."

Tony didn't agree and after a half-hour of screaming at Vanzi, Tony got physical. He leaped at Luigi and grabbed him around the throat. Lloyd and I jumped to the rescue. I tried to pry Tony's hands from Vanzi's neck while Lloyd struggled to pull them apart. Finally, we separated them and got on with the filming. Tony's shot was immediately taken, and we left the bridge.

The last two weeks of filming arrived. We still had to get a sunny exterior shot of four samurai warriors fighting beside a lovely meadow lake. The location was a three-hour drive from Kyoto. The only way to confirm the weather at the location was to have someone there. I ordered my location person to visit the site every morning and report back. With a week left, at 6:00 AM, I got a call. "The sun is out!" I woke up our translator and told him to contact the casting director to get the cast together and to the location for their scene.

We arrived and while the crew was setting up the cameras, I noticed the casting director was acting very strange. Furthermore, I didn't see anyone rehearsing the big fight scene. Vanzi came over to me and said he couldn't find the "samurai" and after chasing down the casting director, he couldn't get a straight answer.

I brought my translator along and confronted the casting director.

"Where are the samurai?"

He muttered a long story to the translator. When he finished, the translator said he was told that the cast would be here soon.

The translator pulled me aside and said, "That's a lie." The cast wasn't coming. The stunt guys playing the samurai warriors had the job because they were cousins of the casting director. They had another job that day and weren't coming. Since they were family, the casting director wasn't going to replace them. We didn't have the cast for the scene we had been waiting a month to shoot. Solution? I fired the casting director, dressed our stuntmen as samurai, found a couple of other actors who could play the part, and shot the scene.

The next day I was called into the executive offices at the studio.

"Mr. Schneider, we are very sorry for what happened yesterday," the head of the studio began. "We know you fired the casting director. He is no longer on your payroll and no longer part of your production. But we do not want him to lose face. He is allowed to come to the studio and sit at his desk. You may see him but you are not paying him. Please don't say anything to him."

At one point Tony, Cerami (he had a crush on my wife), and Tony's stunt double thought it would be a good idea to kiss me. Once again, the talent going after the suit guy. I think I may have grounds for a sexual harassment case.

We were working six nights of filming a week. Off time was cherished. When we got a free moment, we tried to do something to get rid of the stress. We got word of a wedding party being held at a temple in the mountains outside of Kyoto. Everyone was invited.

Upon arrival, we discovered that it was a sex temple. There were two religions that worshiped the male and female genitalia as the givers of life. The wedding party handed out penis-shaped lollipops and pastries and talismans in the shape of male and female genitals.

Religious sex charms closed

Charms open

To hide their affiliation with the religion the charms had the common shape and replication of traditional charms, but hidden compartments built into the trinket showed what they worshiped.

Jane put her hand between the branches in a deep V of a tree that we were told would guarantee she got pregnant. Jane was pregnant when we got back to the States.

Me and my "rock"hard penis.

Finally, the last day of filming arrived. As we were leaving, every employee of the hotel stood in line outside the lobby entrance and respectfully bowed and clapped as we passed. A very sweet and very Japanese custom.

CHAPTER XII

IT'S ALL OVER NOW

After we finished filming in Japan, Jane and I left Tokyo on November 4, 1967, and headed to Italy to finish the film. We stopped on the way for two days in Hong Kong and contacted our tailor. He came by and said, "Because of all the business you sent my way, you will not put your hands in your pockets." Interpreted, "You will not pay for anything." He asked if there was anything in particular we wanted to do. "We want to visit 'Red China'."

He drove us to the border. We stood in a field. Halfway across the field was a twenty-foot-high ten-foot-deep fence made of giant rows of barbed wire. There was a wooden boardwalk passageway through the barbed wire. Guards were posted to check people as they walked through. My tailor explained they were the field workers going back and forth. One side communism, the other democracy. What made one side different than the other? Nothing, except the politicians.

He next took us to a wooden shack. Inside the dark interior were rows of wooden tables similar to those at picnic grounds. It was a restaurant. We sat at a long table surrounded by Chinese workers. The servers brought all forms of food to the tables. In front of me was what looked like a pizza.

"Is this a pizza?" I asked.

"No, it's a fish," he replied.

I ate that and a lot of other things that I had no idea what they were. But they were all delicious.

As we were leaving Hong Kong and going through immigration, I was pulled aside.

"This is Hong Kong and I'm leaving! Why are you hassling me?"

Ignoring my protests, the customs guy began to quiz me. I may have given a wiseass answer since they led me into a small room and asked me to remove my jacket. On the wall was a chart listing items you cannot travel with. The officer pointed at the list and asked if I had any of the items with me.

"I left my gun at home, there's gold in my teeth, and I did all my drugs before I left." They made me strip down to my underwear before they let me go.

Jane and I decided to keep our hotel room keys as souvenirs. To prevent people accidentally taking keys they were unusually shaped or had large objects attached to them. Our hotel key in Kyoto had an 18-inch red plastic attachment. We had to sneak these out via covert operations. By the end of our stays in Europe and Asia, we had a nice-sized barrel of keys.

We also collected hotel and restaurant matchbooks. We packed two giant cardboard expandable suitcases to ship home. We packed the matchbooks in a kitchen trash bag in one suitcase. When we got home and went through our bags, we found all the match heads had been cut off. I pitied the person whose job that was.

We had arrived in Japan with a couple of bags. We thought we could get a great deal on Sony gadgets in Japan, but found they exported most of their products. You couldn't get Sony in Japan. So, when we made our stopover in Hong Kong, we went crazy on gifts. We bought small, round desktop radios that you could touch to turn on and off. We bought cameras and jewelry. Buying jewelry was interesting because the salespeople would say, "You are our first customer and must buy something for good luck." That's great news for a negotiator. We bought an opal ring that was first offered for $120 but was sold to us for "good luck" for $18.

We got to Rome on November 8. I loved the city. The food was spectacular, and the Italians didn't give a shit about anything. Politics, for example. When I was there the communists had just taken power. I was concerned.

"Italy is going to be another communist country," I said, but the Italians just laughed and responded, "Io non ne frega niente," meaning, "I don't give a damn." I would bastardize it and say, "No friggin niente."

I assumed all Italians would respect the Vatican, but I never heard anyone talk about it the way the Italian cab drivers did. They cursed the Vatican, called it the Mafia. Every cab I took to the Vatican had some irreverent complaint. It didn't hurt that I looked Italian. I could get by with a smile and lots of hand gestures.

We got an apartment in Rome for a month at the Residence Palace on Via Archimede and proceeded to start work on finishing the filming and editing of Silent Stranger.

The opening of Silent Stranger was to be shot in Cervinia in the north of Italy, at the base of the Matterhorn on the other side of the mountain from Zermatt, Switzerland. We took a bus with our Italian contingent from Rome to Cervinia.

That bus trip proved to be a microcosm of Italy. The arguing began when they were discussing Cervinia. In a group, they roared that the people in Cervinia weren't Italians; they were French (or at the very least Swiss since they were so close to the border). Then the Romanos (those from Rome) complained about the Sicilians (those from Sicily), and they each complained about the Napolitanos (from Naples) and so on. Each one said the other wasn't a true Italian.

We arrived in Cervinia, checked in to a ski resort, and prepared to scout a location on the snow-covered mountain. We were on the top of the mountain that was supposed to represent the Klondike, and our director, Vanzi, was walking as best he could through the deep snow. He was standing about twenty-five feet in front of us when a frightened look crossed his face. He screamed. He jumped forward spread-eagled onto the snow. We saw the snow fall away behind him as a large crevasse opened like a gaping wound. One of our stunt guys lay flat on the ground, crawled out to him, grabbed his hand, and pulled him to safety.

After that the shoot was fairly routine.

Our month in Rome was spectacular. Tony took us under his Italian wing, and I experienced the city like a local. Most of the time we went to our neighborhood restaurant, Domenico's. The owner was from Abruzzi, Italy. Tony would chide him that every time he went home, he buried more of the ton of money he was making in Rome under his floorboards. We were never given a menu. Domenico would tell us what "Mama" made and ask what we wanted. Even though there were over thirty choices for appetizers, most of the time I picked prosciutto with a sweet slice of melon. For secondos we would order his special house pasta carbonara. There were two types of pasta in the serving, one white and one green—spinach. To these, he added Parmesan cheese, but not the way you think. He took a giant ring of Parmesan cheese before it was totally set, cut the cheese in half, and used the soft unsettled center as the cream sauce for the pasta. Add peas and prosciutto. Oh my god, was it good! My mouth still waters!

Various times while we were eating, Domenico would come to our table with a small plate, "Mama just made this. Here, try it."

After every meal, when it came time for the bill, Domenico and Tony would argue. Domenico would say we owed $6.00 per person. Tony would protest and say it should be $4.00, and so on and so on until they settled in the middle. It was the custom and not a reflection of anything else.

On other nights, Tony would take us on the local tour, visiting different restaurants to enjoy their specialties. First, we went to a restaurant that specialized in simple pasta made with fresh tomatoes from the restaurant's garden. After eating that course, we got up and went to a different restaurant for their special, the best cold salads, and from there we went to the best steak restaurant.

Then we took the Italian restaurant experience on the road. We drove over an hour to the Etruscan caves. We walked into a cave that had a wood-burning fire pit dug into the wall. This place specialized in meat cooked over the fire, known as mixed grill. They asked if I wanted anything special, and I requested garlic bread. They asked how it was prepared. I told them and then I watched them make it. The chef took a big Italian crusty bread and cut off a giant thick slice. He poured fresh olive oil over the bread and cut fresh pieces of garlic. These he placed on the bread. He put the slice of bread on the grill above the fire and after a short period of time, he turned it over. When it was just right, he brought it to me. I took a bite; the oil poured down my chin. It was amazing.

Another thing that made me love Italy: I could eat delicious meals anywhere throughout the country. Just like Domenico's, the restaurants were all family cooking. Nothing was pre-cooked or god forbid, microwaved. They brought the cooking pans to the table and served you right from the pan. There would always be a "mama" cooking in the kitchen and the owner would bring you a bite of "something Mama just made." They weren't hustling you to buy something else; they just wanted to share the good food.

"Here, try the suckling pig," the owner would say as he dropped a small plate on the table with enough for everyone.

On our final night in Rome, Domenico had a party for us. To celebrate our stay, our being friends, and loyal clients, he outdid himself in the spread he laid out. We had our usual appetizers, and some of our guests ordered pasta. When Domenico came out with the carbonara special, the people who had already eaten their ordered pasta dug in and ate this as well, and then the servers came with trays of langostinos (small lobsters) and a giant turbot (fish). This was the best meal sendoff ever.

CHAPTER XIII

ROCK AND ROLL CIRCUS

We returned to the States via England. By the time we left London, we had twenty-one suitcases. The skycap brought our pile of bags to the checkout counter at TWA. After weighing and checking all the bags, they told us we owed $2,700 in excess baggage charges. I carried on about how it would be good hands across the ocean and good publicity if they let us go with no charge. After about twenty minutes, they agreed and didn't charge us for the overage.

I called Pete Bennett in New York and told him we were coming in with over twenty suitcases. Could he arrange our arrival?

"Are you carrying any drugs?" he asked. "No," I told him.

"Don't declare anything and I'll have you escorted through customs."

On the flight, we got the customs declaration forms. I was concerned about not declaring anything. I believed the law was if you didn't declare it, customs could fine you and confiscate it. I didn't want that risk, so I filled out the form and included the pearls from Japan and the fur coat from Greece. I didn't care about the three cases of English China dishes we had gotten.

After we cleared immigration and were going through customs, my guy came over and said, "I told you not to declare anything." I told him my concern of losing the pearls and coat. He handed me another blank declaration form and said, "Fill it out and don't declare anything."

I did and we, and our giant cart of twenty-one bags, were directed out a side door. Once outside, we met our limo driver and went home. They never opened a bag!

In December 1968, I was back in London for the Stones' new album launch of Beggars Banquet. The party was in the stately Elizabethan Rooms of the Gore Hotel in London on December 5. And what a party it was. The Stones were seated on one side of a long conference table and members of the press were scattered throughout the room. Along the walls were tables loaded with cream pies.

After remarks by Mick and cheers and jeers from the rest of the boys, the first pie was thrown. I waded in and began throwing pies at everyone and anyone, managing to stay clean until the last few pies, when it was noted that I was not spattered. I got the most violent pie to the side of my head and saw that it came from Brian. He was ecstatic that he had scored a direct hit.

A few days later, I was on the set of The Rolling Stones Rock and Roll Circus, a special the Stones were filming in a studio in Wembley. The "Circus" had an amazing, talented cast of characters, including the Rolling Stones, The Who, Taj Mahal, Marianne Faithfull, Jethro Tull, and others. When I got to the set, they were filming a classical pianist, Julius Katchen, performing a piece by Chopin. Off to the side, I saw the top model of the time, Luna, waiting beside a caged Bengal tiger. There was a discussion going on about the safety of letting the tiger out of the cage for the performance. The trainer said it wouldn't be a problem; the tiger was sedated, just like many of the musicians and guests.

Then came the Dirty Mac, a group formed by John Lennon, Eric Clapton, Mitch Mitchell, and Keith Richards. When they got to the stage to perform, everyone knew it was a historic moment. They were at the top of their game.

You could see the respect each artist had for one another as the music came from their souls. At one point during their performance, Yoko Ono climbed into a large black canvas bag in a front corner of the stage. While they played you heard her screaming from inside the bag.

Then The Who went on and tore the house down with Keith Moon, powered by jet fuel or something more ingestible. Moon's energy was contagious and transferred to the band and the room.

A friend of mine told me once about a dinner he'd had with Keith Moon. They had walked into an elegant restaurant in London, which was decorated with mirrors. Keith asked the manager how much the mirrors cost. The manager told him they cost about £700. Keith counted out £700 and went about smashing all the mirrors. I don't know if it was true, but it matched with the widely circulated tale that Moon had driven a limousine into a swimming pool, so I didn't discount it.

The original filming of the Rock and Roll Circus lasted until the wee hours of the morning. The incredible amount of talent on the stage generated an energy that drained you. By the time the Stones went on, around 4:00 AM, they were exhausted. Later, after viewing the footage they decided they didn't like their performance and wanted to reshoot. Part of the dissatisfaction stemmed from the energetic Who set and the Stones' exhaustion.

For the reshoot, we came up with a plan for a new Stones closing segment to be shot in Rome at the Coliseum. Tony Anthony got the necessary permissions, and we flew there with director Michael Lindsay-Hogg to plan the filming.

People have an image of the Coliseum being similar to any outdoor sports arena. That was the concept of the shoot, but when we arrived, we went inside and found that it wasn't a flat field. Instead, it was composed of catacombs with narrow jagged pathways. It looked like a maze.

"I don't know how to shoot this," concluded Michael Lindsay-Hogg.

We left, and that was that. Indeed, that was that for The Rolling Stones Rock and Roll Circus as well. Everything was canned until 1996 when the old footage was gathered and re-edited for release on VHS (and later DVD) by Allen Klein's daughter, my cousin Robin. Allen presented me with an embroidered Rock and Roll Circus jacket after the 1996 screening.

CHAPTER XIV

I WANT TO HOLD YOUR HAND

Allen was as giddy as a kid on his first date. He, his assistant Iris Keitel, and I were in his suite at the Dorchester Hotel in London. We had flown in on January 24, 1969, for the meeting he was having with John Lennon and Yoko Ono on the 28th. Allen was on the phone with the hotel chef assigned to the suite going over all the food possibilities. He kept insisting on a tasty vegetarian menu. He believed that John and Yoko were vegetarians and wanted to make sure that the meeting and meal went well. After he'd finished talking with the chef, Allen left Iris and me in the suite and went to the penthouse to meet John and Yoko.

An hour later, he joined us for a brief update.

"It's going great. They appreciated the menu but said they were not vegetarians and would have eaten anything. They want to talk some more. I'll be back."

After the meeting, Allen returned and said they had signed with him and to get ready to work at Apple. To say that Allen was on a cloud would be an understatement. He now had the Rolling Stones and the Beatles signed. For all intents and purposes, he had the two top bands in the world under his management. Only one major element was missing: Paul McCartney. McCartney wanted the Eastmans—his then-girlfriend Linda's father, Lee, and brother, John (both showbusiness attorneys)—to handle the Beatles. He refused to join with Klein. For Allen, all business was personal, and he took it as an affront and a challenge to make Paul love him. However, Paul remained adamant about the Eastmans. Another example of nepotism reigning supreme in the rock 'n' roll world. Or an example of that old song "When A Man Loves a Woman."

The battle lines were drawn when Allen had John, George and Ringo send a letter to Lee Eastman telling him he was not authorized to represent the Beatles. From that point on I was to deal with Paul's legal representative, John Eastman, making Allen's points and John Eastman would deal with me making Lee Eastman's points.

```
Eastman and Eastman
39 West 54th Street
New York
New York 10019                        18th April 1969


Attention Lee Eastman, Esq.

Dear Mr. Eastman,

        This is to inform you of the fact that you are not
authorized to act or to hold yourself out as the attourney
or legal representative of "The Beatles" or of any of the
companies which the Beatles own or control.

        We recognize that you are authorized to act for
Paul McCartney, personally, and in this regard we will
instruct our representatives to give you the fullest co-
operation.

        We would appreciate your forwarding to

        ABKCO Industries Inc.
        1700 Broadway
        New York
        N.Y.

all documents, correspondence and files which you hold
in your possession relating to the affairs of the Beatles,
or any of the companies which the Beatles own or control.

                    Very truly yours,


                    John Lennon

                    Richard Starkey

                    George Harrison
```

We began working full-bore on The Beatles. Allen had me fly back and forth while things were being finalized. I stayed at the Dorchester for a month, spending most of my time working at the Apple Corps Ltd. administrative offices at 3 Savile Row.

I sat with Allen in many a meeting, meetings that everyone knew were more like interviews. Neil Aspinall was the CEO. Neil was a school friend of Paul McCartney and George Harrison who left his accounting job to become the Beatles road manager. He advanced from gofer to manager to chief executive of Apple Corps after the death of the Beatles' manager, Brian Epstein. Mal Evans was an assistant and long-time friend of the Beatles. Klein didn't trust friends doing music business together, especially ones who weren't in the business to begin with. Allen fired almost everyone. He wanted a clean slate and a low overhead (fixed expenses). Lennon told Allen not to fire Neil or Mal. He didn't.

Derek Taylor was a journalist hired by Brian Epstein to be the Beatles' press officer. I liked Derek. He would lean on a desk or table, partially sit, and make his logical points. He was a calming influence when the discussions got heated.

It was interesting to observe the demeanor of the staff at Apple when I walked into the offices on my first day. With my funny American accent and suit and tie, I was definitely an outsider. To them, I looked like the archetypal "ugly American." Days later, after I was assimilated, one of the secretaries told me everyone in the office thought I was a Mafioso.

After being in the office for a couple of hours, Allen came over to my desk and told me to get in the Rolls Royce parked out front and take a drive into the countryside to meet John and Yoko. They were looking for a house and were viewing an estate that had horses, stables, and elegant grounds. Allen wanted me to join them to show that we were there for them. I was to do the same for Ringo weeks later.

After a drive of an hour and a half outside of London, the limo pulled into the long entranceway of this magnificent mansion and parked in front of the Rolls Royce that belonged to John.

I greeted John and Yoko, and we walked together through the house and grounds. The place was beautiful. There were three ponds that were more like lakes, a plush forest of trees, grassy meadows, and horse stables. We talked and walked for about an hour until John said he had seen enough, and it was time to leave. I walked toward my limo as John and Yoko walked toward theirs.

"Do I stink?!" John hollered after me.

I turned, wondering if I had offended them. "No. Why?"

"Why won't you ride with us?"

"I thought you wanted to be alone," I replied. "I have the office car that brought me."

"Come ride with us, Ronnie," John said with a smile.

I got in the car with them.

As we drove back to the city, John talked non-stop about ideas he had: "I want to do a calendar where for each month we…" "I want to film a…" "I need a recording studio that will…"

On and on John went with brilliant idea after brilliant creative idea.

Once in a while Yoko would try and get a word in or express an opinion and John would say, "Shut up!" I would cringe a bit, but it wasn't said in a mean tone, just one that seemed to say, "I'm making a point, don't throw me off." This held true at various times in many discussions. Sometimes John would let her make a point, but overall Lennon was not, as some have suggested, pussy-whipped.

We got back to the Apple offices with the fresh image of the beautiful estate we had just visited—the leafy trees, lakes, meadows, and pastures in our mind's eye.

John and Yoko sat down at one of the tables. I came over and joined them as John picked up a pencil and began to sketch on a piece of paper, Yoko closely at his side.

"What do we really want our house and grounds to look like?" John asked Yoko. Yoko mentioned something about igloos and John said, "Yes, something round with no corners. No sharp edges," and he began to draw.

John sketched out an igloo-shaped house. He drew a high-ceilinged dome shape on the top of the page. Underneath that, he drew a circle within a circle and said as he pointed to the inner circle, "This would be our living room and around the living room, we would have the kitchen, bedrooms, and den." He drew smaller circles between the two circles. He went on, "Instead of painting the outside of the house I think we should cover it with mirrors. When you look at the house," he carefully explained, "you would only see the hills, grass, trees, and sky reflected in the mirrors. You would only see nature."

He wasn't done drawing. Next he drew an airplane in his make-believe sky and added a few clouds. Below that he drew a couple of trees, some hills, and more round houses. He had drawn a small neighborhood.

"With all the houses covered in mirrors a plane could fly over, and you would only see the ground and sky."

"We could do the same for cars," John added, as he became more excited by his idea. "Imagine a VW Beetle driving down the road covered with mirrors reflecting the countryside. With all the houses and cars made that way, you would only see nature."

"John," I reminded him, "you have to be able to see the cars!"

John was always like that. He'd give me a dozen ideas a day, and I would say, "Please just one idea and let's do it."

Later in the day, John walked over to my desk and asked what I thought of his new business card. Everybody at Apple was trying to have a business card that stood out from the usual 2" x 3" card. They'd use gold embossing, ultra-thin, translucent paper, eye-catching fonts, and so on. John's business card was an 8" x 10" glossy head shot. The only info on it was, "I am at 3 Savile Row, most days."

🍎 *I am at 3 Savile Row, most days*

John would have me join him on visits to his son Julian at ex-wife Cynthia's home. I'd sit at the kitchen counter while John and Cynthia would chat while she made us tea and biscuits.

Allen, John, Yoko, and I were in a lot of meetings, working on a plan to get Yoko's daughter, Kyoko, back from her ex-husband, Tony Cox. Cox had custody, but Yoko was doing everything she could to reunite with her daughter. Tony kept disappearing with Kyoko, and no one would know where they were. Allen's concern and attention to this matter show the personal side of his relationships was just as important as the business side.

DAILY MIRROR, *Thursday, March 6, 1969*   PAGE 15

ALLEN KLEIN is the alchemist of pop. He is the one with the jaw and sideboards. He is the show business company doctor who aims to get the Beatles' financial affairs right, and put the rosy glow back into their Apple.

Millionaire Klein, who once wanted to buy out Brian Epstein and take over the Beatles, is shown in this Inside Page picture striding from a Beatles' Rolls-Royce into the Dorchester Hotel, London. With him is one of his bookkeepers.

At 34, Klein, a New Yorker, describes himself as a business ` efficiency expert. Now without any official appointment or contract, he has taken in hand the Beatles' money problems at the boys' own request.

He stands to r e c e i v e a spiffing commission for re-organising their empire, about which John Lennon declared recently: "If Apple goes on losing money at its p r e s e n t rate, all of us will be broke in the next six months."

Klein aims to f i n d o u t whether the Beatles indulge in too much ideology, when it comes to money, and too little business acumen.

Klein has already made a powerful impact on the entertainment world. He is a major shareholder in M G M, and business manager to the Rolling Stones and he holds the recording rights of Dave Clark and Herman's Hermits.

From his initial study of the Beatles' affairs, he has learned they are owed m i l l i o n s of pounds, mostly in r e c o r d royalties from Japan, Russia, Ethiopia, Thailand. And while straightening out those little matters, he intends to clinch new dollar-earning deals in America for them.

3/6/1969. The Daily Mirror misidentifies me. All they had to do was ask. "Jaw and sideboards," "alchemist of pop"—too bad they had only part of it right.

Another time, John wanted to send a cargo ship filled with medical supplies and food, to help in South America. My uncle thought it a good opportunity to get a couple of politicians behind John, in hopes of changing the government narrative on the radical, John Lennon.

Two senators sat with my uncle, John Lennon, Yoko Ono, and me in a semicircular booth in La Brasserie restaurant in Manhattan. After the French onion soup, John explained his humanitarian intent to send the cargo ship. The senators quietly listened.

When John was done one of the senators spoke up. "That's a great idea. I am sure we both can support you. Give us ten thousand dollars each and send the ship off."

John's, Yoko's. and my eyes widened.

"If everything goes well, you can use our names, and we will bring it up on the Senate floor. If there are any problems, you can't use our names, and we keep the twenty thousand."

John's face turned red. "I give you twenty grand and if there's a problem you don't know me?"

"Yes," was the unashamed reply.

My uncle grabbed John's arm to stop him from saying anything further and said, "We'll get back to you."

And we left with disgust in our bellies.

After their wedding on March 20, 1969, John and Yoko decided to embark on a series of publicity stunts to promote their message of world peace. The most famous stunt was the "Bed-In," which basically consisted of the two of them staying in bed for an entire week and inviting members of the press to interview them there. The first Bed-In took place at the Amsterdam Hilton during the last week of March. They had planned to do the second in New York City, but John was not allowed into the States at the time because of his previous year's drug conviction for cannabis possession. After some discussion, we came up with the idea of going to the Bahamas instead. I'd been there before with Jane on our honeymoon. I knew it would be a relaxing vacation, and we figured it was close enough to the States that American journalists could easily make the trip.

Unfortunately, I wasn't able to accompany John and Yoko on the trip so I contacted an old Miami friend, Ronnie Gaines, who had moved to the Bahamas the previous year. I asked Ronnie if he could take care of them. His father was a big builder in Miami who controlled the roof trusses of the Bahamas—you wanted a roof on your house in the Bahamas you had to buy it from Ronnie's father. He had a magnificent house on Biscayne Bay, Florida's Millionaire's Row. I came from the other side of the tracks, but we hung out. One time, after a night of fun and debauchery, I awoke ten steps up on Gaines's living room wooden spiral staircase. I got up and went looking for him, and after a few grunts, I found him in his closet sleeping on his head with his legs up in the corner.

I knew he could handle John and Yoko.

"I'm not sure exactly when I received a phone call from my old friend Ron Schneider, telling me to please pick up John Lennon at the airport," Ronnie Gaines remembers. "At first, I was positive he was putting me on, but I finally believed him. I borrowed my dad's Cadillac and drove to the airport to pick up John and Yoko. I had to laugh at the mountain of luggage they'd brought with them. John treated me with kindness and respect while Yoko was very quiet. I got them checked in to the Lucayan Beach Hotel and when we arrived at the room, John and Yoko jumped straight into bed. Once they were settled, I made sure John had my phone number and left."

As it turned out, the Bahamas was not really the best place to stage a protest. There were no journalists around, and no news coverage. In addition, John and Yoko didn't like the general vibe they were getting from the staff at the hotel. The next day they packed up and headed for Canada. The next Bed-In took place in Montreal. Some people at the time claimed John and Yoko left the Bahamas because of the heat. That wasn't the case: they had air-conditioning. They were after publicity and there was none to be had in the Bahamas.

Forbidden by contract to perform with another group, John and Yoko began recording anonymously as the Plastic Ono Band. "Give Peace a Chance" (released in July 1969) was the first single released under that name. Everyone was asking who the Plastic Ono Band was. Promoters came to me and wanted to know if they could book the band for New York City, at the Lincoln Center for the Performing Arts.

John thought about it and came back with a plan. He would have large Plexiglas platforms built. Each platform would be placed on the stage in front of a microphone where a live performer would normally appear. He wanted to have large reel-to-reel audio tape decks placed on the Plexiglas platforms. John was going to load each deck with a track of a different instrument—one drum track on the Plexiglas stand in the back and so on with the other instruments. And one for the vocals in front. No live people, just tape players.

One promoter was willing to put up $150,000, and it got serious. The idea was we would insist on total anonymity for the band. No one could see them before the show. The drama would build: "What do these guys look like?

Who are they?"

Then John rethought things. If we took the money, the show had to go on. Did he really want to tease the promoters and possibly alienate his fans? John decided not to poke the bear and just be happy that his music was out there being played.

Most of my time at Apple was spent working to keep things running while setting up the operation the way Allen wanted it. My uncle was concerned that people were taking advantage of the Beatles, and he wanted a clean slate. Allen knew that the Beatles had lost over $100 million in licensing fees through bad deals from their licensing company, Seltaeb (Beatles spelled backward). It was an instance where they had relied on lawyers or friends of friends to run an operation they knew nothing about. This meant shedding some of the associated businesses, including the Apple clothing store and restructuring Apple Records. Restructuring Apple Records by getting rid of signed artists. I knew the reasoning, but thought it was a mistake to get rid of such greats as James Taylor.

One day, I was sitting at a desk at Apple Corps on 3 Savile Row in London. I had a plain sheet of white paper on the table in front of me, and George Harrison was leaning over me. He had a pencil in his hand. He turned the paper sideways and began to sketch. First, he drew a wavy line across the middle of the page. "Ronnie," he said, "imagine this is the top of the ocean." Next, he sketched a small rowboat on the wavy line ocean. He drew a circle in the top right corner, obviously representing the sun, then a straight line on the bottom of the page: "This is the ocean floor."

"Ronnie, life is like a rowboat floating on the ocean. You can sit in the boat and drift through your life. Drift until you float into the sunset. Or you can jump out of the boat" — George drew a stick figure— "swim down to the bottom of the ocean, pick up a grain of sand, swim back to the surface, put that grain of sand in your boat, and so on and so on. Your boat fills with grains of sand as you drift into your sunset, your life filled with all these adventures." George was always sharing his grains of sand.

When I wasn't at Apple, I was out scouting recording studio locations, much as I did for the Stones. While I was doing this, the Beatles had a studio being built in the basement at the Apple offices. They were especially proud the studio would have a console from the airport control tower that they were going to convert into a 116-track mixing desk. I took a trip downstairs to take a look at this construction and found Yanni Alexis Mardas, better known as Magic Alex, the name given to him by the Beatles, on the floor under the elaborate console.

"Hi, what are you doing?" I asked.

"I am wiring the board so the Beatles can have the biggest and best recording equipment in the world."

A couple of people in the room smiled at me bemusedly and shook their heads. "He'll never get it to work" and "He's crazy" were some of the surreptitious comments I got later.

Time proved them right.

The Beatles weren't relying solely on our finding recording studios for them or on Magic Alex. On a table off to the side in the main, the Apple office was a large-scale model of dreams of a creative nirvana. The model consisted of a large three-story building in the middle of a park with green grass and trees. From the building, you could follow four separate paths, like points on the compass, finding a large house at the end of each trail: North, South, East, and West. John, Paul, George, and Ringo.

It was explained they wanted to find real estate in the countryside and build a recording studio that had amenities such as a twenty-four-hour restaurant and hotel rooms for recording artists, musicians, and their entourages to stay.

Each of the Beatles would have their own house, just a walk from the studio. It was a nice idea.

While concentrating on the business at Apple, Allen also sent me to the Stone's office to do random audits showing he was still concerned with their business. One day, I would be in the Stone's office and the next day I would be with John Lennon at his ex-wife Cynthia's house. I was next sent to Mellow Yellow, Donovan's house, to deliver papers and hang out with him and his close buddy, Gypsy Dave. My uncle had introduced Donovan to his producer Mickey Most. Allen was concerned that Gypsy was a bad influence on Donovan. Part of my job was to see if that was the case.

After time at Apple, I realized there were many similarities between the Stones and the Beatles. It was the same for both camps: Always looking for a recording studio, stress over album titles, the timing of releases to avoid conflict with each other, stress over album covers, checking the music charts, and fighting with the record companies. And, of course, "Should that be our single?"

CHAPTER XV

CAN'T BUY ME LOVE

Around a small meeting table in Apple Corp sat John Lennon, Allen Klein, Paul McCartney, and myself. In the center of the table was a big glass bowl filled with shortbread cookies. It was a meeting about possible film projects. They were discussing acquiring the motion picture rights to The Lord of the Rings trilogy or The Hobbit. These books by J.R.R. Tolkien were enormously popular at the time. Another choice was a Robert Heinlein novel, Stranger in a Strange Land, a tale about a human raised on Mars and his adaptation to, and understanding of Earth, humans and their culture.

Before the meeting, Allen ordered me: "Just listen! You don't have an opinion. If someone talks about a film, even if you've seen it, you don't say anything. No matter what, don't talk!"

The discussion continued, and points were made: there wasn't a script; it's hard to get a good script; who can play a hobbit? My uncle gave input from his movie-dealing perspective. The conclusion: the special effects technology wasn't there yet. They would not be able to film these stories without having the movie look like a cartoon. They didn't want a cartoon.

After two and a half hours, without a word from me, we stood to end the proceedings. There had been paper and pencils in front of everyone for note taking. John had been sitting across the table from me. He walked around the table and handed me a sheet of paper. He had done a drawing during the meeting. On the left side of the page was a giant apple with a serene looking face penciled in. Wiggling toward the apple was a mop-topped worm with glasses and a beard adorning its face—obviously, John. The worm was staring at a small sign on the bottom right of the apple: "eat me." I knew the shortbread cookies at the center of the table had been tempting me, and it seems they had been calling to John as well. At some point during the discussion, he drew this sweet, funny cartoon of temptation.

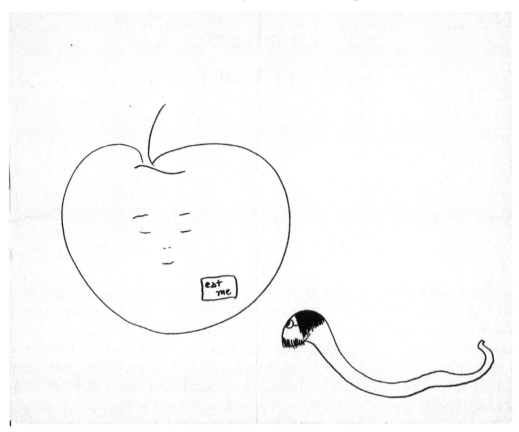

John Lennon drew this and gave it to me Temptation of the cookie?

That would have been enough to make my day, but then Paul McCartney took me by surprise. Paul had been sitting to my right. After John walked away, Paul stood up and handed me a piece of paper. "Here, this is for you," he said and walked away. I looked at it in amazement.

Paul was in the "enemy" camp. He and Linda were opposed to my uncle representing the Beatles. I didn't expect anything from Paul. We were at war. I often chided my uncle when he kept trying to get Paul's acceptance. "He's not going to love you. You say the things you are doing for John, Ringo, and George are great. You're going to make them a ton of money. Do it and stop wasting time trying to win favor with Paul. When the results of what you are doing show you are right, and you make them tons of money, his camp's arguments will weaken. And then—maybe—Paul will change his mind."

Due to this schism, I didn't get a chance to spend much time with Paul, but now he had drawn me. He had doodled a picture. The drawing showed my long sideburns and a Picasso-styled head. I was wearing a uniform soldier's jacket with epaulets, sergeant major stripes on my left arm, my arms crossed across my chest, and a bowtie. This would have been enough if just for the drawing talent, but Paul had gone further. Underneath my caricature were the words "… EMOTION… PICTURE… INDUSTRY."

Paul drew this and captured my silence

John Lennon and Paul McCartney, at the same time, in the same place, and under the same circumstances, had each seen something different. Their artwork blew me away. Of course, I am biased, as they were drawings for and of me, but each is special in its own way. I think it shows how the two artists, separate and equal, together merged to create singular masterpieces, one seeing the humor and temptations in life and the other seeing an uptight business world. I wonder if any scientist, psychiatrist, neurologist, or art expert could look at these drawings and interpret how one artist could write "Imagine" while the other could write, "Live and Let Die," and when they wrote together, would come up with, "I Wanna Be Your Man."

CHAPTER XVI

STARTING OVER

When we became involved in the business lives of the Beatles, Apple was a mess. Apple's business structure was created with the Beatles as directors. Under the laws of the UK, that meant that as directors, they could only draw £5,000 a year. There were millions of pounds in the bank, but they couldn't touch it. They had recently received a royalty statement accounting for over $30 million for the quarter. We had to stop the royalty payment to restructure the company for a better tax advantage.

Apple was broken up to enable the Beatles to take their money. That wasn't what led to the breakup of the group, just the breakup of the Apple entity.

What led to the group's breakup, in my opinion, is the same thing that breaks up marriages; as people grow they change. Responsibilities, needs, and attitudes change. If you grow together (the successful relationship) the dynamic stays the same, but as the majority of examples show, when you are young, the many choices before you lead you to different paths, and often you grow apart.

Many times, Allen and I would discuss the Beatles. He felt the death of Brian Epstein had affected John, to the extent that John stepped back from the band; he became depressed and lethargic. It wasn't until over a year had passed, and he met Yoko, that John came back to life. We both thought that Yoko made John a man again. He resurfaced with a vengeance.

During the time that John had backed away, Paul stepped in to save the band. He had formed the Apple conglomerate and was devoting all of his energy to keeping the Beatles alive. When John came back, his energy and ego took control; he was picking up where he had left off, but Paul must have felt, some might say rightfully so, *What the fuck? I've done all this to keep us going. You can't just jump back in after you abandoned us. Show me some respect and get in line.*

John Lennon was not one to jump into line, behind anyone.

This was not a one-sided opinion on my part. I had many talks with George Harrison where he brought up the topic, and in no uncertain terms, he backed John.

George took me for a ride in his Mercedes-Benz 600. Most people trying to impress had Rolls Royce Phantom V's—they were cool, with cavernous back seats and the immaculate Rolls luxury, everything in good taste—but there was something special about George's Mercedes. Maybe it was the meditation. While we reclined in the back, George's mind would wander off in another direction.

"You know why I don't trust Paul?"

I had never asked that question, nor wondered. Now I did. "Why?"

George, staring intently into my eyes, went on, "We were tripping on acid and Paul started to hallucinate that he was falling down a bottomless well. He was hanging on to the side of the well, gripping tightly with his hands, scared that if he let go, he would fall. I went over to calm and talk him down. I told him to trust me and give me his hand, that I would help him. But Paul wouldn't let go. He wouldn't take my hand. He didn't trust me… That's why I could never trust him."

Weirdly, I related to what George said was Paul's hallucination. As an eleven-year-old kid, I didn't see the logic of living when you were only going to die, especially when you think you are fat and ugly and are being bullied, so I did think a lot about suicide. One morning I was in the shower and out of the blue, a poem fermented in my brain. The minute it came into my head, I knew what it meant. I wrote it down:

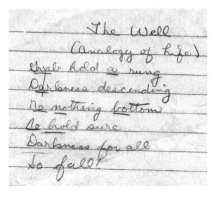

To my little eleven-year-old head, the well was my life. "Grab hold a rung." I seemed to be telling myself to start living. "Darkness descending / No nothing bottom / No hold sure /Darkness for all" — definitely you never knew what tomorrow would bring. There are no guarantees, everyone goes through it, and everyone dies. Then I came to the line in my head, "so fall." I knew that somehow I had made the decision to live; I would never commit suicide. That was a load off!

It was interesting that Paul had a similar experience in his LSD-influenced state with a different result.

George kept talking.

"You know the rumor that John and Paul had a fight, punching each other?" He paused, then said, "It wasn't John. It was me. Paul was having a tough time finishing a song. For days he had been trying to come up with a lyric to continue a line in what would become one of his most successful songs. I came up with the two lines that he was able to use to finish the song, and I wanted a writer's credit on the song. Without those lines the song wouldn't have been the same, but Paul refused. We got into a fight and I punched him."

Later that day, George stopped by my desk and handed me a paperback of *Autobiography of a Yogi*. Inside the cover he had written, "To Ron, best wishes from George Harrison." A little further down he wrote in parenthesis, "(chapter xxxiii)." That chapter title was "Babaji, the Yogi-Christ of Modern India."

AUTOBIOGRAPHY OF A YOGI

To Ron, best wishes from George Harrison.

(chapter xxxiii)

*****

I returned to the States on July 3, 1969. Here I was, this rebel in a suit, with my very large executive office next to my uncle the CEO's office. I had reached my peak at ABKCO. My uncle had a son, Jody, who would surely take Allen's place when he left. Could I be happy always being number two?

Plus, the screaming was taking a toll. We would go over any pending deal or meeting in a mock scenario. Allen would hit me with his point, I would counter with another point of view. Right or wrong he had to win. It was always a competition. He would get personal and use any means to win the argument. He used a sledge hammer of abject faith in what he had to say; he believed his points and would attack, even if wrong. I felt like the sparring partner for a heavy weight. Underneath the bluster, he knew he wasn't always right. I was his testing stone. My only reward was watching the scenarios we battled about, being used in his negotiation, and resolved with my counter points included in the final agreement.

There were other problems. Recently, Allen had me negotiate a large record company deal. He made all the terms, but I was the face of the deal with the other company's representatives. When all the terms of the negotiation were agreed to, we scheduled a sit-down signing of the contract. Allen, one of our attorneys, and I sat at the conference table with the president of the record company. He had come prepared to sign and celebrate.

Allen opened the contract in front of him, scanned a few pages, and then said, "Wait, this says we get a $250,000 advance. It's supposed to be $500,000!"

This was pure nonsense. Allen knew the terms of the deal. I was as shocked as the record company exec but knew what was going on. The other side had probably celebrated the new deal they were doing, and all of a sudden it was blowing up in their face. Klein knew he had the leverage of them wanting to do the deal, and also knew that in the end, it was company money, not theirs. They relented and the deal was done for $400,000

Great for the deal, but horrible for me! I imagined how my word would be treated in the future: "You can negotiate with Schneider, but you can't trust his final deal."

My word not meaning anything was an even bigger problem than my being number two at ABKCO.

There were other problems. A week before leaving London, I was being picked up by a female real estate agent who was researching apartments for the company to lease. She pulled to the curb in a large English cab, and I got in. Just then, Allen came running up to the cab and started screaming at me about something. I was embarrassed and really pissed. I knew that five minutes later Allen would be cool, but this stranger didn't know that, and I looked like a complete loser, so I argued back. The screaming stopped after too many embarrassing minutes and the agent and I took off.

I was still steaming about the way Allen treated me in front of another professional when I got back to the Dorchester Hotel. I was sharing a double room with Harold Seider, one of ABKCO's top lawyers who was there helping with the legal. We worked together, shared the same sense of humor, and played practical jokes on each other. Harold would later become John Lennon's personal attorney. Harold was in our room when I got back and I started complaining about the way Allen had treated me in front of the real estate agent. I vented further about working in the office while fighting off the accusations of nepotism.

"It's only going to get worse," Harold said. "Most of the company business will be litigation. It's not going to be business as usual. Have you thought about leaving?"

"What? No, it never entered my mind," I replied.

"Well, if you're going to consider it, now would be a good time," he confided.

I came back to an office in chaos. Various federal and state bureaus were investigating ABKCO because of the Cameo Parkway Records stock purchase and my uncle's notoriety. There was a negative feeling in the air. Harold had been right.

In addition, Allen wanted me to take a cut in pay because I was no longer in movie production or on the road. He said it riled the office staff that I was receiving more than they. I felt that I worked harder, and my hours were longer. I never watched the clock and resented having to kowtow to the suspicion of nepotism. I also had a wife who resented my long office hours. She was just about to deliver our son, Eric, and she felt I should be out on my own.

Allen called me into his office one afternoon. After I sat down, he looked at me and asked, "Is something wrong?"

I was surprised by the question. "No, why? What do you mean?"
"Something with you doesn't seem right. What is it?"

Part of me realized that I was depressed by the dissension I'd witnessed among the Beatles. Adding to that was the fact that the Stones were upset with Klein. They were being taxed on money Allen had sent them to buy houses. They couldn't pay the tax and couldn't get him on the phone.

There was a lot of backstage ABKCO drama taking place on both sides of the Atlantic. On the drive from Riverdale to the office with my aunt, she said,

"Ronnie, be aware that everyone you think is a friend in the office is not. Some are talking behind your back."

"Who are you talking about?"

"I'm not naming names. Just understand that everyone is not your friend."

Then, she asked if my uncle was cheating on her.

Now, looking at me in his office, Allen must have seen it all written on my face. The door was closing on my fun times at ABKCO.

"I don't know, Allen. I'm not having fun anymore and, as silly as that sounds, you know it means a lot to me. Maybe it's the office politics, the battling with Paul and the whole negative Beatles mess that drained me."

"Do you want to leave?"

"I hadn't thought about it."

"Have you got any plans or money saved to move on?"

"Money?" I laughed. "I owe American Express $10,000, and the baby is on the way."

My uncle leaned across his desk and looked at me. "You should save some money and build a base of clients before you leave. You can still work here while you're doing it."

"That sounds fantastic, but what about when you want me to do something for you when I'm doing something with my own client?"

"Don't worry about it. You just build yourself a base and save your money before you leave."

I was stunned. I knew Allen required 150% loyalty, yet here he was letting me do something independent in the office while working for him. I had a cut in pay from $800 to $600 a week, but at least I was getting paid. All this was counterintuitive for my uncle. He was a control freak, but I figured that his desire to help me outweighed his ego. I could relax a bit and start building a new business for my family. I could hope. This was family: Allen Klein my uncle, not Allen Klein my boss.

Unfortunately, that didn't last long.

On my own, I became involved in a deal with engineer and record producer Eddie Kramer's company, Hampstead Heath Production Management. I also began dealing with the group NRBQ. I set up a company, Libra Management, Inc., and signed NRBQ on July 9, 1969, then immediately helped them get a star guitar player, Al Anderson.

Anderson was signed to another record company, Vanguard, with another group, the Wildweeds. I managed to get him out of that group and the Vanguard recording contract, so he could join NRBQ and begin recording with them.

I put it in my new company Libra Management, Inc.

```
Libra Management, Inc.
4601 Henry Hudson Parkway
Riverdale, New York

Dear Ronnie:

        The following will constitue our understanding and
agreement.

        (1)  You or your company will represent us as Business
             Manager in negotiating and concluding any new
             deals.

        (2)  It is understood that any new Agreement will be
             subject to our approval.

        (3)  It is understood that in compensation for your
             services to be rendered as provided for in para-
             graphs one and two above, you shall receive 10%
             of all monies payable under any new Agreement.

        (4)  It is understood that this Agreement may be
             terminated by either party upon thirty days
             written notice·to the other.

        If the foregoing sets forth our understanding, please
sign where indicated below and this will become our valid
Agreement.

                         Very truly yours,

                         N.R.B.Q.
                         George Thomas Staley
                         Steve Ferguson
                         TERRY ADAMS

Agree to Libra Management, Inc.
                         Frank Hadley
By---------------------------
                         Jody St. Nicholas
```

On July 10, 1969, I started negotiations on behalf of another client who had begun a deal with Playboy to create a Playboy Centerfold jigsaw puzzle. They wanted me to represent other ideas they had: poodle toilet paper, self-portraits on watches, illustrated fortune cookies, scented inks (vanilla fudge, apple), fun badges (private eye, Scotland Yard), frustration toys to kick, Superman suits to hang in closets, baby pajamas in various designs, a TV disapproval kit, high-heeled horse shoes, a doggie bag cookbook, chocolate chessmen, a mirror with a photo taken ten years ago. They had a lot of ideas that they wanted to convert into money-making ventures. As a company, they were utterly insane. I loved them for it.

It was in the midst of one of these meetings in my office having nothing to do with ABKCO that Allen called me to his office. When I didn't come immediately, the screaming began. I knew it was just Allen Klein being Allen Klein, but it was embarrassing and really upset me. Especially with my new client there.

A few days later, Allen called me into his office.

"Ronnie, you doing your own business and meetings here isn't working out. If you are going to keep working here, you will have to give me your full attention."

I had been expecting this problem with Allen, and was honestly amazed I had gotten this far, but as I walked into that meeting, leaving the company was not on my mind.

"Allen, is there any way you can see this working?"

"Yes," he replied. "You keep working here until my birthday (December 18), and then you go out on your own." It was now July 14, 1969.

"What's your birthday got to do with it?" I snapped back. "It's just an arbitrary date that doesn't solve any problems. What happened to, 'Ronnie, you need to build a base and save money'? If anything, leaving in December before the holidays will screw me even more."

At that moment, his phone rang.

Allen snatched it up before the second ring, glared at me, and with his hand over the phone reiterated, "It's your decision. Stay until my birthday or leave now!"

He began to talk on the phone. As I steamed, the call dragged on and on. After about fifteen minutes that seemed like an hour of my mind driving me crazy, Allen gave me a look, turned his back to me, and kept talking on the phone. I was finished business, no further negotiation!

With all the courage I could muster, I slowly stood. A weight seemed to be lifted from my shoulders. I was leaving. Slowly, I walked out of my uncle's office. I had been hoping he would call me back, but he continued talking on the phone. I opened the door, walked through as it automatically closed behind me, and walked out of ABKCO.

I went home to my $10,000 American Express credit card debt, my new baby on the way, my no foreseeable immediate income—and a happy wife, since I was no longer going to be a slave to the company.

As a kid in Florida, I had jumped off the high cliffs of a quarry into unknown water pools below. The fear and weightlessness I felt during those seconds hanging in the air were a good indication of how I felt now. It was scary, but I had a feeling it was going to work out.

When I got home, I found the other positive. My wife supported my decision, and to this day, even though she's now my ex-wife, she never said, "What were you thinking? You had it made."

For me, it all depends on what, "it" is… not waking to an alarm every day; not being screamed at; not knowing what tomorrow will bring; having the trust and love of another; being happy and having fun is "it" for me. Like the Stones, I could rebel. I would counsel, advise, and partner up, but would never be in the backstabbing ladder-climbing corporate world again. I would live my own life. It was a good and final decision, one that I held to, even when I was offered the position of President of Rolling Stones Records.

CHAPTER XVII

EMOTIONAL RESCUE

My uncle was at the right time and the right place for the British Invasion. He was an accountant with a personality and drive that led him to attack the recording business and its inequities in dealings with recording artists. When I came to work for my uncle, Allen Klein, he had just hit it big, and I mean just. I got to the office in time to help everyone wheel file cabinets down Broadway to the new office in the Time-Life Building.

Talent is an energy that propels things and people, but talent can burn only so far, and then it needs money. To get money, talent needs to deal with business. Smart talent understands their limitations. While artist egos may think they can do everything, they usually have an instinctive fear of numbers, and the long, boring boiler plate agreements they would have to read and understand.

For the most part record execs screw the talent with contracts in the same way the sleazy movie producer uses the casting couch. In the record business it's:

"We'll sign you to a recording contract."

"How much do you want to be a rock 'n' roll star?"

"Are you only in it for the money?"

These bromides are mouthed by recording company execs as they place a contract in front of your face where the record company keeps all the money. It's often with a twist of words that a group gets screwed. The record company would say, "We are offering you a deal where you get an advance of $50,000 for signing and a 10% royalty on all records sold. You will record in our studio and we will bill you for it. You will pay us back from your record sales."

"Yeah!" says the group with no money and stars in their eyes.

In the fine print of the document about income would be the little line: "… advances recoupable against your share." If you didn't insert "all costs off the top before accounting for your share" you would see on your statement, for example: "Total income: $200,000. Your share (200,000 x 10%) = $20,000, less your advance of $50,000 plus costs for the recording of the album of $100,000.00."

Presto, you owe them $130,000!

If you knew enough and had a little power, you made sure costs were off the top. Thus $200,000 minus your advance of $50,000 minus the recording costs of $100,000 = $50,000 times your .10 royalty rate and you get $5,000, and your debts are paid instead of owing $130,000.

Then, "behind the curtain," the record companies usually bought off the managers and agents with side deals. The company would appear enthused to sign other groups from the manager; they would promise to book their talent through the group's talent agent.

We've all heard the horror stories of the recording star's business manager or accountant stealing or losing their money. We've also heard the stories of talent dumping their managers once they've "hit it big." One of the best movies I ever saw on that topic was Woody Allen's Broadway Danny Rose. The film features Woody as a talent agent who represents the lowest rung of the entertainment ladder. He is a true manager who helps with his talents' personal lives and stands by them through thick and thin. One of his oldest acts gets a big break, and the minute he is going to get the big money he drops Woody and gets a new agent from a big agency. Typically, the girlfriend of Woody's oldest act is the one who influenced the singer to change agents. It shows that most talent has the loyalty of snakes, and their girlfriends are always in their ear.

My uncle's innovation was a passion for going after the money and assets on behalf of the talent. He got results. He made the record companies submit to audits, found the money they were not accounting for, got it, and gave it to the talent, as he did for Sam Cooke.

I can describe what Allen thought of himself in his own words. We were entering the United Kingdom and had reached the immigration stand at the airport. The agent looked at my uncle's passport, looked up at him, and asked, "What's your occupation?"

Without hesitation, my uncle replied, "Good guy."

"Business or pleasure?"

"Pleasure," replied my uncle.

One of the reasons Klein was hated in the business was because he went after the big-business greed. The top execs didn't like getting beaten, but they realized they needed any act that sold a lot of records. The record company was more afraid of losing the income. Consequently, Allen got them to agree to much better deals than ever before. He almost tripled the talent's income. Better yet, he structured the deals so the artist owned their masters and copyright.

Klein also took care of himself when he took a piece of that artist equity.

To Allen, business was personal and relationships mattered. The way my uncle pursued a band was similar to how one might court a desirable woman. He would charm them, play to their egos and strengths, and then do a job for them. I think he looked at the relationship as an odd kind of virtual marriage; both partners contribute to the household—he, taking care of the business, and them, writing and recording the songs that brought in the business.

Allen often got personally involved in his artists' lives, whether it be trying to help John and Yoko get her child back or fighting to defend the Stones against the drug litigation in the UK or meeting Ringo when he arrived on the QEII. The problem was that Klein was in a lot of virtual business marriages and when his attention and time would be directed elsewhere, the talent would often feel slighted.

In June of 1969, Allen's close friend, Tony Anthony, whom I'd worked with on the Stranger films, warned Allen that he sensed the Stones were upset because they felt ignored after Allen signed the Beatles. I knew the Stones were reaching out to Allen for money. He wasn't taking the calls, and I wasn't given any instruction.

Allen, Ringo, and I, leaving the QE II after Ringo's arrival.

I can speak of one possible fact on why the Rolling Stones hate him: taking a piece of equity as the commission. Allen guaranteed he would always be paid his percentage by taking a piece of the asset—the copyright or master. Instead of only taking a piece of the money earned, he took a piece of the object that made the money. I didn't know this at the time and disagree with the premise, but it definitely got him paid. His survival instinct made sure he made money during the ups and downs of the relationship. His agreements were like prenups: you break up with me, and I still get a piece of the house.

Talent forgets where they were when they first agreed to the deals. Time and money change things—especially your memory.

When I left Allen, I knew he would take it personally. We were very close, so I never doubted that he would be hurt that I left.

It was late 1971 when I next heard from my uncle after he screamed at me in July 1969. He called to inform me that I would be asked to testify in the ABKCO/Rolling Stone's lawsuit.

The members of the band all shared publishing income in a company in the UK called Nanker Phelge Music. With the tax problems of the UK, Klein offered to set up a Nanker Phelge USA corporation and had the band assign their publishing rights to it. Mick, Keith, Bill, Charlie, and Brian all thought the US corporation had the same structure as the UK company. They were wrong. Allen owned Nanker Phelge USA. Prince Rupert had discovered this and the Rolling Stones sued Klein. "You're being called because you witnessed them signing the Nanker Phelge Agreement. Put that aside, Ronnie," he went on. "I would like to speak to Mick about getting the lawsuit settled. Can you conference us together?"

My first thought was, oh, so that's why you called—not a "How you doing?" but a "Here's what I need from you." Whatever. We were talking again. I let it go.

After I put Allen and Mick together, they settled. My only payment for helping settle the $7.5 million lawsuit was $2,000 to cover my phone bill. [1]

Today I am happy to say that once those things were behind us, my uncle and I got along for the last twenty-some years of his life. We spoke at least once a month. Allen took care of my mother (his sister) and helped me and my family as well. When I had to be admitted to the hospital with pancreatitis and didn't have insurance, he came forward with the cash. He did tell me he was sending me a 1099 IRS tax form for the money, so he got the tax write-off, and rightfully so.

---

[1]   I recorded the negotiation telephone conversations to keep everyone honest. I played the tape to Philip Norman for his book on Mick Jagger. The tape has since disappeared.

CHAPTER XVIII

MISS YOU

It was around 2:00 AM on August 20, 1969. Jane and I were in bed in our apartment in Riverdale when she said, "My water broke."

We jumped out of bed and into our car and drove helter-skelter to Lenox Hill Hospital for my son to be born a legitimate New Yorker.

Over a month had gone by, and I hadn't received any cash since my final salary check from ABKCO. I was beginning to wonder, "What next?" Then my phone rang around 1:00 AM.

"Hello, Ronnie. It's Mick. Sorry about the hour, but I'm in Australia shooting Ned Kelly. I need to talk to you."

I was surprised to be hearing from Mick Jagger. I hadn't expected to hear from anyone from ABKCO. I left that behind when I walked out the door.

"Hi, Mick. How are you?"

"I'm well. I only have a minute. Ronnie, we want you to do the tour."

"Mick, I left ABKCO. I no longer work with Allen."

"I know," Mick went on, "but everyone wants you to do the tour. We trust you. Will you do it?"

"Of course, I would love to, but I don't want any problems with the family. The only way I can do it is if Allen gives his okay."

"I'll talk to Allen," Mick said and hung up.

The timing was perfect; I needed the money, and having something to do that I knew boosted my confidence. It didn't hurt that the Stones wanted me. My concern was Allen would say no. I could only wait to see how he felt about it.

It wasn't a long wait. The next morning, I got a call from Allen.

By "got a call," I mean he began screaming at me.

Allen continued screaming until I finally interrupted him. "Allen, if you don't want me to do the tour, I won't do the tour."

He continued screaming.

I interrupted again. "Allen, just say, 'Ronnie, don't do the tour,' and I won't."

He didn't say it, just screamed some more, then hung up.

The next evening, I got a call from Sam Cutler at the Stones' office in London. He explained how he was organizing things for the tour from the UK side, and he was in the meeting with Keith and my uncle. "A deal was reached. You are to go back to the ABKCO office and run the tour out of there."

"This isn't going to work…." I began.

Sam interrupted me. "Keith fired Allen. The boys don't want to embarrass him any further. The deal is that you make it seem that the tour is directed by ABKCO. Everyone knows that you are no longer working there, but for now, you have to keep up the façade. Get to work."

I went back to the office to receive and send telegrams, telexes, and phone calls, have meetings, and assist in the impression that it was ABKCO's tour.

I had done enough touring and visits to the box office that I had an instinctive feel for the bottom line. The Stones would "scale the house." By "scale" I meant we would dictate ticket prices and seats available for sale. Unfortunately for me, in the scaling, Mick insisted that no seats be sold behind the band. In large halls and theaters, this meant we would lose about one-fourth of the potential revenue. This cuts into my profit, which was based on a percentage of income.

"Mick, the fans don't care about being behind you," I told him. "They can look at your butt and be more than satisfied. How about we just don't sell tickets for seats that are behind pillars or anything that obstructs their view?"

"No," Mick answered. "I want everyone to be able to see and hear us. Tell the promoters: no screwing the fans."

I felt the promoters were getting a guaranteed sell-out. Therefore, I wanted a guaranteed 50 percent of the gross sales in advance against a 65 percent to 70 percent fee of the total box office. The percentages were unheard of at the time, but we needed the money. I felt they were fair since I calculated the promoters should end up with a 10 percent net profit. I didn't want the promoters to lose money. I told them I would pay them back for any loss. There were no losses. I did reimburse Frank Field, the Chicago promoter, the cost to have our rug cleaned.

On with the show.

The Rolling Stones had not toured America for three years. Drug busts, legal hassles, and turmoil within the band had conspired to prevent it. That turmoil reached its tragic conclusion with Brian's ousting from the group in June 1969, followed by his death just a few weeks later on July 3, 1969.

The last time I saw Brian was a short time after he was fired. He was upbeat as he played me recordings he made of drumming African tribesmen. He told me he was going in a percussion direction, and leaving the band gave him more opportunities. I felt he was bluffing, but I welcomed the feel-good excuse. He would be dead shortly after. It wasn't a surprise, whether it be the drugs, his asthma, or someone drowning him. He was a flickering candle and burned out. Everyone felt terrible. And his death became a conspiracy rumor... was he murdered or was it an accident?

I liked Brian. He stood out onstage while he existed in his own world. I also respected him. He's the guy who first put the group together. He brought a different kind of music, instruments, and look to the group dynamic.

His replacement was 20-year-old Mick Taylor, previously the lead guitarist with John Mayall's Bluesbreakers. Jagger told me that Taylor was a 'temp hire', and to be paid accordingly. "We'll see if he works out."

I met with Mick Taylor and his girlfriend, Rose. Mick seemed to be a very sweet guy, laid back. Rose was the loyal girlfriend who was watching out for her guy. She paid attention, only listening. It was a low salary and had no complaints. Taylor was appreciative and anxious to get on with it.

With their reinvigorated lineup, the Stones were now ready to begin a new chapter in their story.

The Rolling Stones wanted a tour like no other. They wanted to play with performers they wanted to watch that also had the talent to enhance the show. They instructed me to hire Chip Monck to do the staging and lighting for the tour, as he'd done for Woodstock a few months earlier. Chip was in command of everything you saw. He had to make sure everything was built and ready on time for the show, and the trucks, sets, and crews got to the venue on schedule.

Prior to this Stones tour, it was traditional for the local promoters to put on the show, and they defined its shape and structure. They would hire the big-name band (The Headliners) and then have the local bands, some of whom they managed, open the show. Not for the Rolling Stones on this tour. We insisted there would be no local talent; we would be putting on the entire show—lights, sound, backing groups, staging, everything.

The minute I took over the tour I was given the offers coming in from promoters, from venues, and from people who just thought they had an angle on the Stones that could make them money. The progression of the offers took on a predictable cast. The first letter: "I would like a date to promote the Rolling Stones" became, if they were contacted, "I want three dates," which morphed directly into "Hey, I can promote the entire tour!"

One day when I got back to ABKCO, I found Bill Graham's ego lying on my desk in the form of a four-inch-thick hardcover binder. I opened it to find a press book filled with clippings, letters, photos, and articles about Bill Graham, heralding his heroic life, his vast experiences, and what a great promoter he was. For the most part, it was about the Fillmore West Auditorium in San Francisco, the Fillmore East in New York City, and his representing the Jefferson Airplane and many of the West Coast counterculture bands. Graham wanted to promote the entire tour and was preparing me for his pitch with this four-inch-deep press kit.

I contacted Mick.

"Bill Graham wants to do the tour. He's pitching me in a couple of days. Do you want me to do a deal with him and let him book the tour?"

Before the sentence got out of my mouth, Mick said, "No way! I don't want Bill Graham involved in the tour at all. He can have a couple of dates, but that's it. Ronnie, you have to tell him no. But you can't just say no."

"What?"

"You have to say no, but you can't tell him no. He'll complain that we told him no and backstab us any chance he gets. Come up with something. I know you can do it, Ronnie."

So I had to present the idea of Bill Graham promoting the tour in such a way that he would refuse and the Stones would not be subject to his wrath. Bill was coming to my office on October 1. I had until then to figure out what to do.

When I stepped through the door of my home on October 1, after walking the dogs, my wife greeted me with "Bill Graham is at your office and pissed that you're walking the dogs and not there waiting for him."

Bill turned up at my office ahead of schedule due to the early arrival of his flight. As he saw it, walking my dogs instead of being there ahead of his arrival meant that I had somehow disrespected him.

I got to my office in forty minutes. I charged into the room, apologizing even though he was at my office forty-five minutes early.

"Bill, I'm sorry. I thought your plane was getting in later. I hadn't expected you so early."

He didn't seem to be in a forgiving mood, but that didn't bother me.

How to tell Graham no by not telling him no was going to be another gamble. Bill sent this giant press book; anyone in the business was aware of his background, so why did he bother sending this four-inch tome to me, if not to brag?

"Bill," I said. "I got your press book and was impressed with it."

He smiled.

"But what have you done that's big?"

To say that Bill blew up at that question would be an understatement. His eyes started bulging, and I think I smelt burning brain. By his expression, I knew that he had expected ring kissing and dog walking apologies.

"What the fuck are you talking about?" he hollered at me. "I've done big arenas! And stadiums! And I did Woodstock!"

"Woodstock lost money," I countered.

Graham ranted on, but I knew what the end would be. After getting off to this wonderful start, I made idle chatter for a while to calm him down. I asked him what he had in mind. He started to hustle me with the usual promoter prattle. We talked further about the state of the music industry. Then I took another gamble with his ego.

"Bill, you can do the tour."

He smiled. It was the smile of a hustler who thinks he's hooked a mark. I'd seen it before.

"You will get 10 percent of the gross proceeds…" A logical, but lowball, cut; he didn't blink an eye, nor seem to care about the percentage. I thought he would have wanted at least 15 percent, but he just nodded with that smile on his face, and then I had it: He wasn't in it for the money; he was in it for the name recognition. I saw the theater marquee light up in his eyes: "Bill Graham Presents the Rolling Stones."

"But Bill, you can't put your name on the tour or be associated with the tour in any way. You'll be like an agent booking the dates from behind the scenes."

His eyes darkened.

"My name goes on it, or I don't do the tour," he said.

"Sorry, Bill, That's a deal breaker. No name on the tour or no tour."

"Fuck you." He stormed out of my office.

Bill couldn't wait to complain. When he realized he wasn't getting the tour, he immediately ran out and gave an interview to a reporter, Al Aronowitz, which appeared in the New York Post on the evening of October 2, 1969. "So I finish making my presentation," he told Aronowitz, "and what do you think one of the assistant managers asks me?" He says, "But what have you done that's big?"

CHAPTER XIX

START ME UP

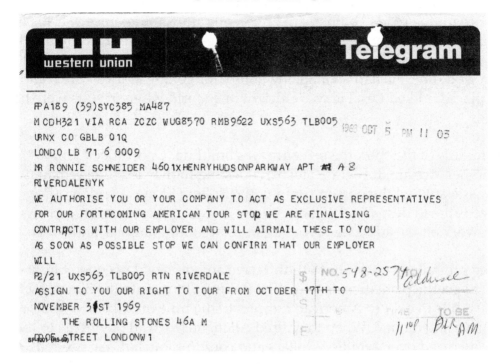

On October 5, 1969, I received a telegram authorizing me or my company to exclusively represent the tour. It was official; I was doing the Rolling Stones 1969 US Tour.

A couple of years later in an interview in Rolling Stone (August 21, 1971), Keith explained why I landed the job:

"Ronnie Schneider we'd known. He's Klein's nephew, but he broke away from him. He's a smart cat. I dig Ronnie. He'd been on a lot of tours with us handling business and hung around with us. He was the only cat we knew in '69 who could handle the Stones tour that everybody knew, that we could leave to get on with it till we got there."

On October 7, I got a telex from the Stones about the itinerary. They felt some of the dates were wrong. Keith wanted the tour to start at a small venue and, at first, suggested San Diego. He didn't want to start the tour in St. Louis or Nashville. He suggested looking into Memphis, Atlanta, or Birmingham. He liked the idea of ending in Miami. They also wanted me to check on Philadelphia as an end date.

Over the next couple of weeks, I would receive telexes from the Stones' office on an almost daily basis with various requests about certain dates, the proposed guarantees, and arrangements for plane tickets, the booking of supporting acts and any number of other issues.

I had to coordinate the UK press with Les Perrin. Les was the classic "Olde Tyme" press guy, and he looked the part. A round man with a one too many "one more for the roads" bulbous red nose. His after-hours office was his local pub. If you wanted to get in touch with Les to cover your ass before the newspapers reamed it, you called the pub. If he wasn't there when you called, he soon would be. He had an amazing ability for getting stories killed, and stories placed. I liked Les. He was efficient in a world where results were hard to judge.

By the middle of October, the pressure was building. On October 15, 1969, I get another "we are desperate" telex requesting money for Jo Bergman, Mick's assistant and the person running the Rolling Stones London office. "She needs bread desperately," Sam wrote. "Please, please get it together so she can work on the advance press, organize accommodations, and so on."

I had the promoter's offers, but I didn't have any money! I needed at least $15,000 to get the plane tickets to get the Rolling Stones into the States. I left ABKCO while in debt to American Express to the tune of $10,000. The Stones didn't have any money. When they fired Allen, he froze all payments to them. They were owed over a million dollars and couldn't touch it. We needed money!

With the onslaught of offers, I began to lay out an itinerary. I wanted to make sure the tour traveled in a straight line. Agents would book you anywhere at any time to make more money. Managers tried to make sure the travel dates made sense logistically so you wouldn't be going from New York to Los Angeles the next day. Especially since we had a large entourage traveling by truck.

I immediately realized a couple of things: I didn't have the money to pay a lawyer to handle the legal implications of the tour, and I didn't have an organization behind me to help with all the paperwork involved. I was spending a lot of time talking to promoters and wasn't confident in what they were saying. They were like guys trying to get a girl into bed. They were promising me everything.

A week into the madness and with apparently perfect timing, I got a call from Steve Leber of the William Morris Agency. He and David Krebs wanted a meeting with me. Klein had signed with them to do the tour. I fired them when I took over the tour from ABKCO.

"Ronnie, we'll be outside to meet you in ten minutes."

I took the elevator down from my office and spotted their limousine parked curbside. I climbed into the back seat, and they did a funny bow while sitting with their hands in the air. "Oh leader, we are here to beg your indulgence," they said in mock subservience.

I told them I was doing the tour myself and already had a drawer full of offers.

And I did have the offers, but nothing was moving quickly because the Stones were still debating on who and where and what. Leber and Krebs were desperate for the Stones business, so I knew I had the leverage. I also knew that I could only get my best deal while they were desperate. I needed their help.

The William Morris Agency had the legal department and manpower to close and organize all the deals, and they also had the money I needed. Paying them would cost me, but it would be faster and cheaper than forming my own army without money. I told them they could do the show, but at a 7.5 percent fee instead of the 15 percent fee they usually charged, and I needed a cash advance to help cover startup costs. They complained and complained but finally agreed. "Don't tell anyone we did it for this commission," they insisted. We shook hands and suddenly I had an army behind me.

Most important, cash! I needed to get the Stones to the States!

Next, I went to the William Morris Agency to see if I could get blood from a stone. I had a meeting with the head of the William Morris Agency, Nat Lefkowitz. He told me they would love to help, and they would "loan" me the money. I had expected at least $50,000.00 but the check he handed me was for $15,000.00. I had over $100,000 in costs approaching, including money to Chip for stage construction as well as guarantees to secure Ike and Tina Turner and the other talent. But that was it; they would only give me $15,000. He told me I would personally have to guarantee the loan. He slid pieces of paper in front of me. I didn't mind signing. I had no assets and nothing to collect against. At least now I could pay for the plane tickets.

I hadn't negotiated the '65 and '66 tour contracts. On the previous tours, I only dealt with promoters in the box office after the deal. This was three years later, and I would be making the deals. I knew the numbers from my box office experiences. I figured the shows would be sold out, and I wanted a 50 percent advance on the shows' possible gross, as scaled by us, in advance as a guarantee against at least 65 percent of the gross sales. By my computation, with those numbers, the promoters should make a 10 percent profit.

As an afterthought, I asked Nat for the contract that was going out to the promoters. I had final approval and wanted to check it and add our rider. I told him I would go over it and give it back with any changes so it could immediately go out. I took the boilerplate agreement they were using and went back to my office to review it. When it came to the line about making the guarantee payments I saw "Make check payable to William Morris Agency," so I changed that to "Make check payable to Stone Promotions, Ltd.," my company. It wasn't subtle; I simply drew a line through "William Morris" and printed "Stone Promotions, Ltd.," above it. I gave them my approved contract and rider and said, "Good luck."

The tour was scheduled to start on November 6. Just in time, I got the money to get the Stones to the States, but what about the rest of the tour?

Chip and just about everyone else was working without getting paid. That would only last so long. I would need to come up with guarantees for the acts that were joining us and money for the set construction, transportation, and the hotels or apartments where the Stones would be staying.

A week later, I got a call from the William Morris CFO. I went to his office. He sat there with a smile and said how great the tour preparations were going and that the promoters were paying but there was a small problem.

"It seems the checks for the guarantee advance from the promoters are made out to your company, Stone Promotions, Ltd. We need you to endorse them over to us. We will take care of depositing these third-party checks to our bank."

I said, "Let me see the checks."

He passed the checks that totaled over $150,000 to me. I looked at the checks and said, "These look fine." I tucked them into my inside suit jacket pocket, stood up, and said, "Thank you."

He sat there with a stunned look on his face.

As I walked out of his office, he called out, "If they fail to play any of the four beginning dates it will be the end of the William Morris Agency and everything."

I left his office for the bank, thanking my lucky stars that now we had money and the tour was on.

Then William Morris agent Steve Leber contacted me with an offer for the Stones to do a closed circuit broadcast of one of the shows. At that time most closed circuit shows were for boxing; the broadcasts played in one hundred and fifty-six equipped theaters. The promoters would put up a $3 million guarantee for a Rolling Stones live closed circuit concert. It had the largest dollar guarantee of any previous musical event. I was excited. Unfortunately, Mick didn't want it. He was concerned because it would be a live broadcast, and he didn't have a director whom he trusted to shoot a live event.

While the tour planning was proceeding, Chip suggested that I meet with a guy who represented Chrysler Motors, John Jaymes. He told me Jaymes said that Chrysler wanted to contribute their cars for use on the tour. I met with Jaymes, and he said the only thing Chrysler wanted at the end of the tour was to have a picture of the Stones in a Chrysler, nothing else. He also volunteered that he would love to help with our logistics and work with us. At the time, I had no one helping me. I didn't have a staff or interns or even an office—I was just working out of my Riverdale apartment—and Jaymes, a heavyset guy, was aggressive and seemed like a good asset.

At the time.

Jaymes said he also had access to great security, former narcotics officers and current New York City detectives who could help us.

It wouldn't be until months later that I would discover Jaymes was a con man who nearly got me killed, and that almost everything he said was a lie.

CHAPTER XX

IT'S ONLY ROCK 'N' ROLL

The Rolling Stones arrived in America on October 17, 1969. I stayed in New York as long as I could while setting up the rehearsal location at Warner Bros and arranging places for everyone to stay in Los Angeles. Sam Cutler and Jo Bergman took care of most of the planning and taking care of the boys.

Jane, our three-month-old son Eric, and I went to California to stay at the DuPont house off Doheny and Sunset in Hollywood. The DuPont house reminded me of a one-story motel with tennis courts. There were many rooms laid out next to each other. People would claim a room, and you had to make sure you locked yours or you could come back to find it occupied by people you didn't know.

There was a large living room with a piano to one side. I walked in one day to find Little Richard sitting and playing. He invited me over. I was pleased to sit beside him as he told me how he discovered the Rolling Stones.

Bill Wyman was accompanied on this tour by his beautiful Swedish girlfriend Astrid Lundström. Bill had gotten together with Astrid in 1967 after separating from his wife. She would be his constant companion for the next 16 years. During some free time, Bill and Astrid asked me to join them on a trip over the hill from Los Angeles to the San Fernando Valley to meet a rock 'n' roll clothing designer, Martine Colette, to have leather outfits made.

We found Martine's house and met the thirty-something hippy clothing designer. She had patterns and leather swatches all over her house. She took our measurements and asked what we wanted. Astrid, in her soft-spoken but I-know-what-I-want tone, asked for vests, pants, and jackets for her and Bill. I pondered for a while, and then, I don't know why, came up with the idea of a leather tuxedo. I wanted it to look like a traditional tux from the front, but have fringe on the arms of the jacket that you could see when I was walking away from you—sort of like a mullet haircut with business in front and party in the back. After Martine took our measurements, she asked us to join her outside.

We walked out the back door of her house into a yard filled with cages of mice and glass tanks with boa constrictors and an anaconda. She raved about her snakes as she picked a small mouse from one of the cages and went over to a large boa in a glass tank and dropped the mouse into the tank. For a brief time, the snake ignored the mouse, but soon the mouse disappeared, forever.

A few days later, we came back for a fitting, and I found that my vision of a leather tux had morphed into a rust-colored suede tuxedo-ish outfit. She had put fringe on the front pockets, which ruined the surprise of the ton of fringe on the back of the jacket.

I still wear it on Halloween.

It was my birthday on October 20, and the Stones took me, along with a small entourage, to an elegant Japanese restaurant, Yamato, adjacent to the Century Plaza Hotel. We sat on the floor with the table recessed in front of us so our legs hung over the side. The Stones presented me with a gift, and I excitedly opened it. It was wrinkle cream. I was 26 years old.

Aside from the band—Mick, Keith, Bill, Charlie, and Mick Taylor—the tour party consisted of Ian Stewart; Bill's girlfriend, Astrid Lundstrom; Charlie's wife, Shirley; Mick Taylor's girlfriend, Rose; tour manager Sam Cutler; Mick's assistant and Stones office rep Jo (Georgia) Bergman; tour photographer Ethan Russell; journalist Michael Lydon, on assignment for the *New York Times*; Stanley Booth, who was writing a book about the tour; our security guy, Tony Funches; transportation, con man John Jaymes; and staging and lighting director Chip Monck. Before the Rolling Stones, or any act, went on, the stage had to be built and the lighting put in place. "General" Chip Monck worked with his crew to create the event. They had to have everything at the location, built, and lit, on time! Chip was ever calm, seemingly. He was at the venues with us but traveled with the crew for the setup and tear-down of the sets.

November 7, 1969: Fort Collins, Colorado, Moby Arena

The Stones wanted a small venue to start the tour, a practice they continue to this day. Fort Collins, Colorado, fit the bill, and they opened there on November 7. Nothing was prepared for the start of the show. The promoter didn't have an announcer, so Sam Cutler, the tour manager, was asked to introduce the band. He had a great voice with the English accent that everyone loved.

I believe it was here that Keith and I began a ritual that we would follow throughout the tour. We were backstage behind the curtain, just before they were going on stage, and Keith asked, "You got a bump?"

"Yes," knowing he meant a hit of cocaine.

I pulled a small bottle of coke and a tiny screwdriver out of my jacket pocket. Just at that moment the lights were turned off and everything went black; I dipped the tip of the screwdriver into the bottle and lifted a small pile of cocaine to Keith's nostril. I quickly repeated the process for his other nostril. Then Sam made the prophetic announcement, "Ladies and Gentlemen, the Greatest Rock 'n' Roll Band in the World… The Rolling Stones!"

Keith strode out onto the stage with the rest of the band, and the show and tour began.

The Rolling Stones are going to the office when they mount the stage. Their job is to entertain, and they do it with enough energy and talent to power a stadium full of people. The second they leave the stage they become Mick, Keith, Charlie, Bill, and Brian or Mick Taylor. They separate themselves from the performer and become a person.

November 8: Los Angeles, California, Los Angeles Forum-Two shows

When we arrived at the LA Forum, the limo driver didn't know where to drop us off, so he left us fifty yards from the complex entrance and just told us to run for it. There were about eighty fans in a clump around the entrance while police security guards tried to open a corridor for the band to run into the Forum. I was following Bill Wyman, and one of the cops grabbed him by his hair.

I screamed at the cop that the guy whose hair he was pulling was one of the Stones. That's when I got "short sticked." The standard-model police billy club at the time was a two-foot-long piece of black-painted wood similar to a small baseball bat, except with a small handle that projected at a right angle. Short sticking was when they tucked the long part of the club under their arm and put their hand behind the handle and jammed the end of the grip into your stomach. I would have gladly not learned this.

I screamed at the cop. He said he thought I was a fan chasing the band. I said,

"Do I fucking look like a fan?" I was dressed in a suit and had short hair.

As with the earlier tours, the Stones decided on their sets a few minutes before the show. "Quick, I need a pencil and paper," we would hear from Keith. He would grab some crumpled piece of paper, a pencil would appear, and he would call out the set for the night, subject to the others' input. Sometimes Charlie would suggest something, and the eraser would come in handy and that was one of the reasons it was done in pencil instead of pen.

Typical Set List
Jumpin' Jack Flash
Carol
Sympathy for the Devil
Stray Cat Blues
Prodigal Son
Love in Vain
You Gotta Move
Under My Thumb
Midnight Rambler
Live With Me
Little Queenie
(I Can't Get No) Satisfaction
Honky Tonk Women
Street Fighting Man

At the show, Chip said we had a problem we had to be on the lookout for. While setting up the stage, Chip found a Nagra tape recorder (a very expensive professional broadcast–quality audio recorder) fastened under the stage and wired to a microphone placed in a perfect recording location for a pirate tape recording.

I had two thoughts immediately invoking "finders keepers":

"Wow! We now have a great tape recorder" and

"Wow! After it records the show we will have a great audio of the concert."

Chip, being my moral compass, quashed those ideas and suggested that we quickly make an announcement. His quote: "Through '69, we walked through the audience and simply cut cables from microphones to recording devices, smiled, and handed the 'offender' a blank cassette after removing theirs. We missed a few. Got many. As we pointed out the statement on their ticket— 'would you care to stay, or be escorted from the building?' It was simple, but effective..."

Over the course of the tour, we constantly had these incidents, and in some instances, we found the recorder during an intermission. I always seized the tape, but relented on the equipment. Some recorders must have gotten through, based on some of the high-quality bootleg recordings that came out of the tour.

November 9: Oakland, California, Alameda County Coliseum-Two shows

After our office meeting in October, I felt a little bad for Bill Graham. Acting in good faith, I gave him the Oakland dates of the tour, but the deals for the shows were the same as with the other promoters: half the house gross up front, as a guarantee in cash against 65 percent of gross income from the concert. Even though it was contracted, Bill didn't pay the guarantee up front and stalled until we arrived to play the dates.

I figured that once again it was an ego thing. I knew he was good for it. We would get paid. Unfortunately, I didn't realize it wasn't good that people knew I would be picking up large sums of cash in Oakland.

It was at the first Oakland show that I had my biggest run-in with Bill Graham; it turned physical.

The first thing we saw when we entered the dressing room in Oakland was a large poster on the wall of Bill Graham giving the finger. The battleground was set. The poster was immediately pelted with food from the snack table until it was covered.

Finding Bill, I immediately asked him why he hadn't paid the guarantee up front like everyone else.

"Hey, I'm paying it now so don't fucking worry about it," he snarled. "I was always good for it."

"Why the asshole poster on the wall?" I asked.

"Because that's what I think of you all," Bill replied. So much for coddling the talent. The first show started at the packed arena, and things were riotous from the beginning. At one point Bill Graham got on the stage and was shoving back the fans who were trying to climb up and get closer to the band. I didn't see it, but was told that Bill had punched a girl and that Mick had reacted by ordering Graham off the stage.

Bill had complained, and Mick said he could stay on the stage if he wore a clown hat like the clown he was.

Graham got off the stage. During the break between the two shows I encountered Bill backstage in front of the Stones' dressing room. We began hollering at each other. I was incensed by his attitude toward the boys and his treatment of all of us.

He screamed back at me while putting his finger in my face, "You have to respect me! This is my town, and I tell you what to do!" He kept pointing his finger at me. A couple of times he poked it into my chest, hard.

Now I was pissed.

"Respect you? You're nothing but a bug, and I should squash you!" (I still have no idea where that came from.)

With the next poke of his finger into my chest, I swung my right hand back; it was holding my briefcase. Then I drove the briefcase forward up into Bill's balls. As he doubled over and before he could swing, Tony Funches, our bodyguard, grabbed him from behind.

In that same instant, Keith grabbed me from behind and pulled me into the dressing room. Strangely enough Keith's was the cooler head on this occasion.

"Funny thing is," Tony Funches told me recently. "Bill and I knew each other. I had worked a few shows for him in LA before I signed on with you guys. He and I remained friends after the farcical fight that night."

While backstage for the second show a couple of detectives and a few uniformed cops came over to me.

"You Mr. Schneider?" they asked. "You the guy with the money?"

I was carrying my old beaten-up briefcase stuffed with papers and money.

"Why?" I immediately asked.

"We got word that the Black Panthers are going to rob you of your cash and use it to buy guns." (The Black Panther Party was a black revolutionary party active in the US at that time.)

As he finished, an officer grabbed my wrist, handcuffed it, and attached the other handcuff to the handle of my briefcase.

"Wait, wait, wait," I said. "Take the handcuffs off! I don't want my hand cut off for stupid money."

The cop took off the cuffs.

"Okay, but when the concert's over, you are going with us. We will take you to the airport. We will protect you."

I walked away from the cops and into the dressing rooms.

"Hey, Ron! Come here," called out Ike Turner, as he stood in front of a typical dressing room locker. I walked over.

Ike pulled me in close. "Ron, if the Black Panthers try to take money from you, come to me and my band." He nodded to his bandmates, and then pulled his coat to the side to show me he was carrying a.45 semi-automatic in a shoulder holster.

"We're all packing and you're safe with us."

Now I felt safe.

During the earlier shows I was in the promoter's office at the start and missed the opening acts. Now I was in time to catch B.B. King. I watched and listened as he spoke through his guitar, Lucille, and heard the blues as they were meant to be played. I always enjoyed listening to this giant of a gentleman.

Then, there was Ike & Tina Turner and the Ikettes. You had your heartstrings tugged by BB, and then you got a kick in the groin from Tina. She could build a song and then go from a singer in front of a microphone to a whirling dervish with legs moving in a blur and a performance that kept your eyes on her even with other girls (the Ikettes) dancing in rhythm behind her. If it was a dancing competition, Tina always won. The audience would usually be drained after she went off the stage, and it was a good thing the Stones were always late. The technical delays of tuning their instruments and getting in the right mind-set gave the audience time to recover. The fans would need all their energy for the kick in the gut from the headliners. "Jumpin' Jack Flash, it's a gas gas gas" — and that gas fueled the audience to let them know the waiting was over.

The band they came to see was leaping onto the stage.

My nickname for Mick was "The Leaper," and I got that from his style, his spastic, jointed rooster strut. The band would usually follow "Jumping Jack Flash" with its Chuck Berry cover "Carol" that was even better when Chuck came to the show. Next came one of my favorites, "Sympathy for the Devil." Since most of the fans were sure that the Stones were in league with the Dark

One it only added credence to the notion, "Pleased to meet you, hope you guess my name!" Then the Rolling Stones would bring it down a bit with "Stray Cat Blues" ("Bet your mama don't know…"), and stay leveled out with "Prodigal Son," a cover of another African-American blues guitarist, The Reverend Robert Wilkins. Then they really calmed it down with "Love in Vain" ("I followed her to the station with a suitcase in my hand….") that put everyone back in their seats, eyes glazed with thoughts of those loves in vain. "You Gotta Move" still kept the kids in their seats listening to this blues guitar driven song.

The pace picked up with "Under My Thumb" ("The girl who once pushed me around—the change has come…"), a good song for the boys who found out the hard way that girls control things, but maybe they had a chance to get them under their thumb. Things exploded with "Midnight Rambler." The music built, and Mick milked the audience.

During the number, Mick pulled off his belt and dropped to his knees. Everyone had to stand to see him. He would lie across the floor of the stage. He used the belt like a whip, smashing it against the stage, building the tension. "You heard about the Boston…! hit and run raper in anger, everybody got to go…!" The audience was now concentrating on the stage totally, not the kid next to them, not the cop in front of them, just the stage and this Midnight Rambler.

Keeping the pace without burning out the audience, the Stones followed with "Live With Me" ("I got nasty habits...") and then another acknowledgment of the influences of Chuck Berry, "Little Queenie," to keep the energy alive.

It was only fitting that the Stones now followed with "Satisfaction." I would remember how it was a battle to get them to play it in 1965, so I was glad to see they did it now, and, based upon the reaction of the fans, they were definitely getting the satisfaction of seeing the Stones play the song that had introduced so many of them to the Rolling Stones.

Time for some "Honky Tonk Women" ("She blew my nose, and then she blew my mind"). Fists were pumping by now, and the kids would sing along. Ever faithful to their image and as a reflection of the time to close the show came "Street Fighting Man" ("The time is right for fighting in the street"). We had worldwide fighting in the streets over the war in Vietnam "but what can a poor boy do, except sing for a rock and roll band." The perfect exit as the fans were charged and ready to go as we ran as fast as hell to get out of there. No encores.

When I left the show, the police insisted I go with them. They maintained it was a serious threat. The Panthers were going for the publicity as well as the money. I got into the car with the cops, and they drove. After about ten minutes, we changed cars. They did some double-back driving, changed cars again, and eventually got me to the airport.

November 10: San Diego, California, San Diego Sports Arena

We would invite our flight crew to see some of the shows. In this shot, we have our "stewardesses." I have my back to the shot and in front of me are Bill and Astrid. To the left (the tall guy) is Michael Lydon.

Chip called me over to the right back corner of the stage, behind the curtain. He handed me a gigantic set of headphones. They looked like the ones you might see airport crew wearing to drown out the sound of the jet engines. "Here, put these on. I want you to say hello to the crew."

I put them on and heard Chip saying, "Crew, this is the guy who signs the checks. Say hello to Mr. Schneider."

There would be headphone voices saying, "Hello, Mr. Schneider." I would say, "Hello, you're doing a great job, guys," and there would be some garbled interchanges. I would hand the headphones back to Chip, and we would all go back to business. Chip did this at a few venues when our paths crossed backstage. He was always bringing management and labor together.

November 11: Phoenix, Arizona, Veterans Memorial Coliseum

After the show in Phoenix, our pilot informed us that the plane wasn't due back until the following morning, and we could stop anywhere en route from

Phoenix to Los Angeles. Boom, Las Vegas! We got off the plane and headed to the Strip. First stop Circus Circus. John Jaymes got the pit boss to let us take pictures (which was against the rules).

From the left corner, Astrid, Bill, Michael Lydon, Jo (Georgia) Bergman, me, Mick, Keith, and Sam Cutler. Behind us with the long blond hair and smile is actor Howard Hesseman. See the article: November 13, 1969, article Chicago Tribune "Doing Vegas with the Stones"

The group would tease me about numbers. Mick Jagger used to poke me: "Eight, Ronnie, the number eight. Does that get you going?"

November 13: Dallas, Texas, Moody Coliseum

Wild stuff always happened in Dallas from the 1965 tour and the creation of the infamous "prune burger," to us being on an escalator in the hotel and a guy trying to punch Mick. And then there was the Butter Lady.

After the Dallas show, we returned to the hotel. There were a lot of fans in the lobby and some had dressed up in Halloween costumes. As I was going to the elevator, Sam brought over two girls who were in costume. One was dressed in a Sheena, Queen of the Jungle, outfit similar to the comic book and TV show, and the other was dressed like Scarlett O'Hara from Gone with the Wind. Sheena went with Sam, while Scarlett and I went up to my room.

We were chatting for a while when there was a knock on my door. It was "Sheena" and she was complaining that Sam had tried to have sex with her.

I asked what she had expected when she had gone to his room after midnight and after a little while, and a lot more talking, both girls were naked in my bed. An hour went by and there was another knock on my door.

Wrapped in a towel and with the two girls in bed, I cracked open the door to see a fully dressed girl standing there with a big black purse in front of her. She opened her purse, and I saw a pound of butter just sitting there. "The Rolling Stones can't come to my city and swing their asses on stage without me spreading butter from the top of their heads to the tips of their toes," she said.

I closed the door.

Our next interruption came in the form of a phone call to the room at 5:45 AM. It was our jet charter. We had a 707 Boeing jet charter leaving in the afternoon that was taking us to Auburn, Alabama. They were calling to tell me there was a schedule change, and we had to get over to the jet by 7 AM. I immediately told them it was impossible. Forget about the girls in my bed, the real problem would be waking Keith. There was no way the plane was going to wait, so at that moment I decided I would not attempt to get everyone together to make the charter. Instead, I went back to the girls. That would cost us $7,000 and prove the attorney Roy Cohn— yes, that Roy Cohn from the Joseph McCarthy hearings—to be a liar.

Prior to leaving for the later Euro Tour, I received a bill for $7,000 for the Dallas chartered jet fiasco. I refused to pay it since the charter left before our scheduled time. They threatened a lawsuit and put me in touch with their attorney, Roy Cohn. I explained to him that I was leaving for the Euro Tour and requested that he put the lawsuit on hold until I returned, as I was going to fight it. He said, "Sure, no problem. Let us know when you get back."

When I got back, I found that during my absence, Roy had sued on behalf of his client Diner/Fugazy Travel, won by default since no one was there to answer; he got his judgment, served it on my bank, and took the money out of my account. So much for "Sure, no problem."

There was only one plane we could find for charter at the Dallas Airport, and the captain explained that it didn't have heat. We had no choice, so we said we didn't care—until we reached altitude, and we were freezing.

Heat rises, and since there was no heat on this small plane that we got in Dallas to take us to Auburn. A bottle of whiskey was all we had to try to warm up.

November 14: Auburn, Alabama, University Coliseum-Two shows

For most of the tour, to alleviate the in-flight boredom, we played cards or Monopoly.

November 15: Champaign, Illinois, Assembly Hall-Two shows

The University of Illinois promoted the Champaign, Illinois, date. I met with the Dean, who was in charge of the event, in an office on an upper level in the

Assembly Hall. He voiced his confidence in his students and the fact that the concert would be a big, peaceful success. Before he gave me the check for our share of the box office, he insisted we go into the hall and see his students. The Dean and I stepped out of his office, walked through a tunnel to the third-level balcony seats in the Assembly Hall, and looked out and down over a nicely dressed student audience waiting calmly for the show to start. He bragged some more about his "kids," and we went back to the office to get the check.

As he gave me the check, we heard the intro to the band and the music starting. I put the check in my jacket pocket and started to leave, but the Dean kept talking so I politely sat and listened as he did a longer promo version of the benefits of the University of Illinois. As I finally stood up to leave, the sound of the music stopped.

"Uh oh, probably a riot," I said as I dashed out of the office.

"Not possible," hollered the Dean as he charged after me.

When we looked down at the stage and audience, it was obvious that everyone was up and dancing or just trying to get closer to the stage. The music had only stopped for a moment as the Stones were getting ready to do another song, and the show was moving forward. It wasn't a riot, just exuberant fans. Unfortunately, the Dean didn't see it that way. He yelled to a nearby assistant, "Turn on the lights!"

"Don't!" I screamed at them.

As much as you would think that turning on the lights at a Rolling Stones concert would calm the fans and make them think twice about rioting, you would be wrong. Turning on the lights only seemed to inflame and embolden the fans more as it put them under the spotlight, as it were, making them as much a part of the show as the group. The Dean and his assistant ignored me, and the lights went on.

The fans immediately charged the stage, and I headed for the dressing room to organize a fast exit for everyone. I left with the image of the Dean's face and its look of disillusionment with his beloved "kids."

November 16: Chicago, Ill, International Amphitheater -Two shows

After I was finished in the box office, I walked down the amphitheater aisle and saw a group of guys on the stage, one of them spouting some kind of political rhetoric into the microphone. I didn't care as I made my way backstage and into the Stones dressing room. In the dressing room, I saw more unkempt people, including Abbie Hoffman of the Chicago Seven. The Chicago Seven were seven defendants charged with conspiracy, inciting to riot, and other charges related to protests that took place in Chicago at the 1968 Democratic National Convention the previous year.

I sat on a table away from everyone to recount the cash I'd just picked up. I glanced up to see Abbie coming my way.

"Mick said to talk to you about getting money for our cause. Will you give us some bread?"

I looked up at him for a second from my counting and said, "No," then immediately looked down to resume my count without losing my place.

"We've got the stage and we're keeping it," he announced.

"No problem; if you're still on the stage when the band is ready to go on, Sam will make an announcement that you guys want to be the evening's entertainment and the Rolling Stones, not being political, will be leaving."

The show went on.

November 18: Taped Ed Sullivan Show to be aired on the 23rd.

The Stones and Ed Sullivan had always had a difficult relationship. After their first performance on his show on October 25, 1964, Sullivan declared, "I promise you they'll never be back on our show. It took me 17 years to build this show, and I'm not going to have it destroyed in a week." Sullivan disliked the band's looks and the way they worked up the crowd. Nevertheless, the Stones became so popular that he booked them again in May 1965.

Then there was the protracted battle on January 15, 1967, over "Let's Spend the Night Together" and Sullivan's subsequent overdub of the audience. I never liked the censorship and that entire episode rubbed me the wrong way. I wondered if we would ever get a chance to right what I considered a wrong.

By 1969, Ed's ratings had dropped, and he needed a boost for the show, so he wanted to book the Stones. I was not that cooperative—our schedule was already full, and this would be an extra add-in. At that point, Ed needed us more than we needed him. I told Sullivan's people that the only place we had the time to film the show was in Los Angeles.

Ed always filmed in New York and was prohibited by the unions from filming in LA. A New York show has to be made using New York unions and the same goes for Los Angeles. The Ed Sullivan Show reached an agreement with the unions, and the deal was struck with a provision that Ed was not to announce that the filming was in Los Angeles.

We set up a date in LA. Not only did they have to come there, another part of our revenge was having Sullivan pitch the album. We insisted he mention it by title, Let It Bleed. Just having Ed utter the very uncharacteristic words "Let it bleed" seemed to balance out the "Spend some time together" fiasco.

During the filming, Sullivan seemed rather distracted and out of it. He went to greet Mick and said, "Hi, Mick, what do you think of Los Angeles?" The director yelled, "Cut!" Ed was reminded that he couldn't mention they were in LA, and they had to reshoot the greeting. Six times Ed said the same thing and six times the director yelled "Cut!" and started over.

The release I signed only allowed for one play of the show.

November 24: Detroit, Michigan Olympia Stadium

Before the show, I had work to do. The Rolling Stones knew they were going to follow the US tour with a European tour. Prior to MTV, the way to promote albums and tours in Europe was via film clips. The Stones wanted to film at least two of their songs and had decided they should be shot at the 1969 Madison Square Garden shows where they were going to record a live album. They wanted me to close the deal for a director and cameraman. They had a couple of suggestions for me, and I went about contacting them while on the road.

First on the list was Leacock-Pennebaker (Richard Leacock and D.A. Pennebaker), who had done Bob Dylan's *Don't Look Back*. Next on the list was Robert Downey Sr., who'd just completed *Putney Swope*, a dark satire about a token black man on the executive board of an advertising firm who is accidentally put in command. For a top cameraman, they asked me to check with Haskell Wexler, director of photography for *Medium Cool*, which was about a TV news cameraman who becomes personally involved in the violence that erupts around the 1968 Democratic National Convention. Wexler also shot *The Thomas Crown Affair*. However, it turned out that each of them had projects they were already working on, so they wouldn't be able to help us, especially at such short notice. Haskell suggested I contact the Maysles brothers. I called them; they were available, and we scheduled a meeting on November 25 at the Plaza Hotel.

November 25: Philadelphia, Pennsylvania, The Spectrum

Prior to leaving for the show, I met with the Maysles. My first impression was a positive one. David was enthusiastic and friendly. We hit it off immediately. Albert was more on the quiet side, listening attentively as David told me of their experience making *Salesman*, a documentary they shot that followed four Bible salesmen as they traveled across New England and southeast Florida. Albert would chime in every now and then in a quiet voice, reinforcing something that David said or to make another interesting point. Their excitement was contagious. If David and Albert could be this excited about Bible salesmen, I could only imagine what they would bring to the Rolling Stones. Also at the meeting was Porter Bibb, their business guy, and as typical artists do, they ignored him, for the most part.

We discussed the requirements. We only wanted two songs for the promotion. The Maysles suggested they go to the Baltimore concert and get a feel for the Stones' performance to come up with ideas on how to capture the songs on film. The next morning, they called me at the Plaza and came back with a suggestion to do four songs that they would film during the three Madison Square Garden shows. David pitched the idea for four songs since he thought we might have a chance of turning that footage into a half-hour TV special. They would give us a thirty-minute rough cut of the show, he said, and it would not be longer than forty-five minutes.

November 26, Baltimore, Maryland Civic Center

Because of a time problem we chartered two six-passenger Lear Jets to fly us to Baltimore. I requested a power-assisted takeoff. It's basically a booster pack for the jet. When they do that kind of take off, they taxi down the runway and launch the jet at a 90-degree angle. You shoot straight up into the sky. It's amazing, if you love to be pinned back in your seat because of the g- forces and heading to the heavens.

After the take off, the two jets were flying side by side when we decided that it would be cool to race each other. We told our pilot to step on it, he said that it was against the FAA rules and they couldn't race, but then he "stepped on it" and we began to race each other. At least the pilots seemed to make it so as each jet leapt in front of the other back and forth as we sped across the sky. Great fun!

When I returned to the hotel I found the Maysles agreement for the Madison Square Garden shoot.

Maysles Films, Inc.
1697 BROADWAY, AT 53RD STREET, NEW YORK, N.Y. 10019 · JU 2-6080

November 26, 1969

Mr. Ronald Schneider
c/o Plaza Hotel
Fifth Avenue & 59th Street
New York, New York

Dear Mr. Schneider:

Following our telephone conversation this morning regarding our filming the Rolling Stones' concert appearances this week here in New York, I am writing to confirm our enthusiastic acceptance of this commission on the terms set out below:

We agree to observe a Rolling Stones concert in Baltimore on November 26, 1969, and to film three concerts in New York City on November 27th and November 28th, 1969. We further agree to provide you with a 16mm color rough-cut of at least 30 minutes (and not more than 45 minutes) in length. This rough-cut will include a minimum of two songs by the Rolling Stones, and partial on-stage performances by B.B. King and Ike and Tina Turner.

For our services, we will receive $20,000, one third of which will be paid upon signing of this letter of agreement, one third upon completion of actual shooting, and one third upon delivery of the completed rough-cut, (delivery to be made not later than January 10, 1970). *of all film materials including original film + track*

We clearly understand that you and/or the Rolling Stones will have free access (and viewing privilege during the rough-cutting of this film) and that the ultimate use of this footage will be as concert sequences in a longer film to be produced by you.

We look forward with great interest to working with you and the Stones on this project and sincerely hope that this collaboration will lead to other possible film ventures.

You shall be responsible for all rights + clearances (including but not limited to ... ... With best regards,
... ... film ... (London) necessary for the exhibition of the film
we are furnishing + shall
hold us harmless in Navis N. Maysles
connection therewith. For Maysles Films, Inc.

_____
For the Rolling Stones

Albert Maysles' birthday is November 26, the same day we signed the deal that led to Gimme Shelter.

November 27-28: New York City, New York, Madison Square Garden-Three shows

November 27, 1969, was Thanksgiving Day and we were in New York City. My wife's relatives lived in Maplewood, New Jersey, about an hour drive, if lucky, and we went there for Thanksgiving. We brought back a "care package" of turkey and all the fixings to our room at the Plaza. Mick Taylor and Rose were hanging out with us, and I offered Mick some turkey. He told me he was a vegetarian and had been for many years. Mick, being the nice guy that he was, said he would share in our holiday celebration and would eat the turkey. He did. Not too long thereafter, Mick got sick and threw up (nice Thanksgiving image). He later told me that after that he went back to eating meat. I still feel a bit guilty.

Before the tour started, Madison Square Garden was a problem. I suggested that we do four shows, and I requested we scale the house and get 50 percent of the gross box office in front, against 60 percent of the gross income. The Garden said they would only do two shows and give us 50 percent of the gross. I countered and said that I would do that deal, but if they asked for a third show, my terms kicked in. They agreed. The two shows sold out in record time and they wanted the third show.

I sent our rider to the contract to the Garden and with that, I went on the road.

Now it was the day before the Madison Garden show, and I still didn't have a signed contract. I contacted William Morris Agent Steve Leber and he told me that the Garden had not only thrown out our rider but was instituting a penalty if the Stones played past midnight. We would be responsible for the Garden crew overtime, which was about $15,000. Leber said that we would have to wait until the night of the show to deal with it.

Now it was the night of the show.

Ike and Tina had just left the stage. I still didn't have a deal. I grabbed Steve Leber and told him that the Stones weren't going on until we resolved the rider and got rid of the midnight restriction. I added that I was going to make an announcement to the crowd, "The Garden doesn't give a damn about you. They haven't paid the Stones, and the Stones are leaving." After that, we'd see what happens to the Garden.

The problem with that strategy was that I had told the Stones to wait for my word before going on, but they gave me the impression that they weren't going to wait. The Stones were going on when they were ready, and I was on my own. However, Steve didn't know that.

Steve went to the microphone and asked for any Madison Garden executives to come backstage, immediately. Two executives appeared, and I repeated my threat with the intensity of a rapidly closing deadline. They agreed to take the Stones rider with no midnight penalty, and the $15,000 would be returned to us. I could pick up the guarantee and overage at their bank the next morning. I told them I didn't trust them and insisted on cash. They reluctantly agreed.

And the Stones went on. And gave one of the best performances of their career. Being at the world-famous Madison Square Garden didn't hurt, and all the grief that was involved with booking this date seemed to be channeled into the energy of the show. All the stars were out, and I watched as they sat or stood and danced just like the rest of the fans. The Rolling Stones played way past midnight...

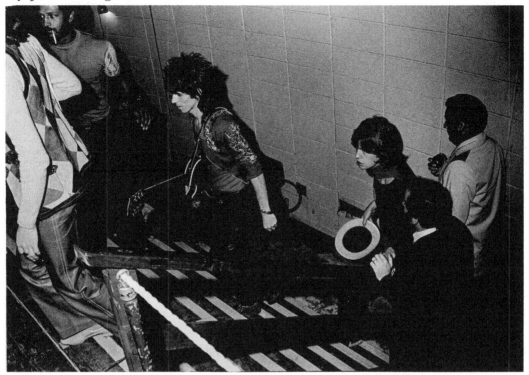

Bill in his leathers, Tony Funches, Keith Richards, Mick Jagger, our NYPD off-duty cop security and me, going to work.

Mick was magnificent as he stoked the audience, energized by their excitement. He not only played to the celebrity-filled front rows, he looked up and sang and strutted to those in the farthest "cheap" seats.

The next morning, I went to the bank at One Penn Plaza to pick up the overdue cash guarantee from the Garden. I took Pete Bennett to act as my security since I was picking up $150,000 in cash. Pete was great. He put his hand inside his jacket like he was an armed bodyguard and stood there looking mean. The Garden brought in the cash. I insisted they count it in front of me since I didn't trust them after their running me around. Pete Bennett and I walked out of the bank with a briefcase full of green.

While we were staying at the Plaza, we had 24-hour limo service. The drivers would park their limos around the Plaza, come in, and hang out in a room we kept for them until someone needed them. This was also the room that the "cheaters" used to surreptitiously hook up with people other than their significant others.

One night, Joey Head of Head Limousine called me. Joey told me that the cops had towed the limos at the side of the Plaza Hotel to the impound lot. Joey was going crazy. "What if Mick needs a car now?" John Jaymes was nearby and said he would take care of it. He made a call, and the cars were towed back. That wouldn't be the last time John would do something to impress me.

Earlier in the day, Keith had been in my room, and we were talking about the tour and how the cities all seemed the same. All of a sudden, he turned pensive.

"Heroin traps you; it's a prison; you're held prisoner by it, kept trapped where you live. You can't just... pick up... pick up and travel anywhere. You need to be able to score, to have a connection unless you're ready to go cold turkey."

I hadn't thought about heroin making you a prisoner. That may have been a problem for the typical junkie, but not Keith. He had connections all over the world just by his fame. Fans would throw drugs at all of us. Even if Keith had wanted to quit, it would be like going to a birthday party on a diet and everybody offering you cake.

November 29,1969 Boston, Massachusetts, Boston Gardens-Two shows

Waiting on the Stones at the Plaza Hotel, NYC.

November 30: West Palm Beach, Florida, West Palm Beach International Music and Arts Festival
We were leaving the Plaza Hotel and New York City. As I was finishing pack-

ing, there was a knock on my door. B.B. King was standing there. "Before you left, I wanted to tell you, I had the best time. The boys, man, they made the world a bigger place for me!" he said, with a big smile on his face. He really liked the Stones. I was smiling as he left. I liked B.B.; he was a gentleman, a pleasure to work with, and an amazing talent.

One hour later, there was a knock on the door. I opened it to find our two tall, suit-wearing, narrow-tied, police-shoe-wearing, Fed-seeming security guys. They had come to say good-bye, and they came bearing gifts. They handed me two aluminum film canisters, the kind used by photographers to hold 35mm film, which, when empty, made nice little contraband containers.

"One is for you and the other is for the boys," he said.

I opened one and saw it was filled with a white powder, pure cocaine, no doubt. Next he handed me a three-foot-long cardboard tube, the kind usually used to mail rolled posters. It was heavy. "Inside are three pounds of high-grade pot for you guys to split. You can guess where we got it from. It's primo."

I figured he meant that it was from big dealer busts and not from some random street pushers. I thanked them, and they went on their way.

David Maysles called me and asked if they could accompany the band to Muscle Shoals to film them recording there.

"Ronnie, I think we might be able to get an hour TV show with the added content," David told me, "and if we don't, I won't charge you extra."

"Sure, no problem," I said.

Our departure to West Palm Beach for the final date of the tour was anything but expected. The date had been on again, off again while we waited for the $100,000.00 cash guarantee to be in the bank. They got the money to us at the last minute. We boarded our little aircraft charter early and were getting ready to leave when we taxied over to an area and told to wait. We started getting story after story as to the reasons for our delay. At first, it was, "We will be leaving in twenty minutes." After a few of these, we were told an hour. We were just sitting there playing cards and trying to wait out the delay. During part of the boredom, I noticed our police security guys smoking hash in a small hash pipe. It was a bit weird. It wasn't until about eight hours later that we left New York for West Palm Beach. We were eventually told that we had been on hold because Richard Nixon was in Miami, and they had closed the airport.

By the time we got to West Palm it was late at night, pouring rain, and freezing cold. There was a long debate as to whether the Stones should go on. Keith is the one who demanded they go on. Which was interesting since he had been the only one electrocuted and our biggest concern was the lightning.

"The fans endured this, staying for us, so we have to play," Keith insisted.

The Stones went on, got soaked, and froze their asses off. It was miserable, but was another example of how much they cared for their fans.

The morning after the Palm Beach show, the Stones and I met on the tarmac of a private airport in West Palm Beach where I had set up a special airplane charter. I had a customized three-tailed Constellation with propeller engines on the runway to take them to Muscle Shoals, Alabama, to do some recording.

We boarded and saw that the interior of the plane had been gutted. Instead of normal airplane seats, they had old leather reclining barber chairs as well as drapes and various other luxuries. It looked comfy. The pilot greeted us and said he was going to warm up the engines and get the plane ready to go. We stood around in the plane talking as the engines began to start, and we watched the propeller start to turn. Began to start being the key words. The outside right engine began cranking and cranking as it tried to turn over. There was a lot of sputtering, smoke, and noise before it finally started. And then it stopped. A minute or two went by, and the pilot tried again. More noise, more smoke, more vibrations, and it started. Same thing happened with the next engine. I noticed that Mick was getting a bit nervous, as was Bill. It was taking too long to start the other engines, and then one sputtered and shut down.

"What's the matter?"

The pilot said it wasn't anything; it just took a while to start. I told the boys, but Mick announced he wasn't going to Muscle Shoals on this plane and walked off. After about half an hour, everybody else decided not to take this charter either and made other arrangements. Off they went to Muscle Shoals.

The tour was over and now I had to write it up. The main difference in maintaining the books then and now would be phone apps. I could see myself keeping a much better record of the costs on the road with the ability to enter it into my phone's database. Then I had to keep pens, pencils, and scraps of paper ready at all times. That wasn't always possible. Most times I had to scramble to get a pen and find a scrap of paper anywhere. Bathroom hand towel roll, pieces of a napkin, a side of a cardboard French fries box, these are all examples of "any space will do" for a handwritten receipt. One thing

I learned from being on the road that you don't learn at a desk is that you usually screw yourself when it comes to your expense report. You forget to get a receipt, and you forget a cab trip you took and you see why you usually come up short as to an actual out-of-pocket cash reimbursement.

I put the money where my mouth is and accounted for the cash that I laid out to them or on their behalf. I salute the Stones because they never hesitated to give me a receipt. As small a feat as that sounds, it's a big deal for an accountant who wants the dollars to be right. I never wanted them to think I had cheated them, so I tried to keep everything in the "sunshine" so they didn't ever have to question me.

At the start of the tour, Mick said that they wanted to see "something" from this tour, and he made me promise that at the end of the tour I would give them some cash. With that instruction in mind, I managed to keep $50,000 in cash on hand at the end of the tour.

Putting the money where my mouth is and getting a receipt from Keith.

I individually wrapped five $10,000 packages in newspaper and called the Stones into our last tour meeting after the West Palm Beach date. I chose newspaper as a little touch of home as the traditional workingman's fish 'n' chips are wrapped in newspaper. I handed each of them a newspaper-wrapped bundle as a partial payment on what the accounting would finally dictate. They loved it; there's nothing like cash to make up for royalty and accounting reports that were just dollar numbers on a page. They preferred the "green" to the black and white of a report.

Paying the Stones cash and hiding it in the expenses presented a quandary for me. What if the auditors, lawyers, or Rupert Lowenstein (their new financial manager) found it and thought that I had ripped them off? I did get receipts for the payment to the boys, but I kept them for myself and didn't include them in the accounting. My fee would show up as less than what I was entitled to since the money would be buried as an expense, reducing the profit I was basing my fee on. Five thousand dollars was and is still a lot of money.

Eventually, I had to tell Rupert because I didn't want to have them find it and then give my story. I was concerned I would look guilty. Ironically, the major auditing firm and the top lawyers who were employed for the tour never found the hidden funds. I wanted to make the point to the Stones that it is important to trust who you are working with since I could have taken the $50,000 and no one would have been the wiser. Rupert understood and did pay me $5,000 as another fee buried in the expenses to cover what I was entitled to.

Mick Smiles

CHAPTER XXI

SYMPATHY FOR THE DEVIL

Back home in New York, I was told that everything was set for a free Stones concert in Golden Gate Park in San Francisco. Other free concerts had been held there; the permit was granted, and everything was a go. The next call I received was a frantic one saying that the permit for Golden Gate Park was withdrawn. The west coast organizers were in a quandary. They didn't have a venue for the concert. John Jaymes volunteered that he could find a new location through his Catholic church and political contacts. John came up with three properties, one of them Sears Point Raceway in Sonoma, California. They chose Sears Point. It was owned by Filmways. I was asked to fly to San Francisco to meet with Dick St. Johns, the president of Filmways, Inc., to finalize a deal for the use of their location at a lease fee of $6,000.

Rock Scully, the manager of the Grateful Dead, Sam Cutler, Emmett Grogan, Chip Monck, and others had already started moving the equipment to Sears Point, and announcements had been made.

Next, David Maysles called, "Can we join you in San Francisco?" "Yes."

I got on a plane and went directly to San Francisco. Dick St. Johns and I met in the lounge in the Mark Hopkins Hotel. We sat facing each other in nice comfy leather chairs. Behind us and mostly out of earshot, due to the noise of the people from the bar, were five of his people. Behind me were the Grateful Dead's crew and some others. It was very cordial at first with an acknowledgment from St. Johns, that they were here to help us put on a free concert. I listened as he spent about ten minutes telling how great this free concert was going to be. I kept hearing him say, "Free, free, and free." Then he dropped the bomb.

He began by demanding a deposit of $100,000 cash to cover cleaning up the location after the event, another $100,000 as a 10 percent payment on a $1,000,000 insurance policy to cover liability, another $100,000 on hand for any other damages or incidentals. He also wanted any and all rights to a film of the event.

"This is supposed to be a free concert," I said. "The Rolling Stones are donating their services for free. I thought you were donating the location for free or at least for the cost of the lease in the spirit of the event. Based on your conditions, this free concert is costing us $300,000 and any and all rights to a film that we don't even know if we'll be making."

I went on to explain that the organizers had agreed to arrange for the cleanup, we already had a large umbrella insurance policy, and that I couldn't under any circumstances give them any film rights.

He countered that they weren't doing it for free. Someone must have misunderstood. "They misunderstood enough to have me fly out."

"They misunderstood enough to begin construction and announcements of the new Sears Point location. Sorry, no deal!", I said. To begin with, I never wanted the free concert. I thought it set up a potentially dangerous situation and precedent. Also, the entire premise of the free concert was based on a lie: we weren't overcharging for tickets. I also felt that fans on the East Coast might feel cheated that the Stones were only favoring the West Coast with a free concert.

From the hotel meeting in San Francisco, I was taken to the Grateful Dead's farm and a meeting about what to do next. I was paranoid about what might happen when I got there. I had heard the rumors that everything at the farm was dosed with LSD. I had never taken LSD, nor did I want to. My natural mind was twisted enough. I was happy with it. I particularly remember being told that the Dead had a five-gallon water dispenser with a stack of Dixie cups next to it. Strangers would take the Dixie cup and get water from the dispenser, feeling they were safe, only to find out that the Dixie cups were laced with LSD.

While everyone was trying to figure out what to do next to make the free concert happen, I'd already concluded there wasn't enough time to regroup. The free concert was dead in the water. I was fine with that.

However, Rock Scully of the Dead, Emmett Grogan, Sam Cutler, Michael Lang, and the other people pushing the event said that too much was underway. The groups, fans, and equipment were already on the move. They wanted to try and make a last-ditch effort to find a new location.

My bigger concern at the time was to go after Filmways for screwing us. I wanted a lawyer to sue them. Our Solters and Sabinson press guy recommended attorney Melvin Belli, and a meeting was immediately set up in Belli's office.

I went back to the hotel and up to Mick's room. Keith and Stanley Booth were there. They were upbeat, just arriving from Muscle Shoals. I sat on the dining room table. Keith took out a tape player, put a tape in, looked over to me, and pushed "play." "Wild Horses" filled the air and galloped to my ears. "What you think?" Keith asked. I smiled. Then out came "Brown Sugar." Mick began elbow flapping, then Stanley and Keith began moving to the rhythm. They all dance advanced on me, snapping their fingers, West Side Story-ish, for my opinion.

I always withheld my opinion because I never wanted to be a judge. I didn't judge their behavior; I didn't judge their personalities; I didn't judge their music. I always felt that I had to be independent of a stated opinion. Talent usually has a giant ego, and I didn't want to threaten it with my input, one way or the other. Now I can say, "The songs blew me away."

Later that evening, I got a call from Keith to come to his suite, immediately! I rushed up to his room; the door was ajar. I walked in and saw no one. Next, Keith and his friend Gram Parsons, then with the Flying Burrito Brothers, called out from the bedroom.

"Come here, Ronnie!"

In the bedroom was a large four-poster bed with tall, carved wooden bedposts on each corner. Keith stood next to one of the posts and said," Ronnie, look!" With his right hand, he lifted his left arm up and straight out from his body and swung it like a baseball bat into the wooden post. His arm hit the wood with a loud thud.

"I can't feel a thing!"

"Bam!" Gram did the same, and they both said they were freaked. They had no feeling in their arms. Yet, they kept saying, "Look!" and smashing their arms into the post.

I called the front desk and had a doctor sent to the suite. Here the doctor-client privilege takes over.

They both seemed fine the next day.

It was Christmastime, and we were escorted into Belli's large personal office. On one of his office walls, he had a giant x-ray image of a person with a scissor left in their stomach after an operation; I assumed it was one of his big cases. He started by telling us how we were special, and that he also was representing some of the Charlie Manson family, but had relegated them to one of the smaller back offices. We had the big office.

At times, I felt I was at another rock 'n' roll circus. Belli's office was the circus. The Maysles' were filming, and one of the local channels, KRON, had cameras following us in his office. Belli loved the attention and had probably called the station.

We went through the details of what had happened and the fact that there were thousands of kids coming from around the country to a site that we no longer had a permit to use. I wanted to sue Filmways and St. Johns for the damages we had incurred by originally believing we had everything for free.

After I agreed to Belli's $10,000 retainer, Belli came up with an $11,000,000 figure to sue for and said that he would have his staff prepare the papers. He added that we had to figure a way to serve St. Johns in San Francisco so that we had jurisdiction. Melvin suggested I call St. Johns and try to get him to come back for further talks, and we could have him served as he got off the plane.

With that part out of the way, Belli's first bit of advice was that we should stay at Sears Point and continue with the event.

"Won't we be breaking the law?" I asked.

"Let them try and make 250,000 fans leave," he answered.

At that moment, I knew we had a problem. I couldn't trust a lawyer who advised me to break the law. I figured Belli was just another self-promoting, blustering buffoon. There was no way I was going to let the Rolling Stones break the law and have the event at Sears Point.

Unfortunately, by now the event took on a life of its own. Deals do that. Just when you think a deal has fallen through it comes back to life. The Grateful Dead people, Rock, and Sam kept this one alive. At the very last minute we were told that another location had been found, Dick Carter's Raceway in Altamont, out in Alameda County, about an hour's drive from San Francisco. Belli got us all on the phone with Dick Carter, and we discussed the venue.

It was now Friday, December 5, and the concert had been scheduled for

Saturday, December 6. The final sticking point was who was going to sign the contract with Dick Carter's Raceway?

I always felt that life is made up of brief moments. Now was one of those moments.

I refused to sign. I could now kill the deal with the legitimate reason of not putting the Rolling Stones or myself in a dangerous legal position.

"The Rolling Stones said they would perform for free, and that's it! They are not the promoters of this event; they are performers. Thank you very much," I said. "Now good-bye."

Then, from behind me, I heard, "I'll sign!"

Up stepped John Jaymes, who announced that he would sign on behalf of his company, Young American Enterprises (never trust any company with the word "American" in the title). That was fine with Dick Carter. He thought he had someone on the hook. I didn't care as long as the Stones and I weren't the ones.

The free concert was on again. Everything and everyone were redirected to Altamont with about 24 hours to go.

Dick Carter, Melvin Belli, me, and John Jaymes, who is pointing to the location on a globe.

That evening after a shower, with only a towel wrapped around my waist, I watched the local evening news broadcast of the "behind the scenes of the free concert," seeing Belli's office madhouse ending with a shot of me. They referred to me as "Mr. Big," the behind-the-scenes guy. I dropped my towel.

CHAPTER XXII

ALTAMONT — DECEMBER 6, 1969

With all the craziness going on, Keith suggested we visit the Altamont site the night before the show. Mick, Keith, Tony Funches, Stanley Booth, and I got into a limo and took the drive to the site. We drove for quite a while with the usual query to the driver: "You know where we're going?" We got the typical disquieting, no response. After driving in total darkness for over an hour, we noticed campfires in the distance. We told the driver to get as close as he could and let us out.

We walked toward the lit stage, about three hundred yards from the road. It was freezing cold, and we stopped at a nearby campfire. The fire was built with broken wooden boxes and anything else handy and flammable. As we stood rubbing our hands in front of the fire, a gallon jug of wine was passed to Keith. He swung it over his shoulder, took a large swig, then passed it to Mick, who did the same. The jug made the rounds and was handed back to the group around the fire. Joints were passed around. The night became mystically peaceful and serene.

We left the fire and walked toward the stage. The area was quiet, except for the distant sound of hammering providing a soft back beat as we walked on. I glanced over my shoulder and was surprised to see a large group of people quietly trailing us. They seemed either respectful or in awe of Mick and Keith. When they saw we had spotted them, a couple came over and asked Mick for an autograph. He wasn't surrounded or hounded, just a couple of "please, may I" and that was it. It was magical. So magical that when Mick said he wanted to get back to the hotel to rest for the next day, Keith said he wanted to stay.

"It's fantastic here, Ronnie. Don't worry, I'll be fine. See you tomorrow,"

Keith said as he wandered off alone into the night.

The Rolling Stones weren't the only band at Altamont. Other acts were scheduled to perform: Santana, Flying Burrito Bros, Crosby, Stills, Nash and Young, the Jefferson Airplane, and the Grateful Dead.

The next day we waited on a pier at the Embarcadero in San Francisco with the Grateful Dead for the helicopters to take us to Altamont. The Dead left on the first helicopter.

Not until I saw the footage from *Gimme Shelter* did I discover that the Grateful Dead returned to San Francisco without performing their scheduled set. Sam Cutler later stated it quite well: "What a bunch of cowards." The fans and Hells Angels were, for the most part, from San Francisco. I would have thought the Dead would have done their best to relate to their hometown crowd and calm the Angels down. Nothing like a very, very long Grateful Dead set to do just that. Instead, they ran.

As the helicopter got closer to Altamont, we flew over what seemed to be miles of abandoned cars leading to the site. And then I saw a giant blot of humanity resembling a dark infection plastered against the hilly Altamont landscape.

We landed.

A young uniformed security guard greeted us and said to follow him. He turned around and led us directly into the crowd. Mick was walking next to the guard, a foot or so in front of me, when a guy leaped up and punched Mick in the jaw. People in the crowd immediately grabbed the guy and pinned him on the hood of a car.

I screamed at our guide, "Where the hell you taking us?" It seemed he was trying to walk us through the audience to the front of the stage.

"We have to get to the back of the stage!"

We turned around, flanked the crowd, and were led to a small trailer surrounded by a crowd of people. The Hells Angels guarded the door.

"Go in, relax, and stay here until you go on," the Stones were told.

We were a short distance from what was occurring on the stage, where the atmosphere was already becoming oppressive. You could cut the tension in the air. As Georgia (Jo) Bergman told me at a later time, there was no way she was leaving the trailer.   No room to breathe.

I left the trailer and walked the twenty-five feet to the back of the stage. The stage was about three feet off the ground, without any stairs going up. In their place stood a Hells Angel pulling people up. I went over, gave him my hand, and I noticed that as he was pulling me up with one hand, he was pulling back his other hand and balling it into a fist. Just then someone called out, "He's with the Stones!" The guy opened his fist to offer his other hand to help me.

Our Fed security guy (you can see him in *Gimme Shelter*. You can't miss him; he's the shorthaired guy in a sports coat at the front of the stage during one of the melees) followed me and offered his hand to the Hells Angel. The Angel took a lit cigarette from his mouth, took our security guy's hand, and made a motion to put it out in the guy's palm. Sonny Barger, Oakland Hells Angels' founder and president, came running over and told the Angel to stop. It seems Sonny knew our Fed. The FBI and the Angels were well acquainted. I was told they worked together on some things.

I heard Sonny also intervened after Tony Funches, our tour in-house security, broke two bones in his hand when he punched out two Hells Angels. I recently asked Tony if it was true, and he replied: "Affirmative, after the two morons were put to sleep, I eventually found my way over to the 'Leader of The Pack' and let him know what had happened and said I pretty much expected to die because of it, but that it was 'just business' ... He answered to me 'Hey man, you was just doin' your job; we got no problem with you.'"

While I observed the stage being readied for the Stones, the crowd in front of the stage pushed forward and shorted out a speaker on the ground, causing a small fire. The Angels placed their bikes in front of the stage as a barrier to keep the fans back and the speakers safe. The bikes were no competition to a crowd intent on getting close to the Stones. The crowds pushed the bikes over, and another series of pool cue beatings took place. The Angels got their bikes out of there, and Chip ordered the speakers placed on the stage.

The Stones went on.

'Stones' in the heart of darkness.

You could feel the tension in the air. Keith began screaming at the Hells Angels to stop beating people. I worried the Angels would go after him like they had Marty Balin, one of the lead singers for the Jefferson Airplane, who they'd knocked out.

Backstage again, I got word that a lighting tower had fallen, and up to forty people were trapped and injured underneath it. I hadn't heard any crashing sounds, but was told it was true and to find doctors to help. I ran out, simultaneously looking for doctors and proof of this fallen tower. After ten hectic minutes of running and screaming, I found it was just a rumor and not real—maybe just part of someone's bad trip.

That was the feeling in the air around the stage: The "forty people may be dead" feel.

I returned to the stage and made plans for our getaway. Earlier, hearing that the helicopters wouldn't fly at night and there was no way we were going to fight traffic to get out of there, I told one of my security guys, "Keep the helicopter for our escape." He instructed the pilot to wait and was told, "We can't fly at night."

Our security guy flashed a gun from inside his jacket and said, "Wait here!"

The pilot waited.

Meanwhile, I corralled an ambulance backstage. All the Stones could jump into the ambulance and escape to the helicopter. That was the plan, until I was told that someone had been stabbed, and they needed an ambulance immediately. I knew where the ambulance was and ran to where it was parked, to find it empty. The driver was gone, even after I had told him to be ready at a moment's notice. I went hollering for the ambulance driver, running blindly along the hillside when I came upon a policeman. He called me over, "You looking for the ambulance driver for the stabbing victim?" I nodded yes. "You can stop running. He's dead!"

I felt gut punched. A guy was dead!

On stage, no one knew what had happened. The Stones played on, just trying to get through this horror of a night.

I knew we were in a scary situation. Usually, Mick had control of the audience and could read how far he could go. We always knew we had the dressing room as a backstop, but at Altamont, there was no backstop. If this crowd rioted, we were in the middle of it. That wasn't good.

The Angels were out of it. There is one moment in *Gimme Shelter* (and also featured in the recent documentary *Crossfire Hurricane*) that shows this crazed-looking Hells Angel pulling his hair out and beginning to puff his lips in and out. It's a scary sight to see and to remember you were near this guy!

The music started and stopped while another beating was being witnessed. Mick tried to soothe the crowd, "Come on, people." Keith would storm forward, finger pointing at an instigator, threatening to end the show. The music would start again until another crowd eruption. The Rolling Stones performed for the fans, even with the sense of dread in the air. They played and in some instances stopped playing during the violence: "Jumpin' Jack Flash," "Carol," "Sympathy for the Devil," "The Sun Is Shining," "Stray Cat Blues," "Love in Vain," "Under My Thumb," "Brown Sugar," "Midnight Rambler," "Live with Me," "Gimme Shelter," "Little Queenie," "(I Can't Get No) Satisfaction," "Honky Tonk Women," and finally, with "Street Fighting Man," it was over.

We ran to the helicopter. Everyone and their friends dove into the chopper. People were lying across laps, and seat belts weren't even considered as we screamed to the pilot to get us the hell out of there!

The helicopter lifted off and simultaneously the pilot called out, "We have a problem." That's not something you want to hear when in the air. "We are overweight. There are too many people on board, and we won't be able to land normally. I have to glide in like an airplane landing, instead of hovering down."

Hell, the Angels didn't kill us, now God might.

We flew a short distance to the airport, and the pilot glided the helicopter in, as we held our breath. We landed hard, but safe and sound. From that point on, no one said a word. Everyone seemed to be internalizing what had just occurred. Not so much the helicopter close call, but the fact there was a death.

We got back to the hotel. I sat on a couch in the lobby with John Jaymes and one of his security guys. They were talking nervously about liability while I sat not saying a word; after all, John Jaymes had signed his company, Young American Enterprises, and himself as the promoter of the event.

A couple of girls joined us on the couch. John turned his attention to them and started to chat them up. A cute, tall girl in a short dress was sitting next to me. I don't know why, but I stood up, still not saying a word, and reached my hand out to the girl. She took my hand, and we walked to my room.

It was only the next day that we learned some of the details of what happened.

While the Stones were on stage performing, 18-year-old Meredith Hunter had been stabbed to death just twenty feet in front of the stage by one of the Hells Angels. It later emerged that Hunter was brandishing a .22 caliber revolver—a fact that was afterward confirmed by film footage of the incident. A rare instance where the person who brought a knife to a gun fight won.

Even though it struck us very hard, I looked through the newspapers in the days afterward, and rather than highlighting the violence, they were raving about the large crowds and how well behaved they had been.

Everyone was sad and shocked and handling it in their own way. A young man had just been killed, and many people were beaten at an event that was supposed to have been a celebration and a gift to the people. The role of the Hells Angels that day remains unclear; I always maintained that the Hells Angels were not hired by the Rolling Stones to perform security for the concert. You only have to listen to Hells Angels leader Sonny Barger's remarks to confirm this. Sam Cutler now says that they were given beer to guard the generators, which was a common practice for the West Coast concerts. I know I never paid the Hells Angels anything! And I was the exclusive representative for the tour.

Factually, the persons responsible for event security are the promoter and the venue. The promoter was John Jaymes and his company, Young American Enterprises; the venue was Dick Carter's Altamont Raceway. Legally, people could have gone after those three entities—Carter had Jaymes indemnify him against claims so the only one that was actually accountable was Jaymes and his company. The Hells Angel had self-defense as his defense.

The story I was told at the time, by Sam Cutler, was the Hells Angels had come to the festival in a bus filled with ice and beer. In *Gimme Shelter*, you see all of them on the top of the bus, and Sonny commented on coming there to enjoy the music and drink the beer. During the day, instead of passing the beer around, they began to throw it. A girl was hit in the head with a can of beer and typical of a head wound, there was a lot of blood. It was very scary. Sam told me he went to the Angels and asked to buy the beer to give to the crew—he didn't want to tell them to stop throwing it (as if you could). They agreed, and he purchased the beer for $500.

For more detail, I asked Albert Maysles, the *Gimme Shelter* director, Hells Angels security questions, and he suggested that I ask the cameramen and woman if they remembered.

When Maysles realized the concert was a go, they called out for filming help and enlisted Peter Adair, Baird Bryant, Joan Churchill, Ron Dorfman, Robert Elfstrom, Elliott Erwitt, Bob Fiori, Adam Giffard, William Kaplan, Kevin Keating, Stephen Lighthill, George Lucas[1], Jim Moody, Jack Newman, Pekke

1   Years later; Albert Maysles told me that he got a call asking if they could put Lucas down as a cameraman on *Gimme Shelter*. Albert checked with the lab, and they told him that the footage George shot came back exposed, with nothing on it. And when viewed, they only saw black with white dust particles… the lab guys teased, they figured that's where George got the idea for *Star Wars*…

Niemala, Robert Primes, Eric Saarinen, Peter Smokler, Paul Ryan, Coulter Watt, Gary Weiss, and Bill Yarru.

I contacted cameraman Eric Saarinen, and he relayed some interesting info to me. First, he told me he was on the stage and had his camera pointed at Meredith Hunter when Meredith pulled his gun. Fearing he would be shot, Eric said, "I took my eye away from the camera and just pointed the camera in the direction of the violence." Later, he would find his footage of the stabbing was out of focus. He was the first person to view the developed footage and saw that another cameraman, Baird Bryant, had captured the stabbing on film, even though Baird didn't realize it at the time.

Eric told me that he and the other camera people were assigned Angels to protect them. I asked if he remembered who assigned the Angel to him, and he replied via email: "I don't recall who assigned the Hells Angel to me. I think all camera positions had an Angel assigned to them. I remember being able to depend on the Hells Angel, who was protecting me."

He made another point in his talk with me. "There was a big, fat, blind, naked guy walking around and when the Angels saw this, they were enraged and took their pool cues and beat him."

I, too, had Hells Angels assigned to help me. Outside the door to the trailer, as I stepped out to view the surroundings, someone assigned two Hells Angels to help me. One was a giant guy, over six-foot-three, wearing a round black hat, and the other was a much shorter, chubby Mexican guy. I was told, "These guys will stay with you." I lost my helpers about five minutes after they were assigned to me. They didn't believe in running and lost me as soon as I dashed off.

The Rolling Stones never hired the Hells Angels. I never paid the Angels for security, but it is obvious they were there to help with the event. My only question that has yet to be answered is when did they start to be assigned to the camera people or anyone? Was it from the beginning or when the violence started? They weren't on the stage all the time. It wasn't until later in the day that they ended up on the stage.

For years, I thought I had seen film footage, at the Maysles, of early in the day when someone crashed the stage and into a drum kit. The band called for help, and the Angels mounted the stage. No one would dare ask them to leave. Unfortunately, all my queries to David and Albert about that footage met with a "no one recalls it or has seen it" so I can't confirm that happened. Either way it isn't an excuse for beating people.

Meredith Hunter minutes before he was stabbed

The Stones moved on without the woulda, coulda, shouldas of those bearing guilt. What was, was, and let's see what today and tomorrow are gonna be. They were pragmatic as hell! Altamont was never mentioned or discussed. It was time for us to leave San Francisco.

Everyone gathered together in a large suite preparing to head home. I entered and noticed that John Jaymes was in a corner with Charlie Watts. John was scribbling notes on a large yellow notepad. He stopped writing, smiled at Charlie, and walked about fifteen feet to Bill Wyman and started talking to him.

Charlie walked over to me and asked, "Do you think it's true?" "Is what true?"

Charlie went on, "John says that Chrysler is giving each of us a car. He's taking our requests now."

I thought about it, since I hadn't heard of that in any of our dealings and said, "I don't know, Charlie, one way or another we will eventually get the truth. If we don't get the car, he's full of shit and if we do get the car, great! All it cost you was talking to John."

John walked over to me with a smile on his face. "Ronnie, I'm taking everyone's order for their gift car from Chrysler. I am putting you down for the top executive car, a Chrysler Crown Imperial. What color do you want?"

"Really, John? They're giving me a car as well?"

"Absolutely," he answered. "You will have it within three months."

In the press coverage in the weeks following the concert, many of the facts were misrepresented. In particular, there continued to be a lot of bullshit emanating from Ralph Gleason of the San Francisco Chronicle. On December 11, he was quoted in an article in Daily Variety that stated, "Any profits from a film of the songfest were announced as going to charity."

I didn't know where he got this stuff;[2] besides not talking to anyone about a film we weren't sure about yet, I never discussed charity. Gleason could have contacted me at any time to fact-check his story. He, at no time did, even though he had the information from Rock Scully, as mentioned in a December 5, San Francisco Chronicle article.

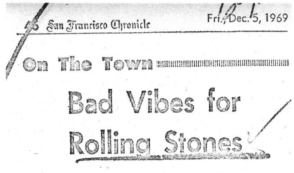

San Francisco Chronicle   Fri., Dec. 5, 1969

On The Town

Bad Vibes for Rolling Stones

Ralph J. Gleason

...we won't go against billyclubs.

The raceway people and Filmways (the giant corporation which owns raceways among other businesses) claimed the Rolling Stones had misrepresented the entire affair. First, that the money from the film (Scully said there were no definite plans for a film) would go to the United Nations Orphanage Fund and now they found that wasn't true. Secondly, that the Stones had agreed to fly in the security personnel from Woodstock and that this wasn't true either.

Scully denied knowledge of any of this and said that a meeting for last night was scheduled with Ron Schneider, the Stones' business manager, and Joe Bergman, Mick Jagger's personal representative, who were en route to Novato from San Francisco.

In another article, Ralph rants that the Stones were only in it for the money, and the free concert was just another way to make money with the film. Nonsense! Plus with show ticket prices in Oakland at $5.50 and hightest at $7.50, I wonder where he got his facts.

2 *I now believe all the false information was gotten from con man, John Jaymes.*

If the Stones only cared about the money, they would have let the promoters sell all the seats in the stadiums, not limiting them to proscenium seating (no one behind them) starting at $20. The promoters wanted it, and we wouldn't allow it. They would have done the $3 million closed circuit pay-per-view. In fact; the Stones (and I, indirectly) paid out over $40,000 to cover some of the costs of the Altamont "free" concert.

And, at the time of the concert, there was no film planned.

I believe Ralph Gleason was under the control of Bill Graham. The ticket price facts proved the concert was based on his misinformation.

A rolling pasture in Alameda County yesterday held Northern California's biggest crowd — 300,000 persons, mostly young and very hip—who came to hear the Rolling Stones, the Jefferson Airplane and the Grateful Dead.

The scene was a hillside alongside the Altamont Speedway. Young humanity was jammed on the dry grass as a lukewarm sun lighted the scene in photo above. Highway 50 was clogged with cars, two abreast, as shown at center left. These autos were moving 10 mph from the Bay Area. Note the lone car driving westward.

The rock-happy crowd was extremely peaceful, sitting and lounging as you see at lower left.

Most brought food and drink, although hot dogs and cokes were for sale. The crowd reached its full size in the early afternoon. It's deportment seemed to follow the theme of the Jefferson Airplane—"We Should be Together."

If you weren't near the stage--"The rock-happy crowd was extremely peaceful, sitting and lounging as you see"

STONE PROMOTIONS LTD.
PROFIT AND LOSS STATEMENT
JANUARY 31, 1970

INCOME:	CONTRACT GUARANTEE	790000 —
	OVERAGE	304001 63
	TELEVISION	15000 —
	SOUVENIR BOOK	15000 —
	POSTERS	9000 —
	INTEREST	3187 50
	TOTAL GROSS INCOME	1136189 13
EXPENSES:		
	AGENCY COMMISSION	88373 07
	PRODUCTION FEE - CHIPMONCK	30000 —
	PRODUCTION EXPENSES - CHIPMONCK	63617 60
	ARTIST EXPENSE — OTHER ACTS	79200 —
	ROAD MANAGER	5000 —
	SECRETARY	3638 21
	TEMPORARY HELP	2322 —
	FREIGHT	13110 25
	LIGHTING	8000 —
	SOUND	5815 —
	EQUIPMENT	4577 03
	TRAVEL	80140 37
	MEALS AND LODGING	37367 28
	COSTUMES AND CLEANING	1607 08
	TIPS AND SECURITY	11938 97
	POSTER PRINTING	5683 98
	MAKE UP	511 75
	PUBLICITY	7566 19
	PHOTOS	5020 08
	TELEPHONE	10275 30
	MEDICAL	327 —
	INSURANCE	6631 W
	REPAIRS AND MAINTENANCE	176 97
	STATIONERY, PRINTING, POSTAGE, AND OFFICE	54 73
	BANK CHARGES	8 —
	MISCELLANEOUS	30 —
	STATE FRANCHISE TAX	15500 —
	CITY TAX	750 —
	TOTAL EXPENSES	487242 15
	NET PROFIT	648946 98

The tour had a net profit of 57 percent. I did it all by hand.

CHAPTER XXIII

THE LAST TIME

In the aftermath of the '69 American tour and the Altamont concert there were a lot of issues needing to be addressed, and still more problems arose in their wake.

I had been going back and forth to London to take care of business with the Stones.

Meanwhile on one of my returns to New York, John Jaymes called me. "Ronnie, you ever been in a casino in Manhattan?"

"No," I said.

"Meet me at 82nd and Park Avenue, East Side, middle of the block."

I spotted John and three black-suited guys in front of a high-end East Side apartment house. John said something to the doorman, and he waved us in. We took the elevator to the eighth floor and got out. John knocked on one of the doors. Inside we were greeted by a hostess in a tight black dress. We were offered drinks from a bar and a seat at any of the three blackjack tables in the living room. "You want to roll the dice, you'll find a craps table in the dining room." There were tuxedoed men, playmate-dressed cocktail waitresses, sharply dressed female dealers, and a few gamblers laying bets. It was a casino in New York City. I wouldn't be placing any bets here. I smiled and had a Jack Daniels on the rocks.

I got another call. John took me to dinner at a Turkish restaurant, famous for their belly dancers. The dancers were feet away on a runway running next to our table. John took a crisp $100 bill, folded it into an airplane glider, wrote a message, and sailed it toward the closest belly dancer. "I invited her over."

With a few of his mafia-looking cohorts joining us, John was trying to impress me.

A month had gone by and I started getting bills for rental cars lost on the streets (we had a couple of those), cars left at the airport outside curbside check-in, towed and left in storage only to be found months later. I gave copies of the bills to John to send to Chrysler for payment.

I started to hear that the bills hadn't been paid. I asked John, "How come Chrysler isn't paying this?" He always had a good story: "The corporate delay is because of a stockholders meeting." And we still hadn't received those "gift cars" from Chrysler: "Because of a delay in customs and importing."

I received more bills that John said he paid, that weren't paid. A couple of months went by.

I began to wonder.

I no longer trusted John Jaymes.

I contacted Chrysler and got a different story than the one John had been giving Chip and me. It was their understanding that he was doing a National Body Painting contest that segued into the Rolling Stones tour. It became clear that John was lying to me; he was on the con. He had hustled Chrysler into thinking he represented the Rolling Stones and us into thinking he represented Chrysler. We now had limo and rental bills totaling over $80,000. Chrysler covered $20,000 for the rentals and $10,000 for the limousines to and from the concerts, but I paid the rest, which amounted to $50,000 to avoid any further problems.

The most upsetting part is that he could have done all the things he promised and been successful. It seems to be a disease with con men; instead of completing the tasks that could make them money, they choose to rip people off. The con in con man doesn't stand for convict, it stands for confidence.

I cut off all contact with John. I never spoke to him again.

Unfortunately, that wasn't the end of John Jaymes and his negative effect upon my life.

One night there was a knock at my door in Riverdale. When I answered, three very large, dark-suited mafia types pushed their way into our apartment. Jane had Eric in her arms; I told her to go upstairs. She hurried up the stairs, but unbeknownst to me, sat at the top listening.

They told me John Jaymes said that he and I were 50/50 partners in the Rolling Stones and he sold them half of his half, 25 percent for $100,000. They had given John $100,000 to pay for the tour expenses he said he was responsible for. For that, he gave them a nonexistent 25 percent in a nonexistent deal.

They were going to be mad. I was scared. I began protesting that I wasn't partners with John. They ignored me.

One guy shuffled over to my desk and grabbed my checkbook. The largest of the three thugs immediately demanded that I write them a check for 25 percent of what was in my bank account.

"He's got a balance of over $40,000," he told his cronies. Then to me: "It's easy; you owe us $10,000. Give us a check."

"I can write you the check, but the Stones' accountant will call the bank and stop payment," I protested. "I'm not partners with the Rolling Stones or John Jaymes."

Immediately all three thugs pulled their guns and pointed them at me. It was surreal!

"Write the check," barked one of them.

The logical (but insane) person in me replied, "The Stones won't go along with this, and I don't own a piece. I can write the check, but I've seen enough movies and TV shows to know the accountant always gets killed. I can't work with you."

One of them stared at me for a long time and remarked, "He's crazy," and they holstered their guns. Now, with the additional facts, I dropped a bombshell: "John ripped you off." John Jaymes had taken $100,000 from the mafia and told them it was to pay Stones bills, and for that, he gave them a piece. "He lied to you; I have the unpaid bills with their threats of collection." I asked if I could get the copies to prove it. They nodded their assent. After taking a long look at the evidence, they stormed out of my apartment.

I smiled as I thought of them visiting John.

Months later, I heard a story from Pete Bennett that he still held to be true when I spoke to him two weeks before he died in 2012. After leaving my place, the mafiosi went to my uncle and threatened to throw him out of his 43rd floor office window. Allen called Pete and Pete made some calls. The mafiosi left Allen alone.

I got word they later got hold of John Jaymes[1] and threw him out of his apartment window, where he fell six floors onto a garage roof.

He was in the hospital for six weeks.

My life went on. As I prepared to pay the last large cash installment to the Rolling Stones, I was informed by the accountants that I had to withhold 30 percent of their income for the US alien tax, and I had to report it to the IRS.

"Can you do anything about this?" I asked. "I want to send them all the money and balance the books."

"We'll see what we can do," said the giant accounting firm's vice president.

A month later the Arthur Andersen VP contacted me and said they had taken the matter to the IRS, and it was ruled that I did not have to withhold the alien tax. I could send all the money. He added that I wouldn't get the opinion in writing, but they were good on their word.

---

1   John Jaymes was an alias of John Clifford Ellsworth, whose aliases in police files include Clifford J. Ellsworth, and Thomas Fiorelia
https://www.washingtonpost.com/archive/lifestyle/1979/12/02/the-mysterious-connections-of-john-ellsworth/6044c556-88b1-480c-b6ce-cc24043a0805/
On July 19, 1979, news show ABC TV "20/20" exposed John Ellsworth, detailing his connection with a national swindle called the International Children's Appeal, a scheme to rip off the International Year of the Child, which conned such people as Rosalynn Carter and Senator Edward Kennedy. The 20/20 program also described Ellsworth's activities as a government informant.
The October 3, 1979, issue of Long Island New York newspaper Newsday also identified Ellsworth as a government informant. The article reported the slaying of two mobsters, which allegedly took place as a direct result of the 20/20 program exposing the International Children's Appeal and Ellsworth.
Ellsworth's Capers During Papal Visit Feed Feds' Anger.
http://articles.latimes.com/1988-05-09/business/fi-1703_1_papal-visit
John Jaymes=John Clifford Ellsworth died in 1994.

CHAPTER XXIV

GIMME SHELTER

A week after returning from Altamont, I got a call from David Maysles, "Ronnie, get over here!" I headed over to his office in Manhattan, next to the Ed Sullivan Theater. There we sat before a Movieola film-editing machine's small screen as he played the footage for me, over and over.

"The cameraman didn't know he had shot it," he explained. "It wasn't until Eric Saarinen, another cameraman, was checking the footage that he found it. Look," he continued excitedly, "if Hunter's girlfriend had on a black dress, we would never have seen the gun. See the gun against her white knit sweater?"

Up until this time, I had only heard the rumor that Hunter had a gun and had thought it was just being used as an excuse for the stabbing. Now, as I watched I couldn't help but be thankful that the Angel was next to the guy.

"See, here they are standing next to each other much earlier in the day," said David, after rewinding the film to that spot. He continued to talk excitedly about the footage and events, and then turned serious.

"I got word that the San Francisco DA is threatening us, you as well, with conspiracy to commit murder and other charges. They guarantee they will drop all charges or threats of charges if I turn over the footage."

David went on to explain he had agreed and suggested I join him. It was one thing to be sued and another to be charged with murder. More bad shit from Altamont.

I had to take care of some of the mess that was left in the aftermath of the free concert. I was going to help pay some of the bills I felt we were obligated to, and also be there on the Stones' behalf. David and I got on a plane heading into a world we weren't part of.

On the flight to San Francisco, David and I sat together and talked about a movie. David had been pitching me on the idea the minute he was finished shooting Madison Square Garden. It had started out as the possibility of a half-hour TV show, then, after Muscle Shoals, a one-hour special. After two weeks of looking at footage, including the events at Altamont, he felt we had a movie.

I asked how much he thought it would cost and he tore out a piece of paper and started jotting down numbers that totaled $113,000 for acquiring the footage less the $10,000 advance.

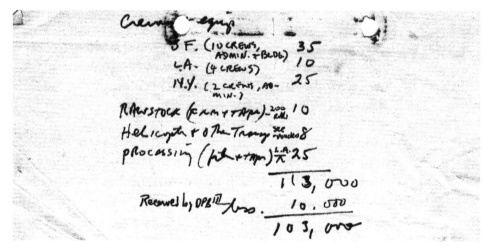

I said, "Okay." I believed him and thought the idea of the film made sense. He needed the money immediately and asked if I could cut him a check when we got to the hotel in San Francisco.

"You know us documentary filmmakers don't have any money," he explained, "and I have to pay everyone for the footage and work before the issue gets clouded."

"Sure," I replied. "I have my checkbook in my bag. When we get to our rooms, I'll cut you a check. Please have simple letter agreements drawn up."

I didn't have the Stones' or Prince Rupert's authorization at this point. I made the decision on my own. The Stones had agreed to the filming for the promo clips, but this was a separate deal not covered by any of our agreements. I hoped they would go along with my commitment.

I wrote out a check to David for $100,000. I had over $500,000 in an account at

Chemical Bank, just not the one I drew the check on.

When I set up the bank accounts for the tour, I didn't want anyone to have to trust me. I suggested that we have a petty cash bank account that I could use while on the road to cover out-of-pocket tour expenses, and a general account for deposits of the guarantees and overages. I was the only signature needed on the petty cash account; I insisted there be two signatures on the general account, with two of the Coudert Brothers attorneys authorized on the account to write the checks to reimburse my petty cash account.

Unfortunately, the plan didn't work in the real world. By the second day on the road, I needed the petty cash account reimbursed with a check from the general account. I called Coudert Bros and was informed the attorneys authorized to sign were out of the office. It took two more days before the attorneys followed through with the check.

By the end of the week, I realized I had to come up with a new plan to keep the operation running. Instead of depositing the overage cash that I was picking up in the general account, I deposited it in the petty cash account. When banks weren't available, I carried the cash on me.

Which is why I wrote the check from the petty cash account, the only account I could sign on my own.

"I just got a check for $100,000 drawn on your petty cash account," my Chemical Bank officer said. "You have to come into the office and make the transfer from your other account."

"I am in San Francisco and won't be back for another week. Can you take care of it?"

"No problem," he said. "I will loan it to you, just come in when you get back."

At the San Francisco District Attorney's office, David turned over the footage; the Angels turned over the gun; and any threat of criminal prosecution for us was ended.

The Stones had acted with the best intentions and got caught up in a whirlwind. I found the costliest bill was for the helicopters and transportation for the groups. It was over $38,000. I figured it would be our contribution, and I could write it off. Not discounting the fact that I figured the helicopter had saved our asses. The Stones had left the States and were on their way to a vacation before beginning rehearsals for their European Tour. David and I flew back to New York. Our flight was uneventful except for the part where David pulled out and lit a joint that looked exactly like a cigarette. He passed it to me, and after we had a couple of more hits in the second row of first class, the flight attendant came over and said, "Sorry, guys. We don't mind, but the captain says he smelled what you are smoking in his cabin and to put it out immediately."

We sucked it into oblivion to make sure there was no evidence.

As requested, David had two separate letter agreements drawn up to acknowledge my payments to him and to delineate between the proposed film and the original request for the Euro promo footage. I made the two-thirds payments of the $20,000, leaving the balance for payment on delivery of the rough cut. At this stage of its development, the film was to be titled Let It Bleed. The $113,000 figure stated in the letter agreement coincides with David's original estimate that he gave me on the plane and also reflects the $100,000 advance I'd paid him. By this time, I had spoken with the Rolling Stones' financial adviser, Prince Rupert Loewenstein, about the film, and he was discussing it with Mick. Mick wasn't as excited about the idea as the rest of us. In fact, he was very apprehensive. He was concerned about the band's image and what the death at Altamont could represent. At the very least, he was saying the murder shouldn't be in the film. Prince Rupert told me he would have to work on persuading Mick of the benefits of proceeding with the film. I pointed out to Rupert that he should stress to Mick that if he didn't want the film made, we still had to pay Maysles and the money would come out of his pocket.

It was soon realized that a film had never been considered in our tour deal. There were no provisions for it. Prince Rupert and the Stones' lawyers said we now had to provide for the film in an agreement. I was an idiot in that I represented myself during these negotiations instead of involving any lawyers. I trusted the Stones and their attorneys. My thinking at the time was that if I approached any lawyers to represent me, they would use it as an opportunity to show how good they were. They would basically stall any negotiations, anger the Stones, and possibly even kill the deal while trying to make a name for themselves. I had seen more attorneys kill deals than make them, and I didn't want that as part of my karma.

Instead of leveraging my ownership position at the time, I went ahead with the transfer of rights.

By January 6, 1970, just a month after Altamont, I was in negotiations with Universal Pictures and Ned Tanen for the film. In their zeal, they made the deal out between my company and the Maysles. Their biggest desire was to get the next, if any, Stones project as well.

We didn't have a completed film, or Mick and the Stones' approval, but we did have a good pitch.

Based on the numbers I was getting from David Maysles, I figured with a $450,000 guarantee we could make the film and have a profit from the get-go. Whatever the film would do in business would be the gravy, and if it flopped, we still were sitting pretty. The incentive of the money would help with getting Mick's approval.

Knowing the stories and having been involved with film distributors, I also required a "gross" deal. I didn't want studio overhead or creative accounting to mess with our profits, if any. I wanted it simple. A dollar comes into the box office, and we get thirty cents. Universal agreed with the numbers.

During the negotiations with Universal, the film changed tentative titles from *Let It Bleed* to *Just A Shot Away* before finally settling on *Gimme Shelter*.

On February 5, things were moving along; I had asked for 30 percent and Universal came back with 25 percent of gross, which I was being told was "amazing." They would quote that the top percentage deal ever done at that time was for 5 percent for Elvis Presley. I didn't care what they thought; I just wanted what was fair. With this new letter, they penciled in the proposed title, *Gimme Shelter*, and tried to deduct the advances out of our percentage instead of collecting it off the top. They were advancing $450,000 and trying to be tricky. According to their original letter, they proposed deducting that advance from our 25 percent of gross. Based on that assumption the film would have to earn $1,800,000 for them to recoup out of our 25 percent. We changed it to taking it from the adjusted gross, not net; therefore, the film only had to earn $450,000 before they were recouped. On that same $1,800,000 we would now make $337,500. I keep telling you I like numbers. I kept battling them on the definition of "adjusted gross."

On February 11, I got the amended agreement from Universal confirming the advance was non-returnable.

In their filmmakers' zeal to tell the whole story, the Maysles set up a meeting with the Hells Angels. Their meeting didn't turn out as planned.

My phone rang. I answered, hearing the high-pitched voice of a scared David Maysles. "Ronnie, Albert and I are with the Hells Angels in San Francisco. They want 10 percent of the film and $100,000 for their appearance."

"No," I said from the safe confines of my house.

David said he and Albert had been threatened by the Angels. David had been punched and kicked in the balls. I was concerned for their safety, but knew there was no way we could partner with the Hells Angels. I stuck to "No" and the Maysles, bruised and battered though they were, got out of there with their skins intact.

Now for their problem with me.

Over the course of the previous month, the Maysles had been changing our deal. I was operating under the "shoot four songs and get paid for it" letter agreement. I was hiring them to make the film, and now I would give them a percentage of the profits. I thought that 25 percent would be more than fair since they weren't paying for anything. When I mentioned that, I was not aware of their artist-director rights.

The Maysles told me they had rights as the directors and wanted the percentage to reflect that. They went from 25 percent to 50 percent.

A basic premise in the independently financed film business is the producer (the money) gets 50 percent, and talent gets the other 50 percent. At this screening, I had had it. I pulled David aside. "I'm pissed! The deal keeps changing, and I'm getting sick of it. Get everyone out of here! We have to settle this before going any further."

Everyone was asked to leave.

It was time to lock in the percentage split. I felt that 60/40 made sense, and that is what I got. Sixty percent for the Rolling Stones and 40 percent for the Maysles. I felt that the Stones were not only the money, but the talent as well. I would be giving the Maysles a good deal if I only charged them 10 percent for the Stones being in the film.

David shrugged and asked what film credit I would like. I said I would settle for Executive Producer for the Rolling Stones on behalf of Penforta, the Stones' company at the time.

Maysles said the final budget to deliver the film would be $350,000. The Stones would be paid back the $113,000 they paid to the Maysles and the $40,000 spent on the free concert. I figured from that point on, we would be playing with house money.

If the film was a success, we were set to win big.

After our meeting, the Maysles made the changes to our agreement. We signed. The hard part seemed to be over.

If only.

The next stumbling block, and it was a huge one, involved my uncle and the music synchronization rights. In order to use the Stones' music in the film, we had to obtain the synchronization rights from the copyright holder and ABKCO had a piece of the copyright. The Stones needed Klein to sign off on the sync license.

My uncle, and by extension his company, ABKCO, was not delivering the sync license. I received a tentative request from Prince Rupert. "Ronnie, do you think you could do better contacting your uncle for the sync licenses?"

"No, I don't."

I felt it best if I kept out of the negotiations. I knew that Allen would delay until the last possible second to do the deal. I didn't want it to become more personal with me entering the fray. Rupert agreed, but time was running out, and we were showing a weakness to Universal. Movie studios don't like rights complications, and they now realized there was some kind of rift between the Stones and Allen Klein. We had been negotiating for over four months, and Universal wanted the deal done.

We started to look for a workaround on the rights and had different attorneys check for loopholes, all to no avail.

By May 11, things were getting testy. Mick and Keith fired off a telex to Klein threatening to sue and use the press unless the sync licenses were signed.

```
WE ARE FED UP TRYING TO REACH YOU WE HAVE BEEN TRYING FOR
ALMOST ONE WEEK. YOUR DELAYING TACTICS ON ASSIGNING OUR
RIGHTS WE REGARD NOW AS HOSTILE. WE WILL RELUCTANTLY HAVE
TO START PROCEEDING AGAINST YOU TO GET THEM IF YOU DO
NOT SIGN YOUR OWN AGREEMENT BY THIS EVENING.  ?

BETTER TELL YOUR NEWSPAPER CUTTING SERVICE TOO.


MICK AND KEITH.
```

Allen responded in kind.

```
KEITH RICHARD
EARTHY STONES
LONDON ENGLAND


1. JUST RECEIVED PENFORTA LICENSE AT 6:08 PM TODAY , MAY
11 1970.

2. JUST CALLED YOUR HOUSE AND LEFT MESSAGE BUT YOUR
WERE NOT IN.

3. THE PENFORTA LICENSE HAS OMITTED YOUR ABSOLUTE RIGHT
TO DETERMINE WHEN AND IF THE FILM SHOULD BE RELEASED.

4. I HAVE BEEN WORKING MY ASS OFF NIGHT AND DAY FOR THE
KLAYT  TWO WEEKS FOR YOU

5. I HAVE AN APPOINTMENT WEDNESDAY MORNING WITH BRITISH
DECCA TO HELP CLEAR UP YOUR PROBLEMS.

SINCE WHEN HAVE YOU FORGOTTEN MY HOME PHONE NUMBER.

ALLEN
```

On May 13, Mick and Keith fired off another telex to Allen. "This is the day, Klein. I have your letter promising the sync license by April 14. If I do not hear from your lawyers that it has been signed by this evening, I will put out our press release of our impending action and aggravation. Get off your ass. Mick and Keith."

```
13.5.70.



THIS IS THE DAY KLEIN.   I HAVE YOUR LETTER PROMISING THE SYNC LICENE
BY APRIL 14. IF I DO NOT HEAR FROM MY LAWYERS THAT IT HAS BEEEN
SIGNED BY THIS EVENING, I WILL PUT OUT OUR PRESS RELEASE OF OUR
IMPENDING ACTION AND AGGRAVATION.


GET OFF YOUR ASS.


MICK AND KEITH.
```

Klein eventually gave the synchronization license. He had done nothing in the making of *Gimme Shelter* or creating the music, but he ended getting a piece of each. I resented seeing the ABKCO fees on my royalty earnings and understood why Mick and Keith were incensed with his sharing their copyright.

Universal was getting skittish.

There was a final review of all the documents, warranties, and guarantees necessary to complete the Universal deal. This is when I first heard of the deal to hire the Angels as security at Altamont. I also learned that the con man John Jaymes said he registered the name "Altamont" and was entitled to the soundtrack from the film.

(1)   An undertaking must be given to Universal that they will be indemnified in respect of any law suit or other action brought against them by the Hell's Angels. Mr. Albert said as far as he knew the Hell's Angels were hired by the Rolling Stones to act as their bodyguards during the concert at Atlamont. He contends that the Maysles have a tape recording of the conversation between members of the Rolling Stones and members of the Hell's Angels regarding their duties at the concert. Mr. Albert suggested that Penforta and Stone Promotions should take joint responsibility with the Maysles for any action which may be brought against Universal by or on behalf of the Hell's Angels. We agreed that it would be almost impossible to obtain a satisfactory release from Hell's Angels. He pointed out that to date three films have been made featuring the Hell's Angels and no release was obtained from them and no action was taken by them (Hell's Angels). It appears that the Hell's Angels have an understanding with the Police in California and he states they were hired by the Rolling Stones on the advice of the Californian Police as they (the Police) refused to give them the protection required. The Maysles would refuse to take sole responsibility for indemnifying Universal in this respect. I said I would confirm with Mr. Schneider whether he had agreed to pay David Maysles' air fare and hotel room in London when he comes for the screening.

(2)   Universal require a release from a person named John James. Mr. Albert contends that John James has put Universal on notice that he has registered the name "Atlamont" and that he claims to have the right to the soundtrack of the film.

Memorandum reviewing Universal deal

On June 1, 1970, Prince Rupert sent me a draft of a letter he needed me to prepare and sign as if I created it. This document would change the reality of what happened to conform to what was contractually needed to happen. The reality was that neither Rupert and his companies, nor I and my companies, had had any rights to make a feature film during the course of the tour. This new document retroactively granted those rights.

```
                              Stone Promotions, Ltd.
                              4601 Henry Hudson Parkway
                              New York, N.Y.
                              U.S.A.


                              June 1, 1970


Prince Rupert Loewenstein
Penforta Limited
31-45 Gresham Street
London, E.C.2
England

Dear Prince Rupert:

     I refer to the concert tour of the United States

by the musical entertainment group known as "The Rolling

Stones" which was conducted pursuant to an agreement

between Penforta Limited and Stone Promotions Limited

dated October 23, 1969.

     At your request, Stone Promotions obtained the

services and materials required to take, process and edit

motion picture film footage of that tour and has incurred

total expenses for those materials and services of two

hundred and ninety-one thousand nine hundred and sixty-

five United States dollars ($291,965). These expenses are

in addition to those incurred by Stone Promotions on behalf

of Penforta pursuant to the agreement mentioned above.

Stone Promotions hereby agrees to release to Penforta all
```

I copied the draft Prince Rupert sent me to provide for the rights to do the film ex post facto.

Finally, on June 13, more than six months after Altamont, the Maysles sent us the agreement to cover the Universal deal. I was getting paid directly, 6 percent to Stone Promotions, Ltd., my company (i.e., I got 10 percent of what the Stones earned, and I got them 60 percent.)

And then the Universal deal fell apart. The delay in getting the sync licenses from Klein was a big factor in this. Prince Rupert was also concerned because Mick had not yet signed his release or viewed the film. Rupert anticipated that Mick would either not approve the film or would suggest major changes. Furthermore, the Maysles' costs went up.

No deal with Universal!

Undeterred, David and I went about trying to find another deal. While the Stones were in dealings with Atlantic, it was suggested I contact Ahmet Ertegun, the President of Atlantic Records. Ahmet suggested Warner Bros. He would set up a meeting.

When we set up the screening at Warner's, I dictated the terms of the proposal. We wanted a gross deal: 30 percent of the gross receipts of the film (without any of the "creative" studio deductions) and a $600,000 advance. I didn't want to wait months while they pondered the decision. We would screen the film, and Warner Brothers would have to decide right there and then if they wanted the film.

David and I went to a Warner Bros screening room, where we were joined by Freddie Weintraub, the former owner of the Bitter End in New York's Greenwich Village and now Executive Vice President of Warner Bros. Woodstock was one of the first films Weintraub oversaw for the studio. Eight other Warners' execs and lawyers accompanied him. Freddie greeted me with, "Performance [a film Mick Jagger was in] is the best film I've ever seen."

We sat down, and David started the projector. Fifteen minutes into the screening I leaned over to Freddie. "Don't forget you guys have to make a decision after the film is over."

Freddie turned to me and said that wasn't possible. He had to take it before the board. I felt like we were getting jerked around again. I stood up.

"David, stop the film, these guys can't make the decision. They're jerking us around. We're leaving!"

David shut down the projector. I walked out of the screening room into the lobby to wait for him. As I was waiting, Ahmet Ertegun entered the lobby. "

Ahmet, they're jerking us around. We're out of here."

"Wait, Ronnie, let me make a call."

Ahmet told the lobby receptionist to get the president of Warner, Ted Ashley, on the phone. They talked briefly. Ahmet said Ted wanted to view it in his personal screening room. We should come over immediately.

We walked into Ted's office, where he sat on his giant, ornate, gold-painted thronelike chair, his feet curled under him. He did a bit of schmooze. We went down and watched the film.

After the screening, Ted said he would like to meet me to discuss the deal at the Polo Lounge in the Beverly Hills Hotel. I agreed and reiterated the deal was a gross deal and to make that an integral part of his offer.

Later that night I arrived at the Polo Lounge. The maître d'hôtel made a point he was taking me to the best seat in the house, Table 1. I joined Ted in the booth.

Ted began by telling me he wanted to get to know me as a person, even if we didn't do a deal. (Schmoozing 101).

"Ron, we're going to do your deal. It will be a gross deal, but we have to take off the costs of prints and advertising."

"Ted, if you are taking off costs, it's not my gross deal."

We went back and forth on this for a while.

"Bottom line, Ted," I said, "any costs off the top make it a net deal."

I walked away thinking they were jerking us around again. No deal.

Sometimes not knowing what you are doing is a good thing. Unfortunately for me, the Stones, and their fans, this wasn't one of those times. What I didn't know was the studios usually split the cost of advertising with the exhibitors, and the prints are the cans of film that are delivered to the theaters. It was an amazing offer for its time, but I couldn't get past the definition of gross.

I feel I made a mistake not taking the Warner deal. We would have had a major distributor and the best film deal for its time. I think David didn't mind passing on the deal because he didn't trust the film companies.

Once again we were on a search for a film distributor.

CHAPTER XXV

1970 EUROPEAN TOUR

"Ronnie, would you like to do the European Tour?" were the first words I heard from Mick Jagger as I answered the phone in June 1970. By this time, Jane and I decided to leave Riverdale and New York City to move to Florida. We wanted our kids to be able to play outside three hundred and sixty-five days a year, unlike our experiences growing up in New Jersey. Miami was great for me as a kid, and I wanted it for our family; plus, instead of a suit and tie, I could wear a bathing suit to work.

I was surprised by Mick's call and reacted with silence as my brain tried to analyze the situation. Would I be an asset? What value could I bring to the tour? I was dealing with Mick, and I had to be straight with him and debate my value as I would with anyone else joining the tour.

"I don't know what I can bring to the tour," I told him. "I don't speak any foreign languages, maybe just a smattering of Spanish, and I'd be working with foreign currencies."

"That doesn't matter. We want you on the tour."

I couldn't argue with that, so I agreed and was brought into the negotiations. I had said I couldn't do the '69 tour, unless they got my uncle's approval, and now I had given reasons why I shouldn't do the European tour. That wouldn't be the last time I said no to a job with the Stones. Sometimes I was my own worst enemy.

After signing on to the European tour, I was updated on the negotiations with the promoter, European Concert Performances. They were promoting the dates in Europe excluding the deal we were making for Paris. When I say we,

I mean not me. I was asked for some input, but Prince Rupert Lowenstein, Mick's financial advisor, now financially representing all the Stones, was putting most of the deal together in Europe. I was informed we were not expected to make a profit from the tour, but to at least break even. The reason for the tour was to increase record sales.

One idea that Chip Monck and I entertained was to incorporate a performance by Le Crazy Horse Saloon dancing girls into the Stones show. Le Crazy Horse Saloon is a world-famous Parisian cabaret known for its stage shows performed by nude female dancers. Chip and I thought it would be a great idea for the Stones' European tour to include the Crazy Horse show. Bring on the naked dancing girls!

Of course, we had to research it. The girls lived at Le Crazy Horse Saloon in a virtual cocoon. We spent time with the owner, Alain Bernardin. He explained his vision for the Crazy Horse: "Magic is a dream. There is no show that is more dreamlike than a magic show. And what we do with the girls is magic, too. It's the magic of lights and costumes. These are my dreams and fascinations that I put on stage."

As for combining his vision with the Rolling Stones, Alain said he liked the idea, but had to think about it. After a short time, he came back to Chip and me and said that even though a good idea, it wouldn't work. "Within two weeks of the girls leaving Paris on the Stones tour, all the wealthy dukes, princes, barons, and so on would come out and basically seduce the girls into leaving with them." Not only would we not have a show; he would lose all his girls.

I still liked the idea of a live broadcast of the Rolling Stones and the Crazy Horse dancers, adding more emphasis to the first part of the sex, drugs, and rock 'n' roll equation, but we got busy and the idea faded.

CHAPTER XXVI

TWO THOUSAND LIGHT YEARS FROM HOME

The tour was set to begin in Scandinavia. We used Copenhagen, Denmark, as our base in the weeks leading up to the tour kicking off. Fifty years ago, Denmark was regarded as the most liberated country on Earth. There was no censorship, and sex was wide open. I had this idyllic image that we were in a place where sex was beautiful, without guilt and the judgment of society. With that thought in mind, we—in this instance meaning the married couples and not the Stones—went to a "sex" club. It was like any nightclub: people dancing, drinking, and sitting at tables, then the announcement, the show would begin. A bed was lowered from the ceiling onto the middle of the dance floor, followed by an announcement in Danish, which we would learn later was something like "Tonight is Thursday, and it's S&M night." Next, a woman appeared in a little nightie, jumped on the bed, and began playing with herself with various toys. Suddenly, a man in a black cape and mask appeared. At this point, I noticed a lot of the hostesses disappeared. The masked man pulled out a cat of nine tails and began whipping the woman.

At first, we all assumed it was a fake—even when we saw blood—but after a while, we realized that even if faked, it had to hurt.

After the whipping, they had sex and then the man carried the woman off. As they passed, we saw the bloody welts on her, which confirmed it wasn't bogus.

So much for love, beauty, romance, and the lack of Victorian rules—Denmark was hardcore.

After the performers had exited, the hostesses came back. I asked one of them why had they left. She replied that most of the hostesses couldn't stand to watch the whipping, but the woman performer loved it and was actually unhappy she had to wait a week between shows. Apparently, it took that long for her welts to heal sufficiently to perform again.

At the sex club, I found out they did a traveling show. As a surprise for Mick, I hired one of the acts—not the S&M couple—to go to his hotel room later that evening. At about 1:30 AM there was a knock on my hotel room door, and it was Mick. He wanted some money to keep the show going.

One evening Bill Wyman and his girlfriend Astrid Lundström came to my room in Copenhagen to ask my wife a favor. Jane wasn't doing the hard traveling as we had our one-year-old son with us. Astrid's sister would be traveling with the group for part of the tour. They asked Jane if it was okay if Astrid's sister roomed with me. Bill and Astrid didn't want her screwing around or—the worst-case scenario—Mick bedding her. Bill said he knew how I was with women and, therefore, trusted me to be with Astrid's sister.

"Fine with me," responded Jane, which I am sure she said to seem sophisticated.

August 30, 1970 – Malmo, Sweden, Baltiska Hallen

The first date of the tour was in Malmo, Sweden. The Stones were tight, meaning the music was a steady stream of excellence. They didn't have the "still getting it together" feel they'd had on the first part of the1969 US tour, caused by a long dry spell without touring. In Europe in 1970, they were fresh off the previous year's US tour, and it showed in their performances. Many Stones fans still regard this particular tour as one of the best the Stones ever played.

September 2, 1970 – Helsinki, Finland, Olympiastadion

We next traveled to Finland. From the hotel in Helsinki, I was told I would be able to see the Russian border and guards walking along the perimeter. I immediately went outside, climbed some large boulders, and sure enough, I saw a uniformed soldier standing in the distance. As an American who was brought up with Russia as the big bad bogeyman, this was a big deal.

This is also the day Keith helped send me on my own trip.

We were taken to the Helsinki Airport and after being ushered through long corridors and up a flight of stairs, we arrived at a large warehouse structure. About 100 yards from us, we saw a group of uniformed police with drug-sniffing German shepherds standing next to our luggage. Obviously a surprise baggage inspection, one of many we would have on this tour.

As the figures began advancing toward us, Keith sidled over to me and surreptitiously put something round into the palm of my hand.

"Ronnie," he hissed. "Get rid of it!"

I looked down at my hand and saw a piece of hash about one inch across with some pieces of white stuff embedded in it.

Life isn't about years or decades; it's those split seconds that make the difference. It's that split second when you swerve to miss that pedestrian you didn't notice; that split second when you didn't duck. It's those seconds, and the one that followed after I saw what Keith had given me, that make life interesting.

Without another thought and the cops advancing, I popped the piece of hash into my mouth and swallowed it. Just as I swallowed it, I wondered why Keith hadn't.

The guards did a walk-through with the dogs, and everything was cleared. I always had my heart in my throat during those inspections. That would be the least of my worries as we sat on the small, loud prop plane on our way to Stockholm.

By the time we were in the air, I was starting to feel strange. Bill was sitting next to me on my right. I was in the aisle seat, and across the aisle from me was Charlie. I started feeling I was getting high, and it was coming on fast.

Bill looked over at me and asked, "You okay?"

"I don't know yet. I'm feeling very high and seem to be getting higher."

Charlie called from across the aisle and asked if there was a problem.

"Ronnie's getting high!" Bill hollered back over the loud noise of the plane's propellers.

"I wish I had what he had," Charlie replied with a straight face.

I needed to get some food into my system and was happy to see the food cart coming down the aisle. The stewardess placed a tray in front of me and asked what I would like to drink. I mumbled, "Hot coffee."

Immediately I knew I had a bigger problem; I tried to pick up the plastic fork. I couldn't hold it. My hands were getting numb. I figured I had better move fast and get some coffee into me to keep me lucid. I used both hands to get the coffee cup to my mouth. I managed a burning sip before the cup tipped and dropped onto the tray. After that I gave up on eating or drinking anything.

I sat back and figured I would try to ride it out, whatever it was. By now, Keith got word of my condition. I had eaten a piece of hash infused with opium. Perfect.

As I sat back in my seat, I started to hallucinate. I was surrounded by the roaring sound of the engines' vibrations and visualized the plane's wings curling up so that the right and left wing tips touched, forming a tunnel, and I was in the middle of it. I flew like that in my little cocoon of sound and wings until they straightened out, and we landed.

Bill helped me stand as Mick came over and asked if I could help him with his bag in the overhead bin. I couldn't talk by then, and Bill said to Mick, "He's gonna need your help."

The guys helped zombie walk me off the plane and into the waiting car taking us to our hotel. I had to sign for the group after they'd registered. I couldn't raise my arm. Bill lifted my arm and hand up to the counter and guided it to make my scrawled signature. Wyman then helped me to my room.

Once there, I fell face forward, onto the bed.

I woke up the next afternoon, fully dressed, face forward, flat out on the bed exactly as I had fallen.

Just another day at the office.

September 4, 1970 – Stockholm, Sweden, Rasunda Stadium

The next night we were in Stockholm at the Rasunda Stadium. By now, all the shows started to blend into a frenzy of fans and outstanding musical performances by the Stones. For the most part, I noted the fans were polite to the opening acts, but couldn't wait for the Stones to mount the stage to vent their enthusiasm.

This show was a bit different due to the fear coming from the police. Mick's gyrations incited the fans to dance in the aisles; because of this, the cops felt Mick was instigating a riot. The security detail kept relaying word to me; they were going to shut down the concert, unless I instructed Mick not to provoke the fans. Mick reacted by telling the police to cool it, but did assuage their fears when he announced, "I'm going to slow this down for a minute while I catch my breath." He and Keith sat down to play "Love in Vain" and the kids followed suit, making for a more relaxed atmosphere in the stadium. The show went on without a hitch after that.

When it was time to leave the hotel the next morning, everyone was in the cars ready to go—except Keith and Anita. Time was running out, and I kept calling from the hotel house phone to get Keith downstairs. Keith finally appeared with his baby boy Marlon in his arms, but no Anita.

"We gotta go," I said,

"Let's go," responded Keith. "If she isn't down in a minute, fuck her, just leave."

I was in a precarious position. What if Keith changed his mind and because we left her, I ended up being the asshole? The last thing I needed was to end up on Anita's shit list.

In the end, none of that mattered. We had to leave, so we left her.

She caught up with us at the next hotel, and life went on. Leaving on time would often be a problem on this tour, and the sole cause of it seemed to be Keith and Anita's relationship. Not their "I love you; I hate you" relationship, but their relationship with drugs. We had to dodge that bullet many times while traveling.

The scariest was when all our bags were placed before us during a customs check on one of our airport arrivals. The police did a search and found a syringe with a small bottle of a clear liquid seemingly hidden in the baby bag Anita was carrying.

"Whose bag is this and why is there a needle with it?" a cop demanded.

Anita jumped forward and said, "It's my bag and the needle is for vitamin shots."

Fortunately for us, that excuse was apparently plausible enough and the cops backed off.

September 6, 1970 – Gothenburg, Sweden, Liseberg

On September 6, 1970, we were in Gothenburg, Sweden at the Intercontinental Hotel. The tour promoter gathered the local politicians and their entourage to join us for dinner at a long table in the hotel restaurant. The Stones and I were at the far end of the table. Directly to my left were Anita, Keith, and then about ten other people. Across from me were Bill, Charlie, and Mick Taylor. It was a while before the other Mick got there.

A waiter appeared and Anita asked, "What is the strongest alcohol traditional to Sweden?"

He went away and reappeared with a bottle of a clear liquid, probably like straight grain alcohol. Anita took the bottle, filled a large water glass with the alcohol, picked up the glass, and chugged it down.

She slammed the glass down in front of Keith, refilled it, and said, "Now prove to me you're a man."

Keith chugged it, and the rest of us "men" proceeded to do the same. By the time Jagger appeared, we were getting quite drunk. He wanted to catch up; he chugged a glass.

By now, things were getting noisy. Keith leaned back in his chair, put his feet up on the table, smashing the plates that were there. We were talking louder. The promoter signaled me over and asked me to try to get our party under control. We were bothering the other customers. I called the boys over and we rugby scrum huddled in the middle of the room. I told them what the promoter had said to me: "Please calm them down. They are getting too drunk and loud. They are causing a scene." I added that he didn't realize how drunk I was, and I was part of the problem as well. We just laughed about it and got louder.

Keith ended up on the floor of the restaurant making out with Anita, at which point the promoter, the local politicians, and the other people left. A waitress came over to pull Keith off of Anita, and Keith accidentally hit her with his elbow. A photo of this was on the front page of the paper the next day.

Another waitress came over to me and said the police had been called and were coming with a paddy wagon to arrest us. She suggested that I get them out of there. I quickly pushed, dragged, and coerced everyone out of the restaurant and over to the lobby elevator to go to their rooms. Anita was still on the floor of the restaurant after her make-out session with Keith. I had to pick her up and carry her.

As I carried Anita out of the restaurant in my arms, she looked up at me and said, "Do me a favor. Take me to your room."

I carried her to the elevator and took her to Keith's room.

"She undulated towards me. Her body swaying to the fast Moroccan beat. Slowly, she drew down her briefs. The elastic left little stripes as it passed her navel, past her glowing, vibrant womanhood, past her toes and right into the trash. Her tongue hesitated before entering my ear, where it wet, moistened and tickled me until I had to hit her with my imported alligator belt. The sting must have been pleasant because instead of stopping me she...."

The preceding paragraph is an excerpt from the Tuesday, September 8, 1970, Rolling Stones Euro Tour call sheet for the Gothenburg, Sweden, departure for Aarhus, Denmark. It was inserted to get the attention of the Rolling Stones and the crew. We had a problem with no one paying attention to the call sheets and people and their bags not being ready for our departure in the mornings. I thought if I added a paragraph of porn, they would read it.

They did.

September 9, 1970 – Aarhus, Denmark, Vejlby-Risskov-Hallen

September 11–12, 1970 – Copenhagen, Denmark, Forum

The original plan was to spend the night in Aarhus after the show on September 9, but for some reason, that got changed, and we went back to the Marina Hotel in Copenhagen. We arrived late, and as I was getting ready for bed, I heard a lot of loud vibrating thumps throughout the room. Although it was 3:00 AM, there was obviously some construction going on in the hotel. Immediately my phone rang, and Keith was complaining that he couldn't sleep.

I went in search of the noise and found a construction crew with sledgehammers tearing out the cabinets in the hotel restaurant. I yelled at the seven large Danes who were going about the destruction to please stop, as we had just arrived and were trying to sleep. I doubt that they understood English since they continued as if I was not there. I got to the house phone and called the front desk, only to have it ring for a long time.

It was around this time Keith appeared with Bobby Keys, our resident saxophone player and friend, in tow. Now it was looking dangerous. Bobby was an instigator, and Keith was a good bud for Bobby during his instigation. Keith began screaming at the large construction guys to stop. They didn't seem to care what anyone was saying; they just sledgehammered on.

I told Keith and Bobby I was ringing the front desk to get hold of the manager. I hoped the phone would wake him if he were sleeping. Eventually, it did. When he sleepily answered, I told him we had a problem in the kitchen and to get here immediately.

Meanwhile, Bobby shook his fist at the construction guys, threatening to get violent. One of the crew started coming toward him with a sledgehammer. I pulled Bobby back. I think the only reason he went with me was because he knew a fist against a sledgehammer was not an even match.

Since the cabinets were being torn out, all the cups, saucers, and dishes were stacked on the tables adjoining the kitchen. Keith picked up a large stack of dishes and said that he would smash them if the workers didn't stop. They didn't. I told Keith to put the dishes down. "We don't want to be the bad guys." Keith put the dishes down.

Bobby went over to a table, wrapped his hands under the bottom of a larger stack of dishes, and lifted them to his stomach. He braced them under his chin and said if they didn't stop he would drop this giant stack. I pleaded with him to stop, as Keith looked on, amused.

Luckily, just then, the manager appeared. Bobby put the plates down, and the manager told us they thought we wouldn't be back that night and had scheduled the construction during our absence. He stopped the workmen and told them to go home.

The manager apologized and told me that to help make up for the disturbance, he would unlock the kitchen refrigerators, and we could help ourselves to any food during the night. Keith and Bobby were happy with that and walked into the giant refrigerator, helped themselves to some snacks, and took them to their rooms.

Late the next afternoon in the Marina Hotel, Keith, Bill, Charlie's wife, Shirley, and I were sitting at a small square table in the hotel cafe, drinking beers. A guy in a white suit walked over from the bar and leaned over Shirley, squatted down, and said something to her. As he continued to talk, he stood up. I thought he was asking for a light for his cigarette. Suddenly, Keith, who was on my left, stood up, and said, "I am sick and tired of you bothering us!" and with that, he picked up an empty beer bottle from the center of the table and smashed it over the guy's head.

As the bottle shattered, I thought for a split second that it was a practical joke Keith was playing on me, using a breakaway stunt bottle. However, in the next second, a shard of glass hit my hand, and I saw blood dripping down the guy's face. I realized it wasn't a joke.

Quickly, hotel security grabbed the guy and took him away. Keith went on to explain he hit the guy because he was bothering Shirley.

One of the hotel staff came over to me. I expected we were in trouble. Instead, he apologized. I was dumbfounded at the apology when he added the guy was a newspaper reporter. Uh-oh, another bad article. The hotel rep said the reporter was drunk and not to worry. The hotel would take care of it.

For our next date, we decided to go by train instead of plane. Trains were adding cars to facilitate their soccer fans, and we got one of them for our trip to Hamburg. It was going to be an overnight trip, and we all had sleeper accommodations.

Jagger had a pretty young female assistant—she was later in Playboy magazine. To avoid intimacy with her boss on the train, she chose to ride with me in my sleeper car. There is nothing more conducive to sex than being on a train; the clickity-clack of the wheels and the rocking motion they bring to the cars might be part of it. But then again, it might be we were just horny.

The only glitch in any train late-at-night long-term lovemaking is when you are crossing borders. Often our amorous adventures would be rudely interrupted by a knocking on the compartment door, followed by "Your passports, please."

September 14, 1970 – Hamburg, Germany, Ernst-Merck-Halle

We arrived at a beautiful chateau, Hotel Schloss Tremsbuttel, just north of Hamburg. It would be our hotel for the night. We felt like guests at someone's castle. The dining room was spectacular. You entered through carved ornate twenty-foot-tall double doors. The room itself had a thirty-foot ceiling with a beautiful crystal chandelier hanging in the middle. It was decided we would all gather to have a "family" dinner in this classic setting.

As we were eating quietly in this serene old-world haven, I suddenly heard raised voices coming from a table on the left side of the room. Keith and Anita were having a loud argument. Again.

Finally, I saw Anita stand up and storm toward the dining room exit. I noticed everyone staring in her direction with a look of horror in their eyes expressing the same thought: Oh no, she wouldn't! Nevertheless, she did, as she walked through the magnificent wooden carved doorway, she slammed the giant doors shut.

It happened like a car accident; in slow motion, the room vibrated with the loud bang and the chandelier swayed. We all watched, waited, and feared it would come crashing down. It swayed, but didn't fall.

Two heartbeats later, Keith arose and ran after her. We didn't see them again until the next day.

September 16, 1970 – Berlin, Germany, Deutschlandhalle

Flying into West Berlin was amazing. You actually landed inside the city, as the Berlin Wall was still up and Germany was divided between East and West. Imagine landing in Manhattan between the buildings. As you descended to the runway, you could look out the windows on either side of the plane into someone's living room.

Berlin surprised me. On one hand, you had the Brandenburg Gate dividing free thought from Communist rule and on the other, you had a lot of erotica shops.

I was walking down a busy Berlin street with Mick's gorgeous young female assistant, when she reached back to her butt and screamed, "That guy came on me!"

I looked to see a man running away down the street. It seems that the guy was walking behind her, jerked off into his hand, and wiped it on her ass. Luckily, he was gone before we could catch him.

September 18, 1970 – Cologne, Germany, Sporthalle

Twice, I was approached by one of our backstage crew members with similar requests: "Can you arrange for me to make a call to my wife in the States? I fell in love with a girl in Copenhagen (Berlin). She's been traveling with me since then and I feel it only fair to tell my wife. I'm going to ask for a divorce."

Before I arranged for the calls through the local switchboard, I cautioned, "You know the tour ends? What are you and your new love going to do when it's over in Amsterdam? It's romantic traveling, but where are you going to live when it's over? Are you willing to destroy your real life?"

They called home. It didn't end well.

September 19, 1970 – Good News

The Maysles had located an investor who stepped up to the plate with an offer of $600,000 for a piece of the film. It was Leonard Holzer, the New York real estate mogul who was married to Andy Warhol superstar Baby Jane Holzer. That took care of the need for money. It got us all even.

However, the film wasn't finished. We still had to find a legitimate distributor.

And Mick Jagger hadn't agreed to any deal.

September 20, 1970 – Stuttgart, Germany, Killesberg

While we were in Germany, Chip tried to arrange a visit for us to the Mercedes plant in Stuttgart. We were also trying to get to the Merck Pharmaceutical laboratories—hoping for samples. Unfortunately, or fortunately, we didn't manage to accomplish either of these visits.

After we had dinner at the Reichsbahn Hotel in Stuttgart, I went to a nightclub directly next door in the hopes of dancing and forgetting about being on the road. The music was great and there was a large crowd on the dance floor. I figured I would just melt in and began dancing on my own when a cute young woman sidled up and started dancing with me. It didn't take long for me to realize she didn't speak or understand English and for her to realize I didn't understand anything she said, but we danced on. We started getting closer and via the international signals of smiling, grabbing, squeezing, touching, and her putting her hands down my pants, we decided to leave the club and head for my room.

In the morning, I left her to meet our entourage for the next day's train travel. The train station was directly below the hotel, and after I boarded the train in the second-to-last car, I looked out the window and saw her standing on the platform.

The train began to pull away, and she started running and waving at me, throwing kisses until the platform ended and we pulled out of sight. I always remember this when I see movies with similar farewell scenes.

I never knew her name.

CHAPTER XXVII

STREET FIGHTING MAN

September 22–24, 1970 – Paris, France, Palais des Sports

The Vietnam War fermented violent unrest throughout Europe. While driving to the Paris show we swerved between rampaging mobs and overturned, burning cars. With this in mind, while the Stones were in their dressing room at the Palais des Sports, I roamed around backstage checking security.

I noticed a door at the back of the stage, opened it, and looked into a room the size of an airplane hangar. Inside were rows and rows of picnic-style tables and seated at those tables were hundreds of black-clothed, riot-geared, armed French police. I quickly backed out of the room thinking how weird it was. Out front sat the VIPs, all finely dressed, waiting for the Stones, and on the other side of the curtain sat an army in battle gear.

It got weirder.

Word reached Chip Monck that there were Hells Angels in the audience. And one of them had a gun. We were especially wary since we had heard, because of Altamont, there was a Hells Angels hit out on us. We were told how to spot the Angels in the audience; they were shirtless with badges pinned into their bare chests.

Chip found them and asked if they had a gun.

An Angel said, "Yes, but it's a starter pistol. I just want to shoot it in the air."

Chip persuaded him to reconsider.

European royalty from various countries, dukes and duchesses, princes and princesses, counts and countesses, came to Paris to see the Stones. It was the best-dressed, jewelry-accessorized audience of any Rolling Stones show I ever witnessed. Mick and Keith didn't like that the Royals took up the front sections. They suspected the titled individuals didn't care about the group or their music and were there just to be seen. Mick and Keith wouldn't have to worry long! Before the show began I was moving through the audience when I heard a roar and a rumble. The kids without tickets had broken through the doors and were now swarming inside.

The Royals looked on in horror as these street urchins in everyday clothes stormed down the aisles. The dukes, duchesses, counts, countesses, princes, and princesses grabbed their jewels and furs and exited the building, leaving their seats to the kids.

When the show started this unruly audience charged to the front of the stage. As I walked along the left front of the stage, I noticed one guy making threatening gestures at everyone on the stage, especially me. He looked pissed, shaking his fist and wanting to fight.

There was tension in the air in this group of fans. I sensed they were going to jump onto the stage. I needed something to stop them. I walked backstage and spotted a large whipped cream dispenser on a food table. It was an 18-inch-high stainless steel cylinder with a long metal nozzle to dispense the whipped cream. I hoped it would be confused for a tear gas container.

I went back to the lip of the stage with the metal canister. The guy looked at me, saw the metal object in my hand, and got even madder. Apparently, he wasn't concerned about tear gas. He stared at me with red eyes and fist pumping, daring me to fight. The audience around him was paying attention.

Knowing the riot police was standing by was not comforting since it only indicated the possible dangers of this crowd and how easily it could spill over into full-blown urban warfare. I didn't want a riot.

Suddenly, the guy made a leap up for the stage. I squeezed the trigger. And a stream of whipped cream hit the instigator full in the face. He was caught midair and dropped back to two feet in front of the stage. In a flash, he realized it was whipped cream and had a lick. He laughed, gave me a "that's cool" look, and the left-side front of the audience relaxed and enjoyed the show.

My highest priority at the shows was the safety of the Stones. Forget about me being the accountant and the money. It was dangerous out there, and I wanted to make sure it stayed as safe as it could. One thing I did was confirm the band had a clear exit from the stage. We had to be able to escape quickly.

While making sure the exit route from the stage was secure, I noticed a gendarme blocking the stairs while chatting up the girls around the stage. A couple of times I came by and asked him to get off the stairs, but he ignored me. Finally, I was so pissed I pushed him off the stairs. He turned around and grabbed my left arm while a couple of other gendarmes grabbed on to help him. Our stage guys came to my aid, grabbing my right arm, and suddenly I was the middle in a tug of war. The cops were trying to pull me into the back to beat me, and my crew, pulling me in the other direction, trying to save my ass.

Chip climbed over the crew guys, eased himself into the middle, and in his soothing Woodstock voice said something to the police that calmed the situation. They let me go and thanks to the crew and Chip, I avoided a beating.

At the beginning of the tours, I made a point with all that I worked for and with the Rolling Stones, not their girlfriends, wives, relatives, or friends. Too often I saw companions and relatives of the stars take on the persona and power of their significant others. I didn't have the time or patience for that. The boys never complained.

At the Paris concert, the girlfriends and wives were told that when the second-to-last song begins, they have to go to the limousines behind the Stones' limo—or in the case of Paris, bus—in preparation for exiting the arena. During the second-to-last song, I went to double-check our escape route and noticed a large group of people on the Stones' escape bus. On board was Mick's recently met love interest, Bianca, and a dozen of her friends. I told them to get off the bus. Bianca got upset. I told her that it was unsafe, and I wanted her and her entourage off. She kept protesting, but eventually they all exited into the limos behind the bus.

She later complained to Mick, and I was happy to hear him tell her, "When we are on the road, we listen to Ronnie. His word is law."

I never had another conversation with Bianca.

A run-in with the gendarmes wasn't the only danger I avoided in Paris. A couple of days into our visit, my wife, our one-year-old son Eric, and I were in one of the fashion salons along Avenue Montaigne. As Jane was looking through the clothes, we heard a bit of a commotion from outside a dressing room.

"I am Marlene Dietrich, and you should come out of the dressing room and let me use it!" an older woman was yelling.

We looked over, and it was Ms. Dietrich. She continued to yell at the dressing room door. Finally saying, "I'll just change here," she began taking off her jacket, then her blouse. She stood there in a bra and skirt; at that moment, Eric waddled over to where she was standing and threw up on her. Jane was embarrassed and apologetic, but it didn't seem to matter to Marlene. She just carried on changing.

That wasn't the problem. When Jane was done shopping, and the clerk presented a bill for over $2,000, I told him I didn't have the money on hand and would have to go to the bank. The clerk asked where we were staying. I said the George V, and he replied he could send the clothes to the hotel, and the hotel would pay for them and put it on our bill.

"Really? Just send it to the hotel?"

"No problem," he said and took our info.

Early that evening, we returned to our hotel room to find Jane's designer clothes hanging in the closet. I called the front desk and asked about my bill. They told me that the dresses were added and gave me my total. Scared to death that some of the other wives and girlfriends might know of this "put it on my hotel bill" procedure, I asked the hotel clerk what the balance owed the hotel was at that moment. He informed me it was over $30,000. Three days at the George V hotel and we'd racked up a bill of over $30,000. The tour wasn't making enough money to afford that kind of expense. I couldn't ask the wives and girlfriends to return the clothes, which were custom-made anyway, and I didn't feel I could make the Stones ask them either.

As fate would have it, that night I was contacted by an executive from Decca Records, the Stones' record label at the time. He wanted to say hello and wish the best to the band. Basically, Decca was testing the waters for the Stones to re-sign with them at the end of their soon-to-expire recording agreement. I told him that one of the things Decca could do, as an offer of good faith, was pick up the hotel bill from the George V.

The next morning, I got another call from someone at Decca and reiterated, "It would be really nice if I could tell the Stones you're paying their bill."

"How much is it?" the person asked. "Five days at the George V," I told him.

Later that day Decca called and said the George V bill had been taken care of, and they looked forward to, at some later date, sitting at a table to discuss a new recording contract.

David Maysles delivered a couple of notes to me while we were in Paris, related to the film. One note asked me to deliver the other note to Mick and Keith. David wisely suggested that I wait until the "right time" to give it to them. The note he wanted me to give to the boys suggested they use Glyn Johns to listen and help mix the music tracks for the film. Knowing how tight everyone was for money, David also volunteered to cover half the costs.

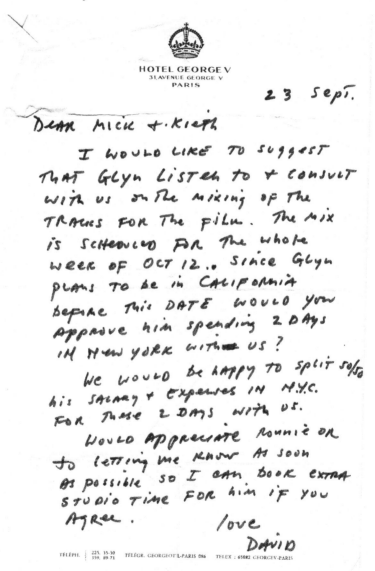

Another close call at the George V occurred one morning when I met Keith on the mezzanine with his infant son Marlon in his arms. Keith had just arrived and there was a photographer standing in front of him snapping pictures. Keith told the photographer to stop using his flash as it bothered Marlon's eyes. The photographer kept shooting and put his hand out to push Keith into a position he wanted for his shot. That did it.

"Ronnie, hold Marlon for a second."

I took Marlon into my arms, and Keith grabbed the photographer. Screaming that he had gone too far, Keith ripped the camera from the guy, leaned over the balcony, and dropped it. The camera fell three flights, crashing through a small wooden box on the ground below. Keith punched the cameraman, who fell down, stayed down, and it was over.

I was later contacted by the hotel: Their only complaint was about the broken box. It was an antique, and they billed us $3,000 for it. I didn't challenge it, and Decca paid for it.

CHAPTER XXVIII

YOU CAN'T ALWAYS GET WHAT YOU WANT

After the Paris shows, I met with Ahmet Ertegun, founder of Atlantic Records. Ahmet had turned a small independent record label into a national giant. The Stones were in negotiations with Atlantic Records for their new record deal.

"Ronnie, how would you like to head up the business end of Rolling Stones Records?" he asked with a big smile on his face.

I was taken by surprise!

Over the course of the last few months, I had been in many discussions with the boys about how to proceed in structuring a new record deal. I had been full of ideas that would take advantage of the leverage the Stones now had. In one instance, we were at Mick's house on Cheyne Walk in London. I started discussing what I was thinking with him, Keith, Bill, Mick Taylor, and Charlie.

"One dollar a record. Screw the percentages and all the other bullshit they throw at you when reporting record sales. I think you can demand a fixed dollar amount for each album sold. You sell a million records; you get a million dollars."

Keith and the rest of the guys were all ears, but Mick said he didn't want to talk about it and went over to his piano and began to play. Keith said that if Mick didn't want to talk about it, it didn't matter as the rest of the band did and suggested we leave Mick to his piano. There was a bit of an argument, and I saw Mick was upset they had chosen to continue the conversation without him. We talked some more, but I felt a problem had developed between Mick and me.

Now Ahmet was offering me the top position at the soon-to-be-formed Rolling Stones Records.

"What about Marshall Chess?" I asked. "I thought he was going to be running the company."

Marshall had learned the record business working at Chess Records, the legendary blues label, founded by his father Leonard and Uncle Phil.

"Marshall will be there for the talent, his name, and studio experience," Ahmet said. "We don't trust him as a businessman with the numbers and running the company. That's why we want you there."

"Do I have to wear a suit and, most importantly, be there at nine in the morning?" I asked.

"Yes!"

As I was imagining myself a record company executive, I flashed back to Allen demanding I always wear a suit. I thought of the corporate ladder and all the backstabbing. If I were on top of the ladder, all the knives would be pointed in my direction. With the memory of why I left my uncle—to be on my own, to live my own life—I decided I did not want to fall into a situation similar to the one I left. I was not corporate-structured record company executive material.

"No, thank you," I told him.

"I don't think it's for me, but thanks again for the great offer."

"You don't have to make your final decision now," Ahmet insisted. "Take some time to think about it."

Months later, Prince Rupert had a meeting with me and proposed that he, Larry Myers (a UK accountant), and I form a company called the Advisors to represent entertainment clients throughout the world. I would represent North America. First client, the Stones: The Stones would pay me $50,000 a year, and I would get a 5 percent commission on tour revenue. There were no tours planned so I had no idea when that would happen, and I found $50,000 a year—knowing the energy I would have to put into the Stones—was not enough.

September 27, 1970 – Vienna, Austria, Stadthalle

In Vienna, Mick asked us to join him for dinner in a glass-enclosed restaurant next to the opera house. The place was gorgeous and reminded me of a high-ceilinged solarium, but at night with chandeliers glowing. I perused the menu, and for the first time I saw pheasant under glass as an entree. I always thought it was a joke, a way to make fun of rich diners, but then Mick told the waiter, "I'll have the pheasant under glass."

He told me I should try it. I ordered it.

Sometime later, the waiter brought two large, glass-covered silver serving dishes to the table. There they were, two dead pheasants. They looked beautiful and tasted exquisite. When we had finished, the sommelier came to the table and suggested we have a glass of an 1800s Napoleon cognac. At $80 a glass I hesitated, but Mick said, "We'll each have one."

About half an hour went by, and I was beginning to wonder what was going on when the sommelier appeared with our two snifters. I asked why it had taken so long, and he replied they slowly warmed the brandy over a candle to the right temperature for drinking. I took a sip and can remember it to this day. It was like liquid gold flowing down your throat.

September 29, 1970 – Rome, Italy, Palazzo Dello Sport

I enjoyed staying at the Parco Del Principi in Rome. It was one of the few hotels in Rome with an outdoor swimming pool, even though it wasn't something that mattered in September.

After the sound check, we left in the limo and pulled out from an underground garage. As we exited there was a loud thump and the car roof above us dented in about six inches. Someone had been standing on a cliff above the garage exit and had dropped a boulder that smashed into the roof. Our driver sped off, and we figured we had dodged another calamity.

October 1, 1970 – Milan, Italy, Palalido Palazzo Dello Sport

We were at the airport in Rome waiting for our flight to board when we heard an announcement informing us it was delayed.

Mick immediately told me he had a bad feeling about this flight and wanted us, instead, to take a train. I remembered how he had balked at flying in the old plane in West Palm Beach, so I tried to calm him.

"Ronnie, you know how many close calls we've had," he said, "and based on the number of flights I've made I'm worried that the odds are one of my next flights will crash."

It was about 8 PM and dark outside. I began worrying about reorganizing the army on the fly and getting them all to a train that matched our schedule.

Bill, Keith, Charlie, and Mick Taylor just wanted to get on the plane and get there. I told Mick to relax, and I would find out what was going on.

"At least they found the problem while the plane was on the ground," I offered in a halfhearted attempt to bolster his confidence.

I searched out the airline personnel and found that a part had to be replaced on the plane, and they were getting the instructions over the phone from Milan.

"Over the phone?" I asked the gate attendant, worriedly.

"Yes, most of the mechanical work is done at the Milan airport so the Milanese mechanics are talking to the Roman mechanics to repair the plane."

I pictured that in my head and wondered how I could tell Mick. My confidence in their repair capabilities got shaky, and I thought more about a train at this last minute.

"It will be fixed in an hour," I was told. "Don't worry, you will get there safely. The pilots won't fly unless it's safe."

I scooted off to calm the troops. The boys agreed that we would wait for the flight even though Mick continued to object. In the end, we were just too tired to run around getting a train. Besides, we rationalized, the pilot wouldn't want to die, so we could count on him to make sure we got to Milan safely.

October 3, 1970 - Lyon, France, Palais des Sports de Gerland

We got back late from the concert in Lyon, France, and I spent a few hours unwinding in my room. It was about 5 AM when there was a loud knock knock on my door. I looked out the peephole and saw the great saxophonist, Bobby Keys.

I opened the door to find Keys, naked with a white towel wrapped around his waist. His eyes had a glow I had seen before, and he said, "I want to rent a car to drive to our next date in Frankfurt. Come with me to my room." He grabbed my hand.

Bobby's room was down the hall from mine, and as we walked to his room, I noticed a row of champagne bottles lining the hallway walls leading to his door. We walked into his room and on an obviously champagne-soaked bed lay a beautiful naked blonde girl smiling at me, her spread-eagled body glistening. "Ronnie," reflected Bobby, "there is nothing finer than being on Owsley windowpane licking champagne out of a pretty young pussy waiting for the sun to rise in Lyon, France. Now rent me a car for this morning. Would you like a hit of Owsley?"

In my head, I was thinking, absolutely no way on either count, but out loud, I said, "Let me see what I can do, but I wouldn't count on it at such short notice. And, no thanks on the acid."

I knew he would eventually pass out, and the thought of a long drive would leave his mind.

He did and it did.

CHAPTER XXIX

THAT'S HOW STRONG MY LOVE IS

October 5–6, 1970 – Frankfurt, Germany, Festhalle

The Stones played two nights in Frankfurt, October 5 and 6. On the first day, I managed to go out shopping. I found a little jewelry store and bought a gold ring with a yellow diamond in it that fit my pinkie.

Mick called later that morning and asked me to join him for a walk in the park across the street from the hotel.

As we strolled together, I sensed something was troubling him.

"Is something wrong?" Mick looked at me, looked down, and mumbled, "I think I was raped."

"What?"

"I passed out drunk, woke up, and my underwear was cut off. I think someone fucked me."

"Is that a bad thing?" I asked. "You really don't know if you got laid, so…?" At the same time, I was wondering, why is he telling me this in secret? This would be a story told around the table with the guys…

Then the other shoe dropped…

"I think it was Astrid."

I may have had a million things going through my mind with the "I was raped" but "Astrid" totally changed the dynamic.

Next I asked the obvious, "Does Bill know?"

"I don't know," Mick replied.

Mick suggested I sit down with Bill and explain how it was a drunken accident. Neither of them intended for it to happen, and it would never happen again.

Returning to the hotel, I went straight to Bill's room and knocked on the door. He opened it and I immediately knew he'd learned what happened. He was visibly upset, but he seemed relieved to have someone to vent to. Despite the weak "we were drunk" excuse, Bill was furious with Mick. He said he wasn't going to tour with him any longer. That was it, he was pissed, and the group was over. I just listened and commiserated with him as he vented, and every now and then would try to interject a touch of logic or reason.

"Bill, how many girls have you fucked with or without Astrid knowing? Has that affected the way you feel about her? Don't you think you are being hypocritical? Finish the tour, and then you can resolve this after you've had time to think about it. They are both sorry and blame it on the alcohol. You know that Astrid doesn't love Mick."

Bill calmed down, after about four hours.

"I'll finish the tour because I committed to it, but I don't know if I can forgive Mick and Astrid."

Part of me felt selfish, since my first goal was to get the tour completed, and another part felt bad for Bill.

In the end, Bill was the bigger man; the tensions eased quickly, and the transgression, to some extent, was forgiven. We went on to our next date, and the band played on.

Finally, a favorite for all of us, Amsterdam.

October 9, 1970 – Amsterdam, Netherlands, RAI Amstelhal

It was a great show and the perfect ending for our European adventure.

CHAPTER XXX

AFTERMATH

A year after Altamont, we had a film distributor. Mick signed when on December 14, 1970, Holzer got the deal with Cinema V's Don Rugoff.

I met Don Rugoff with my uncle many years earlier. We had walked into his office and were greeted by a very large, overweight man who needed a cane to walk. We sat down at his desk, and Don picked up a framed photo of a yacht.

"You see this beautiful giant yacht?" he said, pointing his chubby finger at the picture. "It's moored in my backyard at Martha's Vineyard. I've never been on it."

That was the showman and New York frame of mind guy who would be distributing *Gimme Shelter*.

He did a great job of promoting the film in New York, but that was it. He was a niche distributor, and we had a worldwide product. I longed for the Warner or Universal deal.

Some years after the deal with Maysles, I got a call from the Rolling Stones' litigation attorney, Peter Parcher. Peter said that due to the inaction of the Rolling Stones and Leonard Holzer to perform on the *Gimme Shelter* agreement, the Maysles had taken over all the rights. Peter went on to tell me there was going to be a deposition taken of the Maysles and both the Stones and Maysles requested I attend as an independent observer.

Peter, David, Albert, and I sat at a small round table. Everyone had a legal-sized yellow notepad in front of them, along with pens and pencils. Peter began questioning how everything began while I just sat idly by, feeling a little upset with the Maysles and even more upset with the Stones that they had let this happen.

After three hours of lots of boring back and forth, Peter looked at David, who had been doodling on his yellow pad, and said in a very loud, demanding voice, "What are you writing?"

"Nothing, I'm just doodling."

"I want those papers entered into evidence!" ordered Peter with an accusatory finger pointed at the yellow pad.

All of us were stunned. Peter obviously unsettled David and Albert and they asked for a break from the deposition. Peter said, "Take five," and David and Albert stepped out for a minute.

Peter turned to me and said, "Make the deal. They're scared, and I think they will settle. You have a deal in mind?"

I didn't, but thought about it and came back with, "They have to pay for going against our understanding. I want us to have exclusive control over the sales from Japan, Australia, and the UK. These are the biggest markets for the film and since the US deal has been done, the only money that will be coming in for the next fifteen years. "For my help, I want the right to sell those territories."

David and Albert came back into the room, and the deposition was called off to negotiate the new terms. Peter was right; they had been intimidated.

Even though he was an attorney, I liked Peter. He gave me some of the best free advice I could ever want. I heard when the Stones asked him to negotiate my deal, he told them he couldn't because he respected me too much to battle against me.

In fairness, with my negotiations with the Stones, I did call the attorney's office while I was waiting for a Stones/Schneider negotiation decision and spoke with the lawyer's assistant. I had called a couple of times and had been told they still hadn't heard from the Stones. After the fifth call, the assistant felt guilty and said she had seen a note on her boss's desk about me and the Stones.

"Hold on just a second," she said and put the phone down. A couple of minutes later, she returned. "The note from the Stones says, *Give Ronnie whatever he wants.*"

I enjoyed negotiating with Universal, the Maysles Bros, the William Morris Agency, Warner Bros, and the promoters. I had to reach a middle ground for the benefit of the Rolling Stones. I got them a 60 percent piece, a majority ownership. I think this is when I finally knew what I wanted to do in life.

I wanted to be a dealmaker, a closer. The one who makes the final push that gets contracts signed between CEOs and EGOs. What I did best and what I enjoyed most was making deals, helping make something from nothing. After all, a deal's a deal, and they all have numbers, and I love numbers.

In big deals between business and talent, there are always two things in common: Gigantic Egos and Greed. A chief executive officer has a big ego. Artistic talent has a big ego. Each one wants the best deal for themselves.

A musician takes a piece of metal or wood or animal skin and makes music. The lyricist puts words to the music, and the businessperson turns that music into money. They each speak different languages. I am a buffer between egos, and the interpreter of business speak that puts them together to create that magic of something from nothing for the benefit of others.

I get them to accept a fair split. They can blame me. "Ronnie made me do it." This is acceptable to both egos.

EPILOGUE

SATISFACTION

Many years later, in the late seventies, I was walking up 72nd street in Manhattan about a block from a music industry club owned by Jimmy Pullis called Trax. I had been to the club and met Jimmy many times with my music friends, but Jimmy didn't know my background.

As I got closer to the club, I noticed a black Lincoln limousine stop at the curb in front of Trax. Jimmy got out on the street side and began looking over the top of the car to see who was around. He caught my eye just as George Harrison was getting out curbside. Jimmy had a look on his face that seemed to say, "Yes, that's George Harrison. Yes, I know you. Please don't embarrass me." George got out, looked up, and saw me. I was surprised by what happened next, but not as surprised as Jimmy. George took three steps and grabbed me in a bear hug and lifted me off the ground.

"Ronnie, you were the smart one!" he said.

"What do you mean?" I asked.

"You got out in time!"

Sharing my grains of Sand

Index

Ronnie Schneider